The Impact of Highway

Investment on Development

The Impact of Highway

Investment on Development

By George W. Wilson · Barbara R. Bergmann

Leon V. Hirsch · Martin S. Klein

The Brookings Institution

TRANSPORT RESEARCH PROGRAM

Washington, D. C.

THE BROOKINGS INSTITUTION is an independent organization devoted to nonpartisan research, education, and publication
in economics, government, foreign policy, and the social sciences
generally. Its principal purposes are to aid in the development of sound
public policies and to promote public understanding of issues of national
importance.

The Institution was founded December 8, 1927, to merge the activities of
the Institute for Government Research, founded in 1916, the Institute
of Economics, founded in 1922, and the Robert Brookings Graduate
School of Economics and Government, founded in 1924.

The general administration of the Institution is the responsibility of a self-
perpetuating Board of Trustees. The trustees are likewise charged with maintaining the independence of the staff and fostering the most favorable conditions for creative research and education. The immediate direction of the
policies, program, and staff of the Institution is vested in the President, assisted by the division directors and an advisory council, chosen from the
professional staff of the Institution.

In publishing a study, the Institution presents it as a competent treatment
of a subject worthy of public consideration. The interpretations and conclusions in such publications are those of the author or authors and do not purport to represent the views of the other staff members, officers, or trustees of
the Brookings Institution.

BOARD OF TRUSTEES

Foreword

U<small>NDER A GRANT</small> from the Agency for International Development the Brookings Institution is conducting a major research program on the role of transport in development. One of the important aspects of that program is an empirical investigation of the actual impacts of specific transport investments at particular places and times. The results of selected case studies are reported in this volume along with analysis of the variations in results obtained from transport investments. It is hoped that these cases will help to improve techniques in evaluating future transport project proposals.

Brookings wishes to thank Indiana University for giving George W. Wilson leave of absence to direct the study and to express its appreciation to United Research Incorporated for granting leaves of absence to Leon V. Hirsch and Martin S. Klein to work on field studies. Barbara R. Bergmann, a coauthor, was a former member of the Brookings staff, and is now on the faculty of the University of Maryland.

The initial work in choosing appropriate cases and formulating the field work for the cases done by Brookings staff was performed by Charles J. Stokes while on leave from the University of Bridgeport. James Craig, Antonio Casas, and Inai Bradfield served as research assistants on the project.

A reading committee composed of E. E. Hagen, Massachusetts Institute of Technology; Edward S. Mason, Harvard University; Holland Hunter, Haverford College; A. Robert Sadove, World Bank; and Robert T. Brown, formerly of the Brookings staff, reviewed the manuscript. Marianne Yates edited the volume. Jane Lecht prepared the index.

vii

The Transport Research Program, under the direction of Wilfred Owen, is conducted in the Economic Studies Division, headed by Joseph A. Pechman.

Opinions expressed by the authors do not purport to represent the views of the Agency for International Development or the trustees, officers, or other staff members of the Brookings Institution.

ROBERT D. CALKINS
President

January 1966
Washington, D.C.

Contents

List of Tables

List of Figures

CHAPTER I

Introduction

GEORGE W. WILSON

THE OVERRIDING ECONOMIC PROBLEM of the next several decades is finding effective techniques for accelerating economic growth in underdeveloped nations. After almost twenty years a satisfactory understanding of the development process seems to be as elusive as ever, although there is now a keener awareness of the nature and magnitude of the tasks required to accelerate the pace of economic progress.

Most analyses of growth still focus on the need to raise the proportion of national product devoted to capital formation. If there is any relationship between capital formation and economic growth, there must be some relationship between an important component of capital formation and growth. It may even be that the composition of an aggregate is more significant than the magnitude of the aggregate itself.[1] There is thus some utility in an analysis of evidence that is substantially disaggregated. An approach following Rostow's "organized disaggregation,"[2] as opposed to disorganized aggregation, seems long overdue.

---

[1] The general irrelevance of contemporary, western aggregative analysis to the problems confronting most poor countries has been carefully summarized by Dudley Seers in "The Limitations of the Special Case," *Bulletin of the Oxford University Institute of Economics and Statistics*, May 1963, pp. 77-99. This is further elaborated and more fully examined in a forthcoming volume by Gunnar Myrdal and associates, to be published by The Twentieth Century Fund, tentatively titled, *Asian Drama* (1966).

[2] W. W. Rostow, "Some General Reflections on Capital Formation and Economic Growth," National Bureau of Economic Research, *Capital Formation and Economic Growth* (Princeton University Press, 1955), pp. 635 ff.

Transport is usually an important component of such capital formation. In developed areas like the United States, Canada, and Western Europe, investment in transportation facilities constitutes 10 to 14 percent of annual gross domestic investment.[3] A rough estimate for Canada suggests that the value of its capital assets in transportation amounted to almost 17 percent of total gross capital stock, both social and industrial, in 1955.[4] In underdeveloped countries, the proportion of total public expenditures devoted to transportation and communications generally ranges between 20 and 40 percent;[5] 20 percent or more of total developmental loans made by various United States and international lending agencies have been for investment in transportation.

One reason for singling out transportation is the relative magnitude of this sector in virtually all countries. Since transportation is an important absorber of scarce resources, ill-timed, misdirected, or misplaced investment in this sector can have a serious impact upon the whole economy. Much of the investment in transport is large, indivisible, and long lasting; hence it can tie up vast amounts of resources for long periods of time.

A more important reason for stressing the role of transportation is the frequent claim that, at least in the early stages of development, it is the key sector. E. K. Hawkins asserts that ". . . the one sure generalization that can be made about the underdeveloped countries is that investment in transport and communications is a vital factor."[6] Speaking of the influence of railroads in the development of the United States, Christopher I. Savage asserts that it "can hardly be overemphasized; agricultural and in-

[3] For Western Europe, see J. F. Dewhurst and Associates, *Europe's Needs and Resources* (Twentieth Century Fund, 1961), Table 14-9, p. 457. Canadian estimates from *National Accounts, Income and Expenditure, 1962* (Ottawa: Dominion Bureau of Statistics, 1963), Table 25, p. 40. Estimates for the United States from J. F. Dewhurst and Associates, *America's Needs and Resources: A New Survey* (Twentieth Century Fund, 1955), pp. 1009-21.

[4] William C. Hood and Anthony Scott, *Output, Labour and Capital in the Canadian Economy*, A Study Prepared for the Royal Commission on Canada's Economic Prospects (Ottawa, February 1957), Chapter 6, Appendix B.

[5] For details, see Wilfred Owen, *Strategy for Mobility* (Brookings Institution, 1964), Table 3-1.

[6] E. K. Hawkins, *Roads and Road Transport in an Underdeveloped Country* (London: Colonial Office, 1962), p. 26.

dustrial development and the settlement of the west would scarcely have been possible without it."[7] Similarly, W. W. Rostow claims that the railroad was ". . . historically the most powerful single initiator of take-offs." Again, " . . . the preparation of a viable base for a modern industrial structure requires that quite revolutionary changes be brought about in two nonindustrial sectors: agriculture and social overhead capital, most notably in transport."[8]

These views on the significance of transport to development account in part for the high percentage of total investment devoted to transport. They are reinforced by the fact that a transport base was created prior to, or coincident with, rapid growth in western industrial nations. Ever since Adam Smith argued that the "division of labor is limited by the extent of the market," people have stressed this sequence: improved transport extends the market, which increases the division of labor (specialization), which raises productivity. In their enthusiasm for abridging distance, policy makers seldom realize that the relationship of transport to this sequence is partial and indirect.

If the market requires an enlarged geographic area, transport is relevant. The market might, however, be extended by increasing local purchasing power which requires no investment in transport. The market is also a function of price, quality, the nature of the commodity, sales effort, tastes, and preferences—none of which is necessarily tied to capacity to move the product. The sequential relationship between transportation and growth implied in Smith's well-known dictum may be broken at many points.

Transport is indirectly related because such sequential linear processes are not absolute. Development of any kind requires "clusters of change," which "if they occur together will produce one kind of result while if they occur separately or sequentially, different results will occur."[9] Even if one accepts the implied se-

[7] Christopher I. Savage, *An Economic History of Transport* (London: Hutchinson, 1959), p. 184.

[8] W. W. Rostow, *The Stages of Economic Growth* (Cambridge, England: Cambridge University Press, 1960), pp. 25, 26, 55.

[9] Margaret Mead, "Patterns of Worldwide Cultural Change in the 1960's," in *Social Problems of Development and Urbanization.* Science, Technology, and Development, United States Papers Prepared for the United Nations Conference

quence of Smith, it may be that markets were growing prior to the provision of transport. Or extending transportation facilities may also require other policies to promote their use, such as special stimuli to productive activity along the route, planned or induced migratory movements, and so on. To be successful transport must be part of a cluster of change.

The whole emphasis on transport as a strategic sector is reinforced by two other interrelated factors:

1. The observed correlations between rising gross national product per capita and some index of mobility.[10]

2. The many noneconomic benefits attributed to transportation, such as national cohesion, political and social unity, and the meeting of military and logistics needs. Even where there is considerable doubt of the economic value of new transport capacity, the noneconomic roles can appear to be of overriding importance.

There are many areas with abundant transport facilities but little or no economic dynamism, just as there are many cases where the two coincide. Some amount of capacity for movement of goods, people, and resources is *necessary* for growth, but the cases investigated call into question whether any particular amount is sufficient.

The present study focuses on transportation because of its apparent significance in the process of economic development and its suitability for a disaggregative approach. A major problem will be to examine those other circumstances of sufficiency, the necessary clusters of change that serve to explain the varying results from large investments in particular instances. A search for "other circumstances" that may have rendered particular investments in transport successful or not is the purpose of the analysis of the case studies presented herein.

Another reason for concentrating on transport is that it is uniquely associated with distance. Analysis of economic development has neglected the spatial orientation of economic activity.

---

on the Application of Science and Technology for the Benefit of the Less Developed Areas (U.S. Government Printing Office, 1963), Vol. 7, p. 6.

[10] See Owen, *op. cit.*, Chapter 3 for examples and Chapter 1 for the relationship between mobility indexes and levels of development.

Indeed, economic theory in general has tended to bypass the impact of location and distance or to assume that it is of little consequence. Only in recent years have serious efforts been made to assess the effects of space on some widely held economic beliefs. A discussion focused on transportation, especially in particular instances, will necessarily involve considerations all too generally assumed away.

There is, moreover, another problem associated with the spatial factor. In countries which are not closely bound together economically and which contain within themselves large islands of self-sufficiency and isolation, the meaning to be attached to national aggregates is especially ambiguous.

The Approach

For these reasons a series of case studies involving transportation improvements within relatively small regions of underdeveloped countries is presented and analyzed in some detail. Although there are weaknesses in any case study approach (for details see Chapter VI), it is useful to develop a set of such studies and bring them together in one volume for detailed examination and comparison.

It is important to emphasize that any case study is *a posteriori*. Each transport investment is taken as given and the situation afterwards compared with that prevailing before. The improvement in transport is taken as a datum on the economic scene (whether the action was wise or not in terms of the investment options existing before actual construction). The main concern here is not with the question of whether the investment was excessive, badly timed, poorly located, inadequately maintained, etc., even though these are important questions that affect the outcome. This is a before-and-after analysis that seeks to determine why certain things happened in some cases and not in others following the creation of additional transport capacity. The ultimate aim is to assist in the preinvestment analysis of transportation. If the cases yield useful generalizations regarding the role of transportation in economic development, it will then be possible to suggest in advance the conditions most conducive to a successful outcome.

The General Relationship Between Transportation Capacity and Economic Growth

It is not difficult to show the kinds of relationships between improvements in transportation capacity and economic growth. The following is a brief and highly schematic, generalized discussion of this interconnection.

There are three possible outcomes of improved transportation—(1) a positive stimulus to further development; (2) a deceleration of growth; or (3) an absolute decline in the level of income per capita.

The Positive Case

An improvement in transport capacity permits a more effective abridgement of distance. It makes possible faster, safer, cheaper, and more dependable service which in turn allows a greater movement of goods and people per unit of time. The ramifications of improved transport may range from a dramatic opening up of new regions which could not be developed without it to situations involving improvements in existing rights-of-way or vehicles. In the former case, transport costs prior to "improvement" may be considered infinitely high and thus constitute absolute barriers to change while in the latter case the relative significance of improved transport is less substantial. But whatever the initial situation, improved transport manifests itself through changes in the various service dimensions of speed, safety, cost, and dependability which either induce an expansion of existing productive patterns or create the possibility of entirely new activities. Each of these service features has a somewhat different impact upon mobility and economic growth.

The speed factor permits more intensive use of existing transportation facilities, which is capital-saving in two senses:

1. Less needs to be invested in transport to provide the same amount of service, assuming that depreciation does not rise in proportion to use per time period. In fact, total depreciation may even decline if the improved facility, such as a good road surface, leads to less wear and tear on the conveyances.

2. Nontransportation producers may retain smaller inventories so that a greater amount and variety of real investment is possible. This permits a larger total output per unit of resource input.

The safety factor has both a cost and a psychological dimension. Improvement in safety tends to stimulate use and to reduce the hazards of movement. This brings about greater utilization of the facility per time period and reduced costs in the form of damage, loss, or insurance.

The cost factor refers to the reduced inputs required to move any given quantity of goods or number of people between two points. These released inputs become available for other purposes, permitting greater total output from the same labor force. The surplus product so generated may accrue in pecuniary form to producers (if freight rates are reduced in proportion to the cost reduction), to the providers of transport service (if rates remain the same), or to both, depending upon the degree of competition in the transportation and goods markets. In the longer run, the gains may accrue to consumers of the product, again depending on the degree of competition in the relevant market. The disposition of these pecuniary gains will condition subsequent secondary effects and may range all the way from increased leisure through increased consumption to greater investment in productive facilities.

The dependability factor allows producers to schedule operations more efficiently. This implies reduced costs in the nontransport sector. The potential secondary effects are comparable to, but probably less extensive than, those mentioned above.

In general, improved transport in any of the four service dimensions leads to a reduction in the total resources required to produce and distribute a given volume and pattern of output per time period. How these released resources are subsequently used will determine the crucial secondary effects that ultimately induce changes in the magnitude and composition of output, assuming the released resources are in fact employed.

The Middle Case

The creation of additional transportation capacity may absorb some portion of scarce resources that should, on economic grounds, be employed elsewhere. In terms of opportunity cost, this investment is less productive than some alternative and keeps the growth rate below what it would be if resources were used more efficiently. Essentially this case involves misdirected investment.

Clearly, mistakes in allocating resources can occur in any sector. Cost-benefit analysis, even when properly carried out, inevitably contains many subjective evaluations, such as the price to be put on benefits that are not normally marketed, the appropriate rate of discount, etc. This means that errors are inevitable in the sense that some other allocation would have yielded better results although this cannot generally be foreseen. Alternatively, mistakes may be made in the prior estimate of maintenance or other operating costs of assets actually constructed. This applies to any sector of the economy, but many economists have argued that it is especially likely to happen in the transportation sector for two reasons:

1. The lumpiness, specificity, longevity, and externalities often associated with transportation capital create greater hazards in calculating and specifying future benefits and costs. This makes decisions to invest in transport not as easily reversible nor as readily corrected as those in sectors with assets that wear out rapidly or that can be built in small increments.[11]

2. There is a belief that transport is a "safe" investment in the political sense. For example, Hirschman suggests that "perhaps it is this absence of criteria and of sanctions that has endeared SOC [social overhead capital] so much to the developers. Development planning is a risky business, and there is naturally an attraction in undertaking ventures that cannot be proven wrong before they

[11] Hirschman has argued that investment in social overhead capital, of which transportation is a major item, is "impervious to the investment criteria that have been devised to introduce some rationality into development plans . . . [and that] the absence of *ex ante* criteria is compounded by the weakness of sanctions when mistakes have actually been made." See Albert O. Hirschman, *The Strategy of Economic Development* (Yale University Press, 1962), pp. 84-85.

are started and that are unlikely ever to become obvious failures."[12]

These two factors suggest that the probability of misallocating scarce resources is especially great in transport. Particularly may this be the case with railway transportation. Indeed, Robert T. Brown argues that railroad decisions are structural and in some sense "fundamental." "If they are in error, there is no turning back: the implications of the decisions are far-reaching both in space and in time. They are decisions which involve not five or ten or twenty million dollars but rather hundreds of millions. An erroneous decision of this nature can be classed as a 'disaster' for the economy."[13] In short, these viewpoints suggest that there is a greater chance for scarce capital being invested in transport and that there is a greater possibility of error here than in other sectors.

The Negative Case

An increase in transport capacity may actually lead to a decline in per capita output. The mechanism is relatively simple although there are two variants of it. The first is the simple protectionist argument which suggests that initial industrialization in any area requires the protection of high transport costs as a shield against low-cost competition from other nations.[14] The second is the thesis that in an underdeveloped economy the backwash effects tend to swamp the spread effects and that this detrimental impact on one segment of the economy due to the improved transport is not counterbalanced by equivalent expansion elsewhere. The effects of expansion in one region upon other regions are of two broad types. One is a stimulus to other regions through increasing demand for their products. This raises incomes which imparts a further stimulus to productive activity and so on. But there is a second set of influences that serves to blunt the first. What is expansion in one

[12] *Ibid.*, p. 85. Hawkins (*op. cit.*, p. 359) also makes this point.

[13] Robert T. Brown, "The 'Railroad Decision' in Chile" in Gary Fromm (ed.), *Transport Investment and Economic Development* (Brookings Institution, 1965), p. 247.

[14] See E. F. Schumacher, *Roots of Economic Growth* (Varanasi, India: Gandhian Institute of Studies, 1962), p. 38.

region may be competitive with other regions and drive out some previously established businesses and attract capital, management, and labor away from the others. There are many variations along these lines but the important question is whether the first (spread) effects predominate over the second (backwash).[15] On a more fundamental level of analysis, this latter version also implies that, in the case of additional transport, there will be set in motion a cumulative mechanism of growing regional disparities that may stifle overall development.

Critique of Views on the Relationships of Transportation to Growth

In each of the above cases there is a large element of contingency. None of the alleged effects is inevitable. In every case certain things *may* happen, but again they may not. Furthermore, in the last two cases, the effects can be counterbalanced by deliberate policy. Nonetheless, there is a growing skepticism in some quarters regarding the potential of transport for accelerating growth, and there have been some recent attempts to reinterpret history to show that transport *followed,* rather than preceded, economic dynamism, or that its role in the growth process has been overstated.[16] This is perhaps a healthy reaction to some of the excessive claims made for transport capacity. Each of the three cases, however, tells but part of the story, and each is based upon particular assumptions which, even when not of doubtful validity, are irrelevant in most instances.

In the *positive case* the immediate effect of increased transport is to increase the incomes of producers, consumers, or those who provide transportation services. But much depends on the use they make of the additional income. It is generally assumed that there exists an enterprising, rationalistic environment in which certain entrepreneurial types actively seek pecuniary advantage

[15] For details, see Gunnar Myrdal, *Rich Lands and Poor* (Harper, 1957), Chap. 3, and Hirschman, *op. cit.*, pp. 187-201.

[16] See for example, Paul H. Cootner, "The Role of the Railroads in United States Economic Growth," *The Journal of Economic History*, Vol. 23 (December 1963), and Robert W. Fogel, "A Quantitative Approach to the Study of American Economic Growth," *The Journal of Economic History*, Vol. 22 (June 1962).

and hence respond positively to the decreasing costs that would emerge with improved transportation. Furthermore, the surplus receipts accruing to some groups as a result of reduced costs are employed productively. They end up in business or businesslike hands either directly in the form of excess profits or indirectly, from the increase in household savings made possible by lower prices through a banking system, security exchange, or other financial intermediary. In short, the positive case implies one of two things: a prior dynamism obviously held back by a transportation bottleneck or a set of institutions which may be deemed modern as distinguished from traditional. Neither of these is applicable to most underdeveloped regions. Noneconomic, or institutional, factors—often assumed away—make the impact of improved transportation uncertain. Even assuming "economic man" and an economically propitious environment, however, there must be adequate investment *opportunities* which permit exploitation of *available* raw materials and other resources.

The *middle case* reflects the effects of two assumptions often made about transportation. The first is that transportation is basically different from other industries. Efforts are seldom made to specify in what sense the industry is in fact unique, and when they are,[17] factors are cited which relate as well to a good many other industries. It may be granted that some (but not all) forms of transportation investment are lumpy, indivisible, and durable, but surely this is not a fundamental difference from investment in, say, a steel mill or a power facility. E. E. Hagen argues that even railways can be expanded in bits and pieces and cites the situation in Colombia as an example.[18] Furthermore, except for construction of an entire rail network, it is possible to proceed in stages, to modify the impact of a mistake by relatively small adjustments which do not necessarily require additional capital. Indeed, as Brown points out, the extreme lumpiness is confined to what he calls the "railroad decision" and does not apply to other forms of transportation investment. But even with regard to railroads, the case is overstated, for rail investments are not fundamentally different from others that may be equally large.

[17] See, for example, *National Transportation Policy*, Report of the Committee on Commerce, U.S. Senate, 87 Cong. 1 sess. (June 26, 1961), Part V, Chap. 1. Sec. 1.
[18] Everett E. Hagen, *On the Theory of Social Change* (Dorsey Press, 1962), pp. 45-46.

The second assumption, that transportation is a politically safe investment, is also open to serious question. Steel mills, dams (for example, Aswan), a modern air force, atomic power plants, and so on are politically safe regardless of their economic benefits. Indeed, they are more symbolic of progress in the eyes of aspiring or even entrenched politicians than is a single-track railway or a gravelled road. Transport is a more grubby kind of necessity unless it is lavishly overdone. Even when it is overdone, as it frequently is, transport investment is no more politically safe than is any other symbol. Nor is it true that cost-benefit analysis is less applicable to even an expensive, long-lived piece of transportation capital than it is to major investments in such areas as housing, education, or health.

In short, the "uniqueness theorem" does not stand up. The middle case is based upon dubious assumptions. The chance of misdirected investment in transport is not necessarily greater than it is in many other sectors.

The first aspect of the *negative case*, which is a variant of the infant industry argument, is perhaps the most dubious of all. High transport costs work both ways. While they *may* protect local producers against foreign competition, they disadvantage those industries in which economies of scale exist and reduce net receipts from export trade which are so important for most underdeveloped countries.

As far as the spread and backwash effects are concerned, it is always stressed that these tend to occur only when the market mechanism is operating freely. Even in this case there is no necessary growth in regional inequality over very long periods. Long before regional disparities increase to such an extent that further growth of the entire nation is jeopardized, deliberate policies will be adopted to correct the situation.[19]

Thus, on *a priori* grounds, it is not possible to determine the impact of transport on economic development. Nor does the aggregative approach to the problem appear adequate. Further analysis of this complex interrelationship implies an approach that is disaggregative, specific, and subnational. A series of case studies has therefore been prepared.

---

[19] Hirschman, *op. cit.*, p. 190. Myrdal, however, feels that policy may aggravate rather than alleviate the situation (*op. cit.*, Chap. 4).

Chapters II through V contain a summary of eleven case studies, five of which were made explicitly for the present volume. The rest are previously published reports having many of the features of case studies relevant for present purposes. Following the cases is a critical analysis that attempts to derive some generalizations applicable to development theory and useful for preinvestment surveys in the area of transportation in general, and road transport in particular.

As a convenient frame of reference for the case study countries some data on income and output are given in Table I-1. The figures are of doubtful validity and vary considerably in quality among the countries. The table is presented chiefly to indicate whether or not there is much overall dynamism and to suggest a crude ranking of the countries by per capita income. No significance should be attached to absolute differences. However, obviously Venezuela is by far the best off economically while Uganda, Bolivia, and India are the poorest. All the other countries are somewhere between, probably toward the lower end. Venezuela appears to have had the fastest rate of growth of aggregate output per capita during the fifties—over 4 percent— while Bolivia, India, and Guatemala had the lowest (near the 1 percent level) with the others probably between 1½ and 2½ percent

TABLE I-1. *National Income Per Capita and Rate of Growth of Output in the Case Study Countries*[a]

Country	National Income per Capita[b] (In U. S. dollars)	*Annual Growth Rates of Real Output per Capita*[c] (*In percent*)
Bolivia	80	Under *1*
El Salvador	180	*1.0–2.0*
Guatemala	150	*1.0–1.5*
India	70	*1.0–1.5*
Nicaragua	230	*1.5–2.0*
Peru	120	*1.0–2.0*
Thailand	90	*1.5–2.5*
Uganda	60	*n.a.*
Venezuela	880	Over *4*

[a] The figures are derived from a wide variety of sources, which are frequently conflicting. The estimates above represent crude approximations based on the wide variations observed in published documents from the United Nations, the Agency for International Development, country plans or private studies.

[b] Average for 1958–60.

[c] Decade of the 1950's.

TABLE I-2. *Transport Trends in the Case Study Countries, 1950-60*

Country	Motor Vehicles		Railway Traffic			
	Total Number 1960 (In thousands)	Percentage Increase 1950-60	Total Freight 1960 (In millions of ton-kms.)	Percentage Increase 1950-60	Total 1960 (In millions of passenger-kms.)	Percentage Increase 1950-60
Bolivia	39[a]	197	300[b]	21	236[b]	49
El Salvador	29	244	—	13	—	—
Guatemala	33	161	270[a]	57	—	—
India	529	98	6,921	12	74,519[a]	11
Nicaragua	14	422	23		60	−67
North Borneo	5	391	4		18	—
Peru	144	142	420[a]	4	259[a]	8
Thailand	88	481	1,138	137	2,353	64
Uganda	31	259	—		—	—
Venezuela	369	173	20	18	25	56

Source: Wilfred Owen, *Strategy for Mobility* (Brookings Institution, 1964), Appendix Tables 2, 6, and 7.
[a] 1959 data.
[b] 1957 data.

14

FIGURE I-1. *Trends in Transport and National Income, 1948-60, Selected Countries*

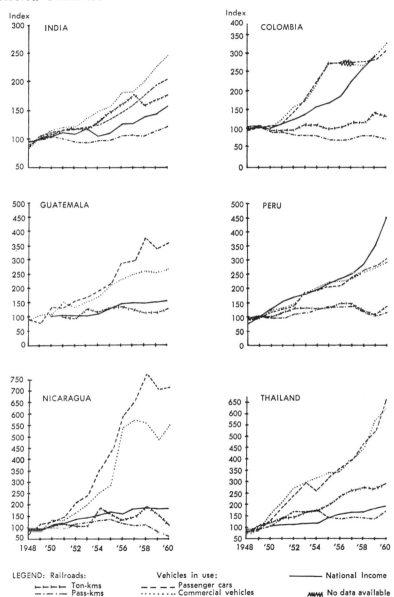

LEGEND: Railroads: Vehicles in use: National Income
         ⊢⊢⊢⊢ Ton-kms   ＿ ＿ ＿ Passenger cars
         —·—·— Pass-kms   ········ Commercial vehicles   ⋀⋀⋀⋀ No data available

Sources: Indexes computed from data contained in the United Nations, *Statistical Yearbook*, New York. Exceptions: (1) G. D. P. Nicaragua, source: Banco Central de Nicaragua, *Primer Informe Anual* (Managua, 1961), p. 55.

Indexes based on average of 1948, 1949, and 1950. National Income, Guatemala based on 1950; National Income, Thailand based on 1950; Net ton-kms, Guatemala based on 1951.

15

a year. If the figures have any meaning at all, they suggest relative stagnation in Bolivia, India, and Guatemala and somewhat more satisfactory progress in the other countries, especially Venezuela, during the period covered by the case studies.

Some information on overall traffic trends in the countries is presented in Table I-2 and in Figure I-1. In all countries motor vehicle registration has increased sharply over the decade of the fifties by amounts varying from about 100 percent in India to almost 500 percent in Thailand. Using a different indicator, the figures show that rail freight has increased at a slower rate, generally less than 50 to 60 percent, except for Thailand. Rail passenger traffic has declined in Nicaragua; it has increased less rapidly than freight in India and Thailand and more rapidly than freight in the other countries for which data are available. The transportation trends during the fifties, shown in Figure I-1 for several of the countries, suggest some relationship to national income although this varies among the countries. Not much can be read into these aggregate trends, nor is there any apparent relationship between economic levels as shown in Table I-1 and the mobility index as defined by Wilfred Owen.[20] This is not surprising and, as previously noted, was one of the reasons for using the case study approach in the first place.

[20] See Owen, *op. cit.*, Chap. 1. Further details on aggregate trends in a large number of countries may be found in Owen's volume.

CHAPTER II

The Cochabamba-Santa Cruz Highway in Bolivia[1]

BARBARA R. BERGMANN

THE GEOGRAPHIC FACTS OF LIFE must dominate any discussion of possible strategies for development in Bolivia and the place of transportation in that development. Bolivia is divided between the cold, highly populated, poverty-stricken Andean highland region in the western third of the country, and the flat eastern lowlands, mainly lush, unpopulated jungles, in the remaining two-thirds. (See Figure II-1). This geography inevitably limits the choice of development policies which are feasible and makes problematical the success of those attempted.

The Background

Bolivia's geography makes transportation between regions difficult, and it also makes the provision of better transportation

[1] I should like to acknowledge the help of Donald S. Green of Robert Nathan Associates, who spent a great deal of effort orienting the writer and suggesting improvements in the manuscript. In Bolivia, Frederick Lowell of U. S. AID was both helpful and kind, and Eric Dodge and Mercelo Peinado of Tippetts-Abbett-McCarthy-Stratton (engineering consultants) gave access to valuable documentary material, including some of their own estimates. In the Junta Nacional de Planeamiento in La Paz, Dr. Smodlaka of the U. N. Technical Assistance Program and Sr. Dalens provided much material of value. Irma Vizcarra of Servicio Agricola Interamericano made the resources of her excellent collection of documents available. Robert T. Brown, formerly of the Brookings Institution, Dwight B. Heath of the Anthropology Department of Brown University, Jacob P. Meerman of the AID staff in La Paz, and Romney Robinson of Brandeis University read the manuscript and made valuable suggestions. Any errors which remain are the sole fault of the author.

FIGURE II-1. *Map of Bolivia*

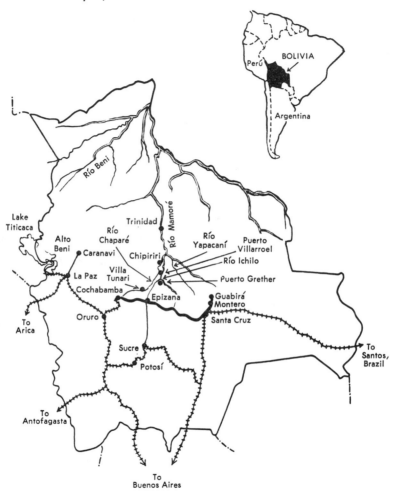

facilities very costly. Whether the cost of linking two such diverse regions can be justified by the benefits is a major question. Bolivian planners see these links as fundamental in their plan for developing the country, and they envisage high economic, political, and social benefits as a result of better transportation.

The highland regions are themselves diverse (see Figure II-2). To the west is the cold, relatively flat Altiplano at an altitude of 12 to 13 thousand feet, with the cities of La Paz, the

FIGURE II-2. *Geographic Divisions of Bolivia*

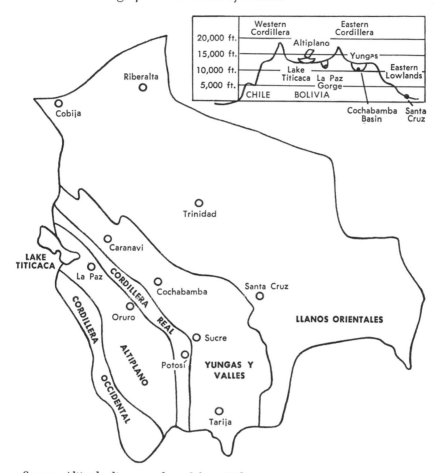

Source: Altitude diagram adapted from *Bolivian Survey*, a special supplement to *The Statist* (Feb. 16, 1962), p. 24.

seat of government, and Oruro. On the east and west, the Altiplano is bordered by bands of snow-covered peaks which contain many mining sites. East of the Cordillera Real, the eastern band of peaks, are range upon range of lesser mountains, gradually descending towards the eastern plains. Among these lesser ranges the population is concentrated in river valleys. The city of Cochabamba, at an altitude of about 8,400 feet, is in the largest valley.

In the Altiplano, the Indian *campesinos* herd llamas and sheep and grow potatoes. Wheat and other cereal crops are grown in the high valleys, such as Cochabamba. The nonagricultural part of the highland population lives largely by mining tin from seams that appear to be playing out. The unrefined metal is sent down to the Pacific coast, and imported food and manufactures are brought up in return. Highland Bolivia is very poor, and agriculturally speaking, very crowded. It contains about 85 percent of Bolivia's population of 3.5 million, and about 35 percent of the land. (See Table II-1.) Income is below $100 per capita. All of the larger Bolivian cities are in the highlands. The European colonization of the highlands took place from the Pacific, and the

TABLE II-1. *Population and Geography of Bolivian Regions, 1962*

Geographic Region	Departments Included	Major Cities	1962 Population[a] (Thousands)	Area (Thousands of square kilometers)	Description
Highlands					
Altiplano	Part of La Paz, Oruro, Potosí		1,610	217	Plateau between two Andean ranges. Has an elevation of 12–13,000 feet.
		La Paz	353		
		Oruro	87		
		Potosí	55		
Yungas and Valleys	Part of La Paz, Cochabamba, Chuquisaca, Tarija		1,391	190	Steep eastern slopes and high valleys
		Cochabamba	92		
		Sucre	54		
		Tarija	21		
Lowlands					
Oriente	Part of La Paz, Pando, Beni, Santa Cruz		501	692	Lowlands of about 500 feet elevation varying from Amazonian jungle in the north to dry plains in the Chaco area of the south.
		Santa Cruz	73		
		Trinidad	15		
Total			3,502	1,099	

[a] Population estimates by Marcelo Peinado for Tippetts-Abbett-McCarthy-Stratton.

Spaniards became the masters of the indigenous Indian population. Full-blooded descendants of the Indians still constitute a major part of the highland population.

Lowland Bolivia, the Oriente, presents an extreme contrast. It is very sparsely populated, averaging 1.4 people per square kilometer. Its climate is tropical, and much of the land is virgin jungle. The Department of Santa Cruz is in the southeastern portion of the lowlands, and its capital, the city of Santa Cruz, is the lowlands' most important population center. White settlers came here from Argentina and Paraguay, and most of the aboriginal inhabitants retreated into the jungle. Therefore, the settled population of the Oriente is largely of European extraction, which allows them the luxury of racial prejudice directed at the highlanders. In the lowlands, the aborigines still roam the jungle, although in greatly reduced numbers and at a lower cultural level than in the precolonial period. They occasionally emerge to attack the "civilized" with bows and arrows.

The rugged, mountainous terrain which separates the Altiplano from the lowlands has always made surface communication between them difficult, time consuming, expensive, and, for motorized vehicles, dangerous. This difficulty in transportation has naturally meant economic isolation of the areas and a tendency towards political separateness. The separatist tendency is of great antiquity. The Inca empire, of which highland Bolivia was a part, covered thousands of miles of Pacific coast and Andean highlands but never extended itself beyond the eastern foothills of the Andes.

Bolivia's fear of losing the lowlands is perhaps made more acute by memories of a long history of territorial losses. In the nineteenth century both Argentina and Brazil took possession of some previously Bolivian territory in the east. In the west, Bolivia's access to the Pacific has been eliminated by the expansion of Chile. Bolivia also lost about 100,000 square miles in the Oriente to Paraguay in the settlement after the Chaco War of the early 1930's. Today, the fact that areas near the city of Santa Cruz have been found to contain petroleum creates added fears that other nations may have designs on the Bolivian lowlands. The current building of railroads by Argentina and Brazil with termini at Santa Cruz has been interpreted as a sign of the interest of these countries in the lowland area that still belongs to Bolivia.

It is a prime objective of Bolivian policy makers to open up the lowlands to exploitation by Bolivians.[2] They envisage the following benefits: that the lowlands will serve as an outlet for the growing population now crowded in the poverty-stricken highlands; that the agricultural products grown in the lowlands will replace imported goods which are now paid for with the dwindled proceeds of the tin mines, supplemented by credit and aid; and, perhaps not least of all, that the danger of losing the area to neighboring countries will be diminished.

The exploitation of the lowlands by Bolivians has required and will require transportation linkage with the highlands.[3] This paper attempts to evaluate the costs and benefits of one such linkage, the Cochabamba-Santa Cruz highway, which was opened to traffic in 1954.

It is hoped that the methodology illustrated by this computation will have applications in other contexts, particularly cases in which the purpose of a facility is to open up an undeveloped and underpopulated area.

In Bolivia, linkages between the highlands and lowlands such as the Cochabamba-Santa Cruz highway are a necessary condition for lowland development and integration with the Bolivian economy, but they are not in themselves sufficient. Other facilities of all kinds in the lowlands themselves are also clearly necessary. Therefore, in attempting to gauge the effects on Bolivian development from a facility such as the Cochabamba-Santa Cruz road, the benefits must be considered a result of costs jointly incurred for facilities of many kinds, not merely those costs incurred for the highway alone.

To illustrate the point concretely, sugar is now traveling from Santa Cruz to Cochabamba along the paved highway towards its

[2] It is still too early to tell what effect, if any, the coup of 1964 will have on Bolivian development policy.

[3] The area might be integrated with the development of Brazil or Argentina, but to consider the economic and political implications of this course would go beyond the scope of this study.

market in the highlands. Before the highway, very little sugar was produced and almost none was supplied to the highlands. It is tempting to attribute the benefits of the sugar supply to the road. Although the highway is clearly a necessary condition to this traffic, so were access roads from the farms to the sugar mills, as well as the sugar mills themselves and the trucks. In addition, it is worth considering what benefits might have been realized if the capital used in building the highway and the other facilities had been used elsewhere.

This means that an evaluation of the Cochabamba-Santa Cruz highway inevitably involves an evaluation of the strategy of Bolivian development, a strategy which is epitomized by a slogan popular in Bolivian governing circles, "In two generations, Bolivia must become a tropical country."

While much of what follows is descriptive, the paper ends with an attempt to draw all of the threads together and to make quantitative estimates of the costs and benefits which allegedly have and will result from the project.

The Strategy of Bolivian Development

Of all possible paths toward development, increasing and developing agricultural production is the one which seems to have caught the imagination of high Bolivian officials concerned with the future of the economy.

The attraction of agriculture as a sector for developmental effort derives from the belief that there is a large quantity of an unexploited resource: the land of the Oriente. One of the most startling contrasts in Bolivia is between the starkness and coldness of the Altiplano and the mountainous areas, where trees and bushes are a rarity, and the lushness of the millions of untenanted square kilometers of the tropics, where, as one official put it, "All you have to do is drop a seed."

The colonization of the lowlands is one of the major strategies of the Bolivian government for raising the national standard of living. The colonists would be drawn from among the low-productivity farmers and miners from the highlands who could, it is hoped, be converted into high-productivity tropical agriculturists. The long-range plan for the Bolivian economy published in 1961 called for the resettling of 100,000 families by 1971.[4] This number would be about equal to the natural increase of population in the highlands. (See Table II-2.)

TABLE II-2. *Projected Rural Population Growth, Bolivia, 1961-71*
(In thousands)

	Altiplano	Valleys	Lowlands	Total
Rural Population, 1961	905	1,479	401	2,785
Natural Increase, 1961–71	+216	+353	+96	+665
Internal Migration, 1961–71	−50	−404	+454	0
Rural Population, 1971	1,071	1,428	951	3,450

Source: República de Bolivia, Junta Nacional de Planeamiento, *Planeamiento*, La Paz, p. 164a.

The feasibility of transplanting the highland population on a large scale has not really been demonstrated conclusively. Past schemes dating back to the nineteenth century to colonize the Oriente from Europe have come to little or nothing. It has been held that highland Indians are even more poorly adapted physically than Europeans for a life in the tropical lowlands. Generations spent in the rarefied air of the high altitudes have produced a breed of men with enormous chest capacity, said to be extremely subject to respiratory infection in the lowlands. However, this pessimistic view of the health situation is not supported by a recent field survey of the colonies conducted by a team headed by Patch.[5]

As recently as 1954, a group of experts from the United States,

[4] República de Bolivia, Junta Nacional de Planeamiento, *Planeamiento*, La Paz (September 1961), p. 164a.

[5] W. Richard Patch and others, *Estudios de Colonización en Bolivia* (Ministerio de Economía Nacional de Bolivia, 1962), Vol. I, p. iii ff., and Vol. II, p. 1b. Of 600 colonists interviewed, 62 percent said they believed that their present situation was more or equally conducive to health than their old location. Of 72 families in one colony, 50 were in good health at the time of the survey, although 46 had, at one time or other, suffered ill health, mainly intestinal trouble usual to those who change residence. These findings are, however, somewhat ambiguous, since more than half of the heads of families interviewed had been born in the Oriente or abroad. Moreover, in view of the high rate of failure, interviewing only those who stayed is bound to give overly optimistic results.

headed by H. J. Henney, tried to throw cold water on the notion that substantial numbers of successful colonists for the Santa Cruz region could be recruited from the highland Indians. They cited "social, economic and climatic factors" including the racial prejudice of the present Cruzenians.[6] Their remarks on the character of the highland Indians display little optimism on the adaptability of the highlanders: "Their [the Indians'] centuries-old traditions and concepts are strong within them, and manifested in their day-after-day adherence to old patterns of conduct and values."[7]

The Henney team concluded that the proper way to develop the Santa Cruz region was by the importation of substantial numbers of Southern Europeans. (This conclusion was perhaps not uninfluenced by the fact that two of the seven team members were employed in a branch of the Foreign Operations Administration concerned with refugees and migration.)

In the past, the major impediments to the expansion of agriculture in the Bolivian lowlands, and to their development generally, were poor transportation links with the highlands and the disinclination or inability of the highlanders to move. This immobility may have been considerably altered by the land reforms which followed the revolution of 1952. It is also probable that immobility and poor transportation are not unconnected and that the improvement of transportation will act as a force dissolving the strong ties holding an individual to his birthplace.

On the other hand, advantages of transportation are relative. Oriente agriculture had a cash market in Cochabamba until the railroads linking the highlands to the Pacific coast were built.[8] The Cochabamba-Santa Cruz highway regains some lost advantages for the Oriente.

To a certain extent the Cochabamba-Santa Cruz highway and improvement of the other trunk roads from the highlands to the

[6] Homer J. Henney and others, *Report of Santa Cruz Area Development Mission* (U.S. Foreign Operations Administration, September 1954), p. 2.

[7] *Ibid.*, p. 7.

[8] J. Colin Crossley, "Santa Cruz at the Cross-Roads: A Study of Development in Eastern Bolivia," *Tijdschrift voor Economische en Sociale Geografie* (August/September, 1961).

lowlands can be thought of as occupying the same position in Bolivian development strategy as the Aswan Dam does in Egyptian strategy. Both the dam and the road represent an effort to increase the agricultural potential and relieve population pressure through a huge capital investment which increases the amount of land under cultivation. Naturally, the analogy should not be carried too far, since the road is potentially richer in beneficial side effects. Use of the analogy does spotlight a problem: Should a grossly underdeveloped country with a population problem devote a large part of its capital investment to increasing the amount of arable land, or should the capital be used in nonagricultural projects to give a new turn and texture to the economic life of the nation?

Of course, there are considerations other than the allocation of a sum in hand to its best uses. Most of Bolivia's new capital is donated and its investment planned by nonprivate agencies, whose preconceptions and ways must be taken into account. A request for $40 million for a road may meet a better response than requests for $40 thousand for each of a thousand smaller projects.

It is worth looking briefly at alternative uses for the capital that Bolivia is devoting to development of roads to the lowlands and facilities there. Two other spheres in which advances in productive activity might be possible in Bolivia are mineral extraction and manufacturing. Table II-3 shows their importance in the Bolivian economy in 1958, the latest year for which comprehensive data are available.

The problems of the Bolivian tin mines include fluctuating prices in world markets, past lack of reinvestment and exploration, exhaustion of some seams, poor labor discipline and featherbedding. Some investment and reorganization are being attempted under the *Plan Triangular,* a joint United States (AID), German, and Inter-American Development Bank assistance arrangement. However, reform of labor practices poses human and political problems which are very difficult. Moreover, the organization running the nationalized mines, Corporación Minera de Bolivia (COMIBOL), loses money, and this is sometimes misinterpreted as an indication that the mines are "unprofitable" to Bolivia. Thus, there may be some tendency toward undervaluation of the possible contribution which mining may in time make to the de-

TABLE II-3. *Bolivian Production and Foreign Trade, 1958*

(In millions of U. S. dollars)

Sector	Gross Value Added	Gross Production	Imports	Exports	Percentage Change (*Real Gross Value Added, 1958–62*)
Agriculture	96.2	112.4	3.2	3.3	+12
Mining	25.9	37.3	—ᵃ	34.3	+ 9
Petroleum	11.3	19.4	1.5	4.0	0
Manufactured food products	7.4	17.5	11.2	— ⎫	+22
Other manufactures	24.1	51.7	42.3	.08 ⎭	
Electricity	3.3	4.1	—	—	+48ᵇ
Transportation	23.8	36.2	9.8	—	+23
Commerce and Finance	35.8	42.7	1.0	.9	+ 1
Construction	3.2	5.8	—	—	−46
Other services	25.8	30.8	2.8	3.3	+17
Totalᶜ	256.5	—ᵈ	71.6	45.9	+12

Source: República de Bolivia, Junta Nacional de Planeamiento, *Planeamiento* (La Paz, September 1961), p. 48a. (Conversion to dollars at the rate of 12,000 bolivianos = U. S. $1.00.)

ᵃ Less than $.5 million.

ᵇ Percentage change between 1958 and 1961.

ᶜ Columns may not add to totals because of rounding.

ᵈ Total not of significance as it would include double counting.

velopment of national income. Nevertheless, it is probably correct to assume that if Bolivia is to improve her economic position significantly, other sectors must make major contributions.

Manufacturing activity has apparently never completely recovered from the shock of stabilization measures taken late in 1956. The purpose of these measures was to stop the inflation which had advanced the price levels by 7,900 percent in seven years. There is considerable manufacturing capacity not being used. Industrial production in 1961 was about 10 percent below production in 1952.[9] Some of what is now excess capacity was created under the artificial conditions of the inflationary period and might not be viable under any relatively normal circumstances. Low demand is probably another major reason for the present low activity, and this, plus a reputedly poor climate for free enterprise, are

[9] U. S. Agency for International Development/La Paz, *Economic and Program Statistics* (October 1963), p. 12.

among the factors which weigh against expansion. As we shall see, a vigorous development of the Oriente might result in a larger and more varied domestic supply of raw materials and higher demand for manufactured goods. These in turn might provide opportunities for new manufacturing activities and for the expansion of the old. However, most observers consider it unlikely that manufacturing could provide a major developmental push without improvements in other sectors.

It would be difficult to conclude, without a great deal more analysis than can be done in this short study, that the capital which has been devoted to opening up and developing the Oriente might have been better used in mining or manufacturing. Moreover, as shown later, the return from the Oriente investment has probably been positive, and it is not certain that mining and/or manufacturing would even give a positive return.

Development of the Oriente and the Roads into the Area

There are three major lowland areas (see Figure II-3) in which development is now taking place: the Caranavi-Alto Beni area, which is about 170 kilometers northeast of La Paz; the Chaparé area, which is about 200 kilometers northeast of Cochabamba; and the Santa Cruz area, which is about 500 kilometers east of Cochabamba. It should be noted that Cochabamba is 212 kilometers by road from Oruro, the large city nearest to it on the Altiplano, and 436 kilometers by road from La Paz.

Most of the development effort for the lowlands has been concentrated in Santa Cruz. Of the routes down to the lowlands areas, only the road down to Santa Cruz is a good one; indeed, the Cochabamba-Santa Cruz-Guabirá highway is the only paved interurban road in Bolivia. The sugar and rice processing facilities have all been erected in the Santa Cruz area. However, considerable colonization effort has been made in the Alto Beni and the Chaparé, and plans are afoot to improve the roads into these areas.

Whether it is appropriate to try to develop all three of these

FIGURE II-3. *Diagram of Principal Routes of Land Transportation, Bolivia, 1964*

(Distances in kilometers)

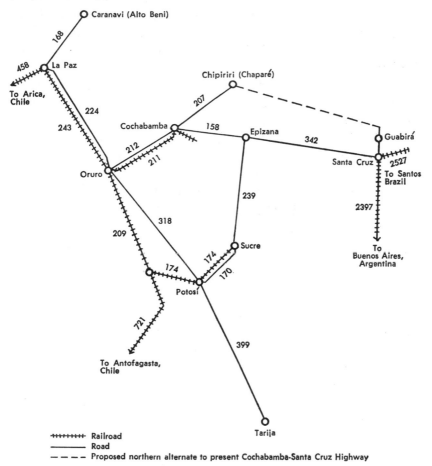

Railroad
Road
Proposed northern alternate to present Cochabamba-Santa Cruz Highway

areas at once is an interesting question. From the point of view of space for colonization and cultivation, any one of them would offer enough. Clearly the Alto Beni area has the advantage of nearness to the populated centers of the Altiplano, which would constitute its market.

There are, however, cogent arguments against relying exclusively on the Alto Beni area. A considerable part of the population pressure is in the Cochabamba valley, and the Cochabamba *campesinos* allegedly could not be induced to settle in the Alto

Beni, which can only be reached via La Paz, and is a long two-day journey from their homes. The Chaparé region is nearer to Cochabamba than the Santa Cruz area, and moreover, the road to the Chaparé will eventually be part of the route by which it is envisaged cattle, lumber, and other forest products will travel from the lower reaches of the Mamoré River to Cochabamba and the Altiplano.

The argument for the development of Santa Cruz, aside from the political ones,[10] probably rested mainly on the fact that the city of Santa Cruz and its surrounding cleared area represented a base on which, even with little augmentation of its pre-road population, agricultural production could be increased fairly rapidly. This has proved to be the case, but it is not clear that the costly development of this area will prove to be a project with longer-run justification in terms of the opportunity cost of investment in the other lowland areas.

In regard to the competitive claims of the Chaparé and Santa Cruz areas to priority in development, a better resolution of the competition might have been achieved by building the Cochabamba-Santa Cruz road as an extension of the road from Cochabamba to Chipiriri in the Chaparé. One might make a strong argument that the Cochabamba-Santa Cruz road was built in the wrong place—too far south through difficult terrain, most of which is either barren or good only for subsistence farming. This means that little development can be expected along the route. A more northerly route, although it would present severe drainage difficulties, would run through land with far greater agricultural potential.

When the present Cochabamba-Santa Cruz road was planned, this more northerly route through the Chaparé was largely *terra incognita*. The costs involved in exploring the northern route would have been extremely high, and the drainage problem would have meant somewhat higher construction costs. An extended cost-benefit study of the various routes which weighted their various defects and advantages might have resulted in building the road which was actually built, but it is worth observing that the best route on which to build between two points is not

[10] There seem to be two distinct political arguments for the development of Santa Cruz: (1) the geopolitical—that geography is against keeping the area in Bolivia and links had best be forged while there is still time; and (2) the pork-barrel type of political consideration.

necessarily the one which minimizes the maintenance and construction costs. A procedure which allows the decision in choosing a route between two points to depend entirely on engineering grounds may result in lower benefits than if the economic impacts of activity along the route are taken into account.

The more northern link between Cochabamba and Santa Cruz will come into existence in the not too distant future.[11] The completion of this northern route, when it occurs, will divert considerable traffic from the present road.[12] The distance between Cochabamba and Santa Cruz on the two roads will not be very much different. The present road crosses numerous mountain ranges and requires much climbing and descending. In contrast, along the northern alternate a truck leaving Santa Cruz could travel most of the way on flat land until it started its almost continuous climb to Cochabamba.

Financial History and Geography of the Cochabamba-Santa Cruz Highway[13]

Studies for a road between Cochabamba and Santa Cruz began back in 1928, and work was started in 1931. More work was done during the Chaco War in 1933, to facilitate movement of soldiers and supplies. In 1941 the Mission for Inter-American Cooperation

[11] In various stages of planning and construction are roads from Cochabamba north to Villa Tunari (on the Chaparé River which flows into the Mamoré), from Villa Tunari to Puerto Villarroel (on the Ichilo River which also flows into the Mamoré), and from Guabirá to Puerto Grether (also on the Ichilo River). A paved road already exists going north from Santa Cruz to Guabirá. The missing link in the northern alternative road between Cochabamba and Santa Cruz is a road from Puerto Grether to Puerto Villarroel. This latter link is being considered as part of a "marginal highway of the jungle" that would eventually run through the piedmont belt of Colombia, Ecuador, Peru, and Bolivia.

[12] It is curious, but perhaps to be expected, that the news story in the *Washington Post* (June 25, 1964, p. C-2) which announced the AID financing of segments of this more northern route as "a dramatic road project designed to open the way to an economic revolution in Bolivia . . . the most expensive single development project yet financed by the Agency for International Development under the Alliance for Progress" did not mention the previously financed Cochabamba-Santa Cruz road which is to some degree competitive.

[13] Much of the material in this section is condensed from the "Cochabamba-Santa Cruz Highway Supplement" of the *Andean Air Mail and Peruvian Times* (Lima, July 16, 1954).

TABLE II-4. *Estimate of Number of Vehicles Leaving Santa Cruz, December 1961-September 1962*

Type of Cargo	Cocha-bamba	La Paz	Oruro	Sucre	Potosí	Tarija	Area North of S. Cruz	Area So. West of S. Cruz	Others	Total
Food Products	4,992	958	179	484	243	22	70	79	33	7,060
Sugar	3,944	213	72	283	207	4	1	54	13	4,791
Rice	367	359	49	95	26	11	—	5	5	917
Corn	369	332	45	58	5	2	2	1	1	814
Fruit	83	41	13	45	5	5	3	1	5	201
Other food	28	12	—	3	—	—	61	14	9	127
Livestock	201	1	—	—	—	—	3	5	—	210
Raw Materials	855	546	91	12	17	—	1	2	1	1,508
Wood	661	461	91	9	17	—	1	2	1	1,226
Cotton	81	81	—	—	—	—	—	—	—	162
Seeds	76	1	—	—	—	—	—	—	—	77
Fodder	37	3	—	3	—	—	—	—	—	43
Manufactured Goods	225	348	189	4	17	—	184	10	14	991
Soles and leather	1	15	—	—	—	—	5	—	1	22
Alcohol	113	208	189	4	17	—	—	1	1	533
Gaseous drinks	—	—	—	—	—	—	40	—	—	40
Construction materials	29	9	—	—	—	—	11	1	9	159
Explosives	1	6	—	—	—	—	11	1	—	18
Fuel	—	—	—	—	—	—	8	7	—	15
Machinery	11	52	—	—	—	—	9	1	3	76
Bottles	70	58	—	—	—	—	—	—	—	128
Other	829	341	43	144	22	9	6,073	252	150	7,863
Passengers	268	93	14	33	6	3	80	104	27	628
Unloaded	273	72	9	40	6	2	5,831	93	78	6,404
Other	288	176	20	71	10	4	162	55	45	831
Grand Total	6,901	2,193	502	644	282	31	6,328	343	198	17,422
Mean weight of cargo per vehicle										
Sugar (in metric tons)	7.9	7.7	7.3	6.5	7.1	3.7	—	4.7	3.7	
Rice (in metric tons)	7.7	6.1	5.4	4.3	5.0	5.4	—	1.4	2.3	

Source: República de Bolivia, Jefatura Departamental de Tránsito de Santa Cruz (Registro de Salida de Vehículos), compiled by: Junta Nacional de Planeamiento.

TABLE II-5. *Estimate of Traffic on Segments of the Cochabamba-Santa Cruz Highway, 1959*

Highway Segment	Length (Kilometers)	Mean Daily Vehicles
Cochabamba-Tolata-Punata	45	413
Tolata-Epizana	113	100
Epizana-Comarapa	112	80
Comarapa-Santa Cruz	249	60

Source: República de Bolivia, Junta Nacional de Planeamiento, *Programa Preliminar de Transportes* (La Paz, 1963), Table 191.

made a study, and in 1943 an agreement between the Corporación Boliviana de Fomento (CBF) and the U. S. Bureau of Public Roads provided for a survey of the best route. The survey took five years and cost $2,363,000. In 1942 CBF had obtained a loan of $10,300,000 at 3½ percent from the Export-Import Bank and by 1945, 65 kilometers had been completed. The loan was used up and work was suspended in 1948 with grading completed only for 90 kilometers east of Cochabamba. In 1949 a loan of $18,400,000 in U. S. dollars at 3½ percent was obtained from the Export-Import Bank, and an additional $8 million in local currency was pledged by the Bolivian government. The road, most of it unpaved, was opened for traffic in 1954. In 1955 a loan of $4,700,000 at 4¾ percent was obtained from the Export-Import Bank and paving was done by 1957. The total eventually expended in construction amounted to $42 million, or about $50 million in 1962 dollars.[14]

The road is 502 kilometers long and a minimum of 7 meters wide. It starts at Cochabamba at an elevation of 8,500 feet and descends irregularly to Santa Cruz at 1,500 feet. It reaches a maximum of 12,500 feet, with no less than a dozen separate stretches of climb.

Traffic on the Highway

The most conservative estimate for traffic on the Cochabamba-Santa Cruz highway is one derivable from data in Table II-4,

[14] Using the deflator for highways in the United States Gross National Product

which gives 25,200 vehicles per year, in the 1961-62 period, in both directions. However, this number refers only to the traffic which has Santa Cruz as terminus, beginning, or transit point.[15] Table II-5 gives estimates for segments of the highway and yields a mean density for the entire highway of 104 vehicles per day or 39,000 per year in 1959. (The daily mean is computed by using the lengths of the segments as weights.) A CBF estimate for early 1962 is 120 vehicles per day[16] or 44,000 per year.

Some underestimation of traffic may derive from the fact that the control points are in operation about ten hours a day and do not count official vehicles. At any rate, the wide variance in these traffic estimates, all of them from government sources, is testimony to the difficulty of understanding past events and projecting future ones in Bolivia.

Effect of the Highway on the Santa Cruz Area

The relative ease and cheapness of movement between Santa Cruz and the highlands which the highway has brought about have had a very dramatic effect on agricultural production, marketing, and population. As to conditions prior to the opening of the road, we have the interesting testimony of an American observer, Olen Leonard, who described life in the province in the 1940's:

Isolated, almost inaccessible during long stretches of the year, many ancient and well-preserved estates remain as aloof and as indepen-

gives $48 million, while the implicit price deflator for the entire United States GNP gives $52 million. Neither of these price indexes is perfectly satisfactory, since for cost-benefit calculations, both cost and benefits should be in terms of Bolivian purchasing power. However, since most of the equipment and higher level personnel used in building the road were imported from the United States and, since in the longer run, the different movements in United States and Bolivian prices are reflected in the exchange rate, not too much harm is done by this procedure.

[15] This estimate is derived by taking the 17.4 thousand vehicles reported leaving Santa Cruz in the ten-month period, subtracting those going to the north and southwest of the city. The remainder was multiplied by 1.2 to arrive at a yearly total and then doubled to get traffic in both directions.

[16] Alfonso Balderrama, *El Transporte por Carretera* (La Paz, Consejo Nacional de Caminos de Bolivia, Departamento de Relaciones Públicas, 1962), p. 32.

dent of the outside world as in the period following the Spanish conquest of the area in the sixteenth century.[17]

In the 1940's, during the short dry season, a truck might go to Cochabamba from Santa Cruz in from two to four days, with good luck. In the rainy season the time required was extremely uncertain and might extend to twenty days or more.[18]

Before the opening of the highway, bringing a cargo from Santa Cruz to the highland cities even in the dry season was about three times as expensive as bringing it up from the Pacific coast.[19] Comparatively little agricultural activity in the Santa Cruz area was oriented toward a cash market because of the high shipping costs to the urban consumption centers of the highlands.[20]

Present shipping tariffs (see Table II-6) show that now a ton of cargo can move considerably more cheaply from Santa Cruz to Cochabamba than from the Pacific coast to Cochabamba, but that movements from Santa Cruz to Oruro and La Paz are somewhat more expensive than from the Pacific coast to those cities.

Agricultural Production

The principal result of the cheaper linkage and other facilities has been the expansion of agricultural production documented in Tables II-7 and II-8. Bolivia is now, or will soon be, self-sufficient in sugar and rice, and the Santa Cruz area accounts for all but a small proportion of the country's production of these two products. Sugar, for which we have the most complete time series, increased tenfold in physical volume of production between 1954, the year the Cochabamba-Santa Cruz highway was open to traffic, and 1962. In 1962 domestic production accounted for 83 percent of consumption. Rice production is said to have tripled between 1958 and 1963.

[17] Olen E. Leonard, *Santa Cruz: A Socioeconomic Study of an Area in Bolivia,* Foreign Agriculture Report No. 31, Office of Foreign Agricultural Relations (U.S. Department of Agriculture, 1948), p. 8.

[18] *Ibid.,* p. 9.

[19] *Ibid.*

[20] *Ibid.,* p. 33 ff. Of the farms Leonard visited, 179 had no acreage in sugar, 28 had less than 5 acres, 15 had between 5 and 25 acres, and only 4 had more than 25 acres. Rice was more common, although only 31 of the farms visited planted more than 2.5 acres of it; only 54 sold any.

TABLE II-6. *Freight Charges Between Important Points in Bolivia, 1963*

Points Connected	Form of Connection	Distance (Kilometers)		1963 Freight Rate[a] per Metric Ton-Kilometer (U. S. cents)	Freight Cost per Ton (U. S. dollars)
Arica-La Paz[b]	Rail				20.25
		Chilean part	209	6.40	
		Bolivian part	249	2.76	
La Paz-Caranavi	Road		168	5.70	9.58
La Paz-Oruro[b]	Rail		243	2.05–4.21	4.98–10.23
	Road		224	1.90–2.60	4.52– 6.19
Antofagasta-Oruro[b]	Rail				16.51–34.76
		Chilean part	444	1.53–3.45	
		Bolivian part	486	2.00–4.00	
Oruro-Cochabamba	Rail[c]		211	2.56–5.21	5.40–10.99
	Road		212	1.97–2.80	4.53– 6.44
Cochabamba-Santa Cruz	Road		500	2.89[d]	14.45
Cochabamba-Chipiriri	Road		207	4.30	8.90

Sources: Truck freight rates quoted from *Plan Bienal 1963–1964*. Bolivian rail freight rates from *Programa Preliminar de Transportes*, and Chilean rates from C. H. Zondag, *Problems in the Economic Development of Bolivia*, La Paz, 1956. Other information compiled for the author by: Ferrocarril La Paz-Antofagasta (Sección Boliviana), Agentes Administradores, La Paz.

[a] Road rates vary by season and direction. Both rail and road rates vary by type of cargo.

[b] Rates averaging somewhat lower than the figures given in this table for the railroads serving Bolivia from the Chilean coast are quoted in a booklet issued by the Chilean government. The price for transporting sugar from the coast is given as $15 per ton from Antofagasta to La Paz and $13 a ton from Arica to La Paz. República de Chile, Ministerio de Relaciones Exteriores, *Facilidades de Libre Tránsito que Chile Otorga a Bolivia*, Santiago, (1963).

[c] Not operating in 1963 because of washout.

[d] 2.0 cents is the rate quoted in the *Plan Bienal*. Other sources give rates up to 4.0 cents per ton kilometer.

Production of rice in 1962 about equalled what national consumption was estimated to be in 1958.[21]

Details on cargoes leaving Santa Cruz are given in Table II-4. It is clear that, in terms of physical volume, sugar is by far the most important export of the area, with wood second, and rice third. In physical bulk, corn is almost as important as rice.

An interesting question for the future is the extent to which the

[21] Maldonado San Martín, Gonzalo, *The General Agricultural Marketing Report of Bolivia* (La Paz, Servicio Agrícola Interamericano, 1959).

TABLE II-7. *Production, Consumption, and Import of Sugar, Bolivia, 1949-62*

Year	Domestic Production	Imports	Domestic Production Plus Imports[a]	Estimated Consumption	Value of Domestic Production	Value of Imports	Total Value Domestic Production Plus Imports[a]
	(In thousands of metric tons)				(In thousands of U. S. dollars)[b]		
1949	.2	33.4	33.6	N.A.	$32	$4,321	$4,353
1950	1.2	36.8	37.9	N.A.	161	5,122	5,283
1951	1.5	43.5	44.9	N.A.	233	6,905	7,138
1952	2.3	33.1	35.4	N.A.	350	5,069	5,419
1953	3.0	51.6	54.6	N.A.	332	5,768	6,100
1954	4.5	50.1	54.5	47.8	439	4,925	5,364
1955	4.3	42.8	47.1	48.3	409	4,046	4,454
1956	4.4	41.2	45.6	48.8	447	4,148	4,596
1957	8.7	66.7	75.5	49.3	859	6,557	7,416
1958	15.5	33.5	49.0	49.9	1,550	3,362	4,912
1959	17.5	46.1	63.6	52.3	1,629	4,278	5,906
1960	24.5	26.5	50.9	54.7	1,996	2,156	4,151
1961	41.2	20.0	61.2	57.2	3,412	1,658	5,070
1962	49.2	20.5	69.7	59.6	4,205	1,755	5,960

Source: *La Industria Azucarera en 1962*, Boletín Económico No. 4, Ministerio de Economía Nacional (Bolivia) (May 1963), La Paz.
N.A. Not available.
[a] Rows may not add to totals because of rounding.
[b] Current dollars at official rates.

37

TABLE II-8. *Rice Production, Bolivia, 1958-63*
(In thousands of metric tons)

Year	Amount
1958	12.5
1959	19.5
1960	23.3
1961	24.0
1962	24.0
1963	36.0

Source: República de Bolivia, Ministerio de Agricultura, quoted in *Economic and Program Statistics* (U. S. Agency for International Development/Bolivia, October 1963).

agricultural productivity of the Santa Cruz area has been the temporary result of mining the fertility of the virgin soil. Tropical soils are notoriously difficult to manage, and the Santa Cruz area is subject to winds and droughts which may cause considerable erosion. At the present time, it is apparently more economical to clear fresh land than to resort to fertilizers. In the case of sugar at least, this must change eventually because sugar mills represent a large capital investment, and the sugar fields must be close to the mill that serves them. One rough estimate made by a local agricultural expert is that within ten years, fertilizer to the value of about $50 per hectare (2.47 acres) of sugar per year will be needed, a figure which represents 20 percent of the value of the processed sugar derived from a hectare.[22] Whether farmers of the Santa Cruz area may find that sugar and rice are not profitable in the future depends to a large extent on the degree of protection from foreign competition the government chooses to give these commodities. All agricultural experts who have surveyed the possibility of the Santa Cruz area, including those who are pessimistic concerning the long-term future of sugar and rice, have been optimistic concerning the continued profitability of growing cash crops and do not foresee a reversion to subsistence farming or autarchy for the area.[23] Soybeans, citrus, cotton, and livestock are cited as the most likely possibilities.[24]

[22] In 1962 the $4.2 million worth of refined sugar was produced on 16,328 hectares. Ministerio de Economía Nacional, "La Industria Azucarera en 1962" (La Paz, 1963), p. 21.

[23] See also, U.S. Department of Agriculture Mission to Bolivia, "Bolivian Agriculture: Its Problems, Progress, Priorities, and Possibilities" (1962), pp. 61-63.

[24] An excellent summary of the agricultural situation and prospects, including a discussion of the fertilizer problems, is in J. Colin Crossley, *op. cit.*

Population Growth

The city of Santa Cruz is estimated to have grown in population by almost 70 percent between 1950 and 1962, a rate of growth more than triple that in Bolivia as a whole. (See Table II-9.) Some of the

TABLE II-9. *Population of Bolivia and Santa Cruz, 1950 and 1962*
(In thousands)

| | Population[a] | | Average Annual Percentage Increase, 1950–62 |
	1950	1962	
Bolivia	3,109	3,556	1.4
Department of Santa Cruz	286	327	1.1
City of Santa Cruz	43	72	4.4

[a] Compiled and partly estimated by Marcel Peinado of Tippets-Abbett-McCarthy-Stratton, for the author.

smaller towns nearby, such as Montero, the site of a sugar mill, have also grown rapidly. The rate of growth in the Department of Santa Cruz, however, is estimated to be even smaller than that in the rest of Bolivia. The large rise in agricultural output of the Department has been accomplished with only a modest increase in the agricultural labor force. In the highlands, with a slightly higher rate of increase in labor force and the investment there of considerable U.S. aid funds, the production of the major crops (such as wheat, corn, and potatoes) has been growing, if at all, at a much slower pace.[25]

A small part of the increase in urban population in Santa Cruz results from the activity of petroleum extraction groups that have been at work there. Their activity would presumably be going on regardless of the condition or even the existence of the Cochabamba-Santa Cruz highway. The recent move of the administrative headquarters of the petroleum operations from Cochabamba to Santa Cruz might not have occurred without the ease in surface communication which the highway allows. Increased commercial activity resulting from the agricultural boom no doubt

[25] Estimates by U.S. Agency for International Development/La Paz. One of the factors clouding the estimates of agricultural production is the probably improved eating habits of the *campesinos* since the revolution which would reduce the amount of food coming to the towns.

TABLE II-10. *Characteristics of Some Colonies in the Santa Cruz Area*

Characteristics of Colonies	Settled by Bolivians				Settled by Foreigners		
	Sponsored by CBF[a]			Sponsored by UN			
	Aroma	Cuatro Ojitos	Huaytú	Cotoca	San Juan (Japanese)	Okinawa	Mennonites
Year of foundation	1954	1957	1957	1955	1955	1954	1954
Area (thousands of hectares)	3.6	17.0	12.0	9.6	35.0	20.0	1.9
Number of families (1961)	240	626	165	100	130	245	38
Average size of family	3.3	3.5	3.3	3.8	5.0	6.0	6.7
Allotment per family (hectares)	15	20	20	10	50	50	50
Total area cultivated, 1960 (hectares)	874	1,865	846	158	800	2,300	340
Average cultivated area per family (hectares)	3.6	3.0	5.1	1.6	6.1	9.4	30.9
Value of agricultural product in 1960 (thousands of U. S. dollars)	135.2	195.0	82.0	28.9	133.3	293.0	19.2
Average value per family of agricultural product in 1960[b] (1960 U. S. dollars)	563	312	497	298	1,025	1,195	1,738
Average investment per family (1960 U. S. dollars)	313	718	718	4,118	3,000	1,855	N.A.

Source: Casto Farragut, *Principales Características de Las Colonias Agrícolas de Bolivia y Sugerencias para una Política de Colonización* (United Nations Food and Agriculture Organization, 1961).
N.A. Not available.
[a] Corporación Boliviano de Fomento, an agency of the Bolivian Government.
[b] A conversion rate of 12,000 bolivianos to the dollar was used.

40

accounts for most of the city's population increase. The rice or sugar processing factories tend to be built outside of the city of Santa Cruz.

Colonization in Santa Cruz

It is often alleged by Bolivian government officials that one of the principal purposes of the Cochabamba-Santa Cruz highway is to enable colonists to travel down it from the highlands to their new farms. To anyone raised on American western movies, the need of new settlers for paved roads may not seem to be great. In fact, however, many observers believe that the influence of the road on the willingness to move has been substantial. The relative ease of movement has meant a good flow of information westward to the effect that the Santa Cruz area is not a tiger-infested jungle. Carriers of this good news are frequently relatives of the colonists who come down from the highland areas to visit or help with the harvest.

The opportunity for colonists to make a cash income is due, of course, to the highway which is the connecting link to the large markets. Similarly, the highway lowers the cost of transporting to Santa Cruz goods manufactured elsewhere, and thus raises real income in Santa Cruz. This benefit, of course, applies to all Cruzenians, not merely the colonists.

So far, the colonization program in Santa Cruz has met with what might be termed moderate success. At the end of 1962, Santa Cruz had about 3,000 of the nation's 15,000 colonizing families, of whom about 10,000 were in the Chaparé and 2,000 in the Alto Beni.[26] In 1961 a survey was made of conditions in the Santa Cruz area colonies (see Table II-10). Among the Bolivian colonies sponsored by the Corporación Boliviana de Fomento (CBF), annual production per family ranged from an estimated $312 in a colony which had been founded four years previously, to $563 per family in a seven-year-old colony.[27] One projection which has

[26] These estimates appear in Tippetts-Abbett-McCarthy-Stratton, "Proposed Highway: Yapacani to Puerto Grether and Yapacani River Bridge" (Cochabamba, April 1963).

[27] Casto Farragut, *Principales Características de Las Colonias Agrícolas de Bolivia y Sugerencias para una Política de Colonización* (United Nations Food and Agriculture Organization, 1961), p. 9.

been made of gross sales in the ninth year of a farm northwest of Santa Cruz, with only limited sponsorship, puts them at $1,037.[28] There seems little doubt that the successful colonists have raised their standard of living perhaps by a factor of two or three.

The colonization movement in the Santa Cruz area seems to be picking up momentum, and the proportion of colonists who do not give up and go home is rising. One of the original colonists at the CBF colony of Aroma, north of Santa Cruz city, told the present writer that of the twenty-one men who had come with him to found the colony in 1954, only six were still there. The local representative of CBF estimates that 80 to 85 percent of the new colonists coming now are staying. Possibly the selection process for those who are coming to the organized colonies has improved. Now many of the new colonists are coming spontaneously rather than as part of government-arranged groups, and among these there is a high proportion of success. It may be also that the presence of so many who have succeeded now makes those who face an initial setback willing to try again.

The most interesting phenomenon relating to Bolivian development observed in the Santa Cruz area, is that many Bolivian colonists are very progressive. The myth that the highland Indians, even if given opportunities, do not and will not share the widespread human tendency to "truck, barter and exchange" is as prevalent now as in the days of the Henney Report. Yet the new Indian colonists of the Santa Cruz area are extremely interested in entering the money economy with the large-scale production of a cash crop—far more so than the white villagers whose families have lived in the region for generations.

The Indian colonists I visited were growing sugar in sizable fields for sale to modern, mechanized sugar mills. In the one village of old-line residents visited, only small patches of sugar cane were grown, and after harvest the cane was crushed in the village by a wooden grinding mechanism of antique design powered by oxen.

The Bolivian colonists observed were also able and willing to save and form capital. In one new village some saving was a col-

[28] Tippetts-Abbett-McCarthy-Stratton, *op. cit.* This estimate was made as a part of a benefit computation for the feasibility study for a road and colonization project.

lective wages fund of rice to pay for the building of a school. Some of the colonists were investing in brick houses, a form of construction previously unknown in the area and not indulged in by *campesinos* of any other area in the country. Others were going into the local trucking business, the demand for which is increasing as agricultural production grows. The new truckers buy Japanese trucks for which they get a loan they must pay off in two years. A successful trucker becomes the owner of a much depreciated, but still substantial, capital good at the end of that time.

One would expect the colonists to be above average in progressive tendencies. They had the energy to migrate in the first place and the energy to exploit the opportunity successfully; they are thus a highly selected group. But there are probably additional factors at work. Their new environment makes day-after-day adherence to old patterns of conduct impossible, which necessarily makes them alert to new things. The relatively easy entry into the money economy which Santa Cruz offers is probably a factor. Moreover, a colonist is forced to save and invest, at least in his first years. Perhaps saving, investing, and alertness become habitual. The theory of "the vicious circle of poverty"[29] is clearly inapplicable to a nation which has a frontier.

Effect of the Highway on Population and Production in the Highlands

The migration to the Santa Cruz area so far has slightly relieved crowding in the Cochabama valley and has probably raised average productivity of labor in agriculture. The city of Cochabamba is less prosperous now than previously, but this is mainly because of factors which are unconnected or only indirectly connected with the highway, such as the outmigration of expropriated landlords and of the administrative headquarters of

[29] R. Nurkse, *Problems of Capital Formation in Under-Developed Countries* (Basil Blackwell, 1953), Chapter 1. For the opposite point of view on saving ability, see Albert O. Hirschman, *The Strategy of Economic Development* (Yale University Press, 1958).

oil exploration groups. The city of Cochabamba probably derives some trade by acting as entrepôt of the goods traffic between Santa Cruz and the Altiplano, and this will presumably increase in the future.

There are other potential effects on the highlands from development of the lowlands which could be highly significant. At least some of the increase in demand occasioned by the higher total and per capita agricultural incomes in Santa Cruz, and higher per capita agricultural income in Cochabamba, may stimulate increased production of manufactured goods in the highlands. Another potential benefit is a supply of raw materials flowing from the lowlands. The importance of nonagricultural industries to successful development was well expressed in 1956 by C. H. Zondag,[30] who was not entirely pessimistic at the prospects:

> If Bolivia's plans for economic diversification are to be a success, industry and particularly those industries using domestic raw materials—will have to expand along with agriculture.
>
> In spite of all the talk about internal migration, it will not be possible to move a substantial part of its population on the high plains to the lowlands within the very near future. . . . As agriculture in Bolivia will gradually become less "biblical" and more mechanized, industry will have to provide new opportunities for those forces which will be released from agriculture.
>
> For the expansion of Bolivian industry there are abundant domestic raw materials available while the Bolivian worker shows great promise in working at manual and mechanical jobs. What is lacking, as we have seen above, is internal markets and an adequate investment climate.

Effect of the Highway on the Bolivian Balance of Payments

The agricultural boom in Santa Cruz is in products which formerly were imported. In 1950 sugar and rice imports were worth over $6 million or 11 percent of the value of Bolivian com-

[30] C. H. Zondag, *Problems in the Economic Development of Bolivia* (U. S. Operation Mission to Bolivia, 1956), p. 124.

modity imports (see Table II-11). Private imports of sugar and rice are now forbidden. Production in Bolivia of sugar and rice is currently running about $8 million annually. Total merchandise imports were between $70 and $80 million in 1961.

However, the net effect on the balance of payments of the Santa Cruz boom is by no means $8 million. Underdeveloped countries have large appetites for foreign goods, and no matter how fast new foreign exchange is released by rice and sugar crops it will not cease to be in short supply. Growers of cash crops have a tendency to spend much of their cash on manufactured goods, most of them imported. This means that some of the foreign exchange formerly spent on sugar and rice is now spent on rewards to domestic sugar and rice growers. However, some of the "rewards" are in the form of capital goods such as trucks which may improve the economy's performance.

It must also be noted that the protection against imports affects the distribution of income among Bolivians. The highland Bolivian, who now buys rice grown by a Cruzenian rather than a foreigner, may be paying a premium (as the necessity for protection hints) which the Cruzenian is using to import a transistor radio. On the other hand, the probable overvaluation of Bolivian currency in terms of foreign exchange tends to cause the import substitute to be undervalued.

Self-sufficiency in food is probably a valuable national political asset to a nation with as shaky a source of foreign exchange as the Bolivian tin mines seem to be, but the ability to finance nonfood imports is entirely accounted for by the increase in food production. To take separate account of the effect on the foreign accounts would be double counting.

Summary Calculation of Cost and Benefits

We shall use the internal rate of return as a measure of benefit over costs. In this method a discount rate (internal rate of return) is chosen which equates the present value of the stream of costs with the present value of the stream of benefits.

TABLE II-11. *Bolivian Imports and Exports of Commodities with Potential or Actual Importance in the Oriente, 1950, 1955, and 1961*

(In thousands of current U. S. dollars)

	1950	1955	1961
Imports:			
Sugar	$ 5,122	$ 4,046	$ 1,720
Rice	1,149	1,392	524
Edible fat	937	50	6
Meat	—	—	12
Cattle	1,967	4,330	89
Edible oil	968	561	333
Crude petroleum	1,484	250	402
Gasoline	334	1,063	5
Aviation gasoline	534	672	879
Lubricant oils	382	647	496
Kerosene	60	161	11
Cotton	615	1,501	334
Lard	905	1,180	2,575
Wood	496	N.A.	83
Vegetable oils	120	N.A.	552
Total, listed items	15,073	N.A.	8,021
Total imports	55,843	82,394	77,686
Exports:			
Rubber	979	661	948
Brazil nuts	153	369	1,563
Leather	1,019	359	359
Cocain leaves	385	191	191
Coffee in grain	—	59	815
Cattle	183	10	98
Wood and wooden sleepers	595	N.A.	394
Crude petroleum	49	N.A.	1,908
Gasoline	—	N.A.	227
Total, listed items	3,363	N.A.	6,503
Total exports	98,435	102,374	76,136

Sources: 1950—*Comercio Exterior* (Dirección Nacional de Estadística y Censos de Bolivia); 1955—*Boletín Estadístico No. 77* (Dirección Nacional de Estadística y Censos de Bolivia), pp. 49 and 53; 1961—Dirección Nacional de Estadística y Censos leaflets.

N.A. Not available.

In calculating the costs, we must take account of the fact that the benefits of the Cochabamba-Santa Cruz highway would have been smaller had it not been for the investment in feeder roads, in sugar mills, rice mills, and so on, which have been made in the area surrounding the Santa Cruz end of the highway. It is, in fact, impossible to separate out the benefits due to the highway alone and it is best to consider all of the investments as a cost "package." The cost of the highway and associated investment in Santa Cruz (without discounting) is estimated to be between $73 and $83 million (see Table II-14).

The next step is to estimate the present annual flow of benefits and to make some estimate of their future course.

Benefits, present and future, can be expected under the following categories:

1. *Net increase in production for which the highway was a condition.*

2. *Higher standard of living available to those remaining in highlands because of higher average (and marginal) productivity.* This benefit need not be explicitly estimated if one makes the simple assumption that production does not drop in the areas from which Santa Cruz is drawing population. (This assumption is implemented by not deducting anything from the estimated increase in production as in [1] above.)

3. *Benefits from colonization, excluding present production of agricultural goods included in [1].* The benefits from colonization not already counted under [1] are social and political. This makes it difficult to give them a dollars and cents value, and is not attempted here. It should not be assumed, however, that the value of these benefits is zero.

4. *Stimulation of manufacturing because of higher demand and raw material supply.* At present, this benefit is probably small.

5. *Balance-of-payments benefits.* These benefits have been already counted under [1] and the additional benefit over and above this is very low or zero.

The key element in computing benefits is to get a numerical estimate of benefits under category [1].

The first step in a numerical estimate of the current flow of benefits is an attempt at arriving at the Gross Regional Product (GRP) of Santa Cruz as shown in Table II-12. Column (1) of that table gives estimates of the value of production by sector. Some estimates were arrived at by collating published data on local production by type for those categories in which data are available. Other items were estimated by taking percentages of national totals, and some are rather sketchily based on transportation records. One source of error in the estimate is that no allowance is made for products produced and consumed by farmers without recourse to the marketplace. On the other hand, "other

TABLE II-12. *Estimates, Annual Gross Regional Product (GRP) and Portion Attributable to the Highway and Other Investments, Santa Cruz Department, 1962*

(In millions of current U. S. dollars)

Sector	Physical Volume	(1) Value of Production	(2) Value Added per Dollar of Production[a]	(3) Value Added (GRP)	(4) Approximate Value Added Attributable to the Highway and Other Non-petroleum Investments[b]
Sugar	49,000 metric tons[c]	4.2[c]	.85	3.6	3.2
Rice	24,000 metric tons[d]	3.8[d]	.85	3.2	2.8
Timber	4,329 thousand board feet[e]	.3[f]	.85	.3	.2
Alcohol	6 million litres[c]	1.0	.85	.9	.7
Cotton	3,000 metric tons[g]	1.5[h]	.85	1.3	1.0
Other agricultural products		1.0[j]	.85	.8	.7
Interurban road transport	11,000 round trips of 7,000 ton-kms. each[i]	1.9[i]	.66	1.3	1.2
Petroleum	500 million litres[k]	6.0[l]	1.00	6.0	—
Other Activities		8.0[m]	.80	6.4	3.2
				23.8	13.0

[a] Derived from the ratio of value added to production shown for 1958 by *Planeamiento, 1961*, Table 6, except for petroleum.

[b] See text for explanation.

[c] *La Industria Azucarera en 1962.*

[d] Publications giving (conflicting) production estimates include "Estadísticas Agropecuarias," Ministerio de Agricultura, La Paz, 1962, *Datos Estadísticos Del Departamento De Santa Cruz*, Oficina de Programas, USAID, La Paz, 1962 (mimeo.), and a CBF memorandum, *Influencia del Camino Cochabamba-Santa Cruz en El Desarrollo Del País*. The latter also gives a price estimate as do SAI reports, from which Santa Cruz prices have been extracted.

[e] From a tabulation for 1961 made by the Director Forestal for TAMS, reported in Eric D. Dodge, *Preliminary Summary of Bolivian Economy and Transportation*, Cochabamba, 1962.

[f] CBF, *op. cit.*

[g] *Ibid.*

[h] Price on United States markets used in estimation.

[i] Estimate.

[j] Estimated by the author on the basis that about 15 percent of the trucks leaving Santa Cruz for Cochabamba carrying food and raw materials carry cargo in this category. (See Table II-4.)

[k] USAID, "Recent Trends in the Bolivian Economy," (mimeo, undated).

[l] Estimated by applying to the estimated value of refined petroleum a multiplier equal to the proportion of value added by the petroleum industry attributable to crude production in the United States.

[m] The city of Santa Cruz has about 9 percent of the nonrural population of Bolivia. This figure is derived from taking 9 percent of Bolivian value added, exclusive of agriculture, mining, petroleum, and manufacturing.

activities" includes commerce and was estimated to be the same proportion of national activities as the region's population to national population. This category may be overestimated because the capital city, La Paz, probably has much more than its share.

Since Santa Cruz industries buy goods both from each other and from outside the Department, the values in column (1) include double counting of local productive activity and also include productive activity taking place elsewhere. Hence there is a downward adjustment in the numbers of column (1) made by applying the ratios in column (2) to get an estimate for each sector's contribution to GRP in column (3). The ratios were derived from the 1958 input-output table for Bolivia. The final sum for the 1962 estimate of Santa Cruz Gross Regional Product is $23 million, about 6 percent of Bolivia's Gross National Product.

Not all of the production in the Santa Cruz area is attributable to the highway and associated investments, so some of it must be subtracted to arrive at the gross benefits of the highway. In column (4) the amount of productive activity attributable to the effect of the highway and other investment has been estimated on a somewhat arbitrary basis. For example, none of the value added in petroleum has been included, on the ground that this activity would have occurred without the highway. Similarly, about half of the residual category "other activities" (mainly services of all sorts rendered by the urban population) has been excluded.

What part of the $13 million of the productive activity attributed to the road can be considered as net benefit? From the income side of the ledger, GRP, or value added, can be broken down into wages, profits, and depreciation.[31] It is a fair assumption that wage payments in Santa Cruz did not replace wage payments which would have been made in other areas of the economy, had the Santa Cruz developments not occurred. This does not mean that the men working in Santa Cruz are assumed to have been unproductive in their previous occupations, but rather that their place was taken by others who were much less productive or nonproductive, so that little output was lost on this ac-

[31] For purposes of this discussion other shares such as interest, rent, and so on are neglected.

count. A similar assumption can be made concerning profit, considered as a reward to entrepreneurs. Our treatment of depreciation assumes that a capital good could produce value equal to its depreciation in any Bolivian region, and therefore, an estimate of depreciation is subtracted. Another way of thinking about depreciation is to consider that the wearing away of (imported) capital is a flow input from outside the Santa Cruz economy, and that this stream of imports should be subtracted for the same reason that imported raw materials would be.

It might be argued that such items in the income account as interurban transport should show up as a cost rather than as a benefit, but to argue in this way would be to go against the logic of income accounting. The products which are transported include in their value the cost of that transport, but their production, transport, and final purchase mean that the benefit derived from them can cover production and transport.

The nonlabor part of the cost of upkeep on the Cochabamba-Santa Cruz highway should be entered as a negative item in our benefit account. Total annual maintenance costs are estimated at $333 thousand per year,[32] once past neglect has been made good. Nonlabor costs of maintenance are estimated at 14 percent.[33] These maintenance expenditures are assumed to be sufficient to insure perpetual life to the highway.

These calculations are summarized in Table II-14. The net benefits, which we have calculated as currently running at $11.3-$11.8 million per annum cover benefit categories both [1] and [2] above, since no loss of production in other regions has been assumed.

The benefit that Bolivia now derives from the extra-economic improvement of the lot of the colonists and from their example to others is difficult to calculate in a way which would gain general agreement. But, as noted earlier, the difficulty of calculation should not be resolved by the implicit assumption that the best

[32] República de Bolivia, Junta Nacional de Planeamiento, *Programa Preliminar de Transportes* (1963), Table 237. In terms of costs per kilometer, the Cochabamba-Santa Cruz highway is the most expensive in Bolivia to maintain, despite the fact that it is paved. Volume of traffic cannot account for the high estimates. (See Table II-13.)

[33] *Ibid.*, Table 158.

TABLE II-13. *Estimated Maintenance Cost,*
Major Bolivian Highways, 1963

Segments	Surface	Lengths[a] (Kilometers)	Estimated Annual Cost of Maintenance[a] (Thousands of U. S. Dollars)	Estimated Maintenance Cost per Kilometer (Dollars)	Mean Number of Vehicles per day in 1960[b]
La Paz (El Alto)- Oruro	unpaved	224	$109	$500	123
Oruro- Cochabamba	unpaved	212	85	400	140
Cochabamba- Santa Cruz- Guabirá	paved	555	333	600	135
Sucre-Epizana	unpaved	239	72	300	22

[a] República de Bolivia, Junta Nacional de Planeamiento, *Programa Preliminar de Transportes* (1963), Table 237.

[b] Computed by taking average density reported for various segments and using length as a weight factor. The basic data are reported in *Programa Preliminar de Transportes,* Table 191.

estimate of the colonization benefits is zero. The future benefits from this source will depend, of course, on the extent of the colonization.

Determining what proportion of the benefits from colonization of the Santa Cruz area can be imputed to the Cochabamba-Santa Cruz highway is difficult. One crude way of dealing with this question is to compare the success of the Santa Cruz colonies with those of the Chaparé and Alto Beni, where road connections to the highlands are poor. The available information seems to indicate that the Santa Cruz colonists are in somewhat better shape than those in the other areas,[34] but, of course, many factors besides the highway may have contributed to this result.

As to benefits to manufacturing and the balance of payments, little need be added to the discussion above.

Looking ahead, some trends in the flow of benefits can be discerned fairly easily. It is most probable that agricultural produc-

[34] A higher proportion of Santa Cruz colonists are reported in the Patch colonization survey as giving answers which indicate good health and a belief in the permanency of their present residence. Richard W. Patch and others, *op. cit.,* Volume I, pp. iii-xii.

TABLE II-14. *Estimated Capital Costs and Current Flow of Benefits of Cochabamba-Santa Cruz Highway and Associated Investments*

(Millions of 1962 U. S. dollars)

Investment	
Building of Cochabamba-Santa Cruz Highway	$50
Other Investments in Santa Cruz Area	
United States dollar aid[a]	10
United States aid given in bolivianos[a]	12–22
Trucks	1
Total (undiscounted)	$73–83[b]
Current Annual Benefits	
Net Benefits Relatively Easily Estimated:	
Annual value added attributable to highway and other investment	13.0
Less estimated nonlabor cost of annual upkeep of Cochabamba-Guabirá highway	c
Less depreciation[d]	1.2–1.7
Total	11.3–11.8

Benefits Difficult to Estimate:	
Colonization benefits	Now moderate, but potentially enormous.
Improvement in demand and in raw material supply for manufacturing industries	Now small, but potentially large.
Balance-of-payments benefits not included elsewhere.	Approximately nil.

[a] Includes sugar mill, rice processing facilities, experimental farms, access roads, industrial and agricultural credit, expenses of establishing colonies, etc. The source of investment data is *United States Contribution to the Development of the Santa Cruz Area*, (Program Office, USAID/Bolivia, La Paz, June 1962). This publication has some ambiguities concerning the size of aid in local currency. Hence the range shown in table.

[b] Except for the included investment in trucks, all of the investment included was with funds lent or given by the United States. Thus some investment by the Bolivian government, international agencies, or by private citizens is not included.

[c] Less than $0.05 million (14 percent of $.333 million).

[d] Computed as 5 percent of "Other Investments in Santa Cruz Area" shown above.

tion in the area will increase, although the emphasis may shift to other crops. Hopefully, the rate of colonization will also increase, but it is unlikely that labor in excess of a natural increase in highland population can be drawn away indefinitely to the lowlands without a decrease in the production potential of the highlands. Later, production increases resulting from migration of labor to the lowlands will not be all net gain.

One foreseeable interruption in the flow of benefits from present facilities is the shift of traffic to the alternative northern route which will connect Cochabamba and Santa Cruz.

Relating the "easily estimated benefits" listed in Table II-14 to the investment also listed in that table results in the "minimal" annual rate of return of 8 or 9 percent, a figure which might be termed respectable. This figure was computed by assuming that the annual benefits of 1962 would continue as a perpetuity and that benefits from the road in the earlier years were related to those of 1962 in the same manner as was sugar production. The costs were roughly distributed through time, and the discount rate found which brought the sum of the discounted costs and benefits to zero. This rate of return is "minimal" in two ways: it leaves out colonization benefits and other benefits difficult to measure, and it does not allow for the highly probable future increase in the stream of benefits.

Conclusion

It is usual in such discussions to compare the computed 8-9 percent rate of return with rates in alternative uses of the funds. In this case, such alternative uses might be investment in manufacturing, in mining, in social overhead facilities in the highlands, or investment in lowland areas nearer to the highland markets such as the Alto Beni or the Chaparé. There is, of course, no easy way to estimate what the results might have been, but it is probably true that the benefits could not have been realized quickly, and might well have been below the costs.

This leads to the general conclusion that, whether the road between Cochabamba and Santa Cruz was necessary and desirable for political reasons, it appears to have been a worthwhile investment from the economic point of view.

Larger questions were raised earlier about the wisdom of the "Aswan Dam" strategy of Bolivian development implied by large investments in transportation to the lowlands and in other overhead for such areas. It is clear that the most important part of the answer lies in those benefits which we have not attempted to estimate numerically. It is unlikely that by increasing agricultural production alone a country in the geographic situation of Bolivia can gain for its population a standard of living characteristic of even the poorest of the presently developed countries. If the agricultural development of the lowlands encourages economic activity in other sectors and social change in the whole population, this strategy will deserve to be called successful. It is now too early to tell, but some of the signs are faintly encouraging.

CHAPTER III

The Atlantic Highway in Guatemala[1]

MARTIN S. KLEIN[*]

Between 1951 and 1959 the Atlantic Highway was built to link Guatemala City with Puerto Barrios, Guatemala's major foreign trade port. In addition a new port was constructed at Matías de Gálvez, near Puerto Barrios on the Caribbean coast. The cost of the port and a major portion of the construction cost of the road were borne by the government of Guatemala. The remaining cost of the highway was financed by a series of grants from the U. S. International Cooperation Administration and by a portion of a loan from the International Bank for Reconstruction and Development.

The Atlantic Highway parallels, for most of its length, the tracks of the International Railways of Central America (IRCA). (See Figure III-1.) The new government-owned port of Matías de Gálvez is a scant three miles from the older port, Puerto Barrios, which is owned by the railroad.

The Background

Guatemala has the largest population of any Central American country—about 3.9 million people—concentrated largely in the valleys and plateaus of the highlands in the southern part of the country. Table III-1 depicts the population distribution in detail.

Its territory is mainly mountainous; the mountains that run through Central America cross Guatemala along the narrow

[1] This study is based upon field work in Central America in 1963.
[*] United Research Incorporated.

Pacific coastal plain and cover most of the south-central part of
the country. There are many high volcanoes in this area, and
earthquakes occur frequently. The northern third of the country
is low, tropical, and covered with thick forests. The rivers are not
generally used as waterways. Those flowing down the Pacific side
of the mountains are short, swift, and shallow. The only river of
any commercial importance is the short Río Dulce, which flows
from Lake Izabal (Guatemala's largest lake) to the Caribbean.
The climate varies from hot and humid in the lowlands to cool in
the mountains.

FIGURE III-1. *Guatemala: Principal Cities and Transport Network*

TABLE III-1. *Population of Guatemala by Department, 1961*

Departments	Number of Inhabitants	Major Cities	Number of Inhabitants
Alta Verapaz	263,668	Guatemala City	407,401
Baja Verapaz	97,077	Quezaltenango	50,750
Chimaltenango	165,432	Cooan	42,302
Chiquimula	166,365	Zacapa	41,786
El Progreso	70,537	Puerto Barrios	30,983
Escuintla	181,462	Mazatenango	26,120
Guatemala	624,734	Antigua	23,719
Huehuetenango	291,346		
Izabal	85,142		
Jalapa	109,120		
Jutiapa	209,989		
Petén	23,500		
Quezaltenango	253,704		
Quiché	247,823		
Retalhuleu	92,314		
Sacatepéquez	80,224		
San Marcos	322,155		
Santa Rosa	163,890		
Sololá	105,007		
Suchitepéquez	165,501		
Totonicapán	132,165		
Zacapa	101,783		
Total	3,952,944		

Source: *The Statesman's Year Book, 1963–64*, S. H. Steinberg, ed., (St. Martin's Press, 1963), pp. 1091–92

The economy is chiefly agricultural, and in its dependence on banana and coffee exports Guatemala resembles several other Central American countries. Coffee is the country's most valuable export. Cotton has recently replaced bananas as the second most valuable export. Chicle, and citronella and lemon-grass oils are also exported, while corn, sugarcane, rice, beans, and wheat are grown for domestic use. The chicle, as well as some mahogany and other fine woods, are the products of the forests, which cover 60 percent of the country's territory. Lead and zinc are mined, but are relatively unimportant. Manufacturing consists chiefly of the processing of agricultural products.

Principal imports are machinery and vehicles, textiles, petroleum products, foodstuffs, iron and steel manufactures, and clothing.

Previous Transportation Facilities[2]

In Guatemala, unlike other Central American countries, railroad construction began many years before establishment of the banana industry. By 1885, 20 miles of track had been laid from Guatemala City toward the Atlantic, and by 1904, 136 miles of track had been laid inland from Puerto Barrios. In that year the Guatemala Railroad Company was formed to lay the 61 miles of track necessary to cross the mountains and complete the link between Guatemala City and the sea. Since no road ran from the city to the coast, the railway was the first means of surface transport over the route. In 1912 the company acquired the Western Railroad linking Guatemala City with the Pacific Coast and El Salvador, and the company's name was changed to the International Railways of Central America (IRCA).

Completion of the rail link between Puerto Barrios and Guatemala City opened up for exporters of Guatemalan coffee a shorter and quicker route to markets in the southern and eastern United States and in Europe, while the Pacific coast area of Guatemala was opened up for the large-scale production of bananas. Similarly, importers in Guatemala received the benefit of shorter routes and more frequent service from Europe and the United States.

Beginning of Highway Competition

No significant highway competition developed in Guatemala until the early 1930's, when several trucking concerns began operating between San José (Guatemala's major Pacific port) and Guatemala City. Intense price competition characterized the industry over the following years, and the railroad was forced to lower tariffs in order to maintain its tonnage. Within a few years virtually all of the major truckers had either gone into bankruptcy or withdrawn from business. By 1933 it had also become apparent that the railroad could no longer continue profitable

[2] The material in this section has been drawn from Stacy May and Galo Plaza, *The United Fruit Company in Latin America* (National Planning Association, 1958) and from a memorandum prepared for the Brookings Institution by the International Railways of Central America (IRCA) in August 1963.

operations with its prevailing volume and type of traffic. With major obligations falling due, IRCA had no liquid funds with which to purchase needed new equipment. Furthermore, the continued survival of the railroad was menaced by the terms of an existing agreement between the Guatemalan government and the United Fruit Company.

Under the agreement United Fruit received concessions for the cultivation of bananas at the Tiquisate plantation near the Pacific coast, but was obligated in return to construct the first major deep water port on that coast. Such a port would have had dire implications for IRCA, which derived a major portion of its gross revenues, and an even more significant portion of its net revenues, from the long-haul transportation of coffee and other commodities from the Pacific side of the country to the nation's major foreign trade outlet at Puerto Barrios.

IRCA convinced United Fruit that it would be practical to ship the bananas from its Tiquisate plantation over the railroad and through Puerto Barrios, and the company in turn persuaded the government to release it from its obligation to build a Pacific port.[3] United Fruit then undertook to salvage the railroad from its financial difficulties. In 1936 the company obtained 42 percent of the stock of IRCA and invested heavily in banana cars and other equipment for the railroad.

Under the terms of several agreements United Fruit paid less per carload of bananas hauled over the line than did its competitors. It is beyond the scope of this study to determine whether the differential was actually justified, as IRCA claimed, by the low rental paid by IRCA for its banana-hauling equipment and by the fact that United Fruit assembled its trains for delivery to the railroad at Tiquisate, while IRCA was responsible for the assembly of competitors' trains. It is clear, however, that this policy, among others, led to a very pronounced hostility toward the railroad on the part of the Guatemalan public.

The Situation in 1951

The railroad retained its monopoly of surface transportation

[3] As a result, Guatemala still lacks a deep water port on the Pacific. At both San José and Champerico ships lie at anchor and are loaded and unloaded by lighter.

between Guatemala City and the Atlantic coast. An unpaved road had been built from Guatemala City to Los Amates but there was no usable link between Los Amates and the sea. (Figure III-1 indicates the location of the points mentioned in the text.) Widespread belief that IRCA was not serving the national interest led to plans for building a major highway parallel to the railroad. The Arbenz regime, in power at that time, showed a marked antagonism toward the United States,[4] and the government threatened openly to confiscate major United Fruit holdings.

The transportation situation between the capital and the Atlantic coast as of 1951 may be summarized as follows:

1. Through traffic and traffic originating or terminating north of Los Amates was generally confined to the railroad. There was no through highway. Air service was provided between Guatemala City and Puerto Barrios.

2. Puerto Barrios (owned by IRCA) handled over two-thirds of the country's international trade.

3. Local traffic between Guatemala City and Zacapa was handled by both road and rail.

4. There was a small and primitive port facility at Santo Tomás near Puerto Barrios. Historically this port had served the small community of settlers, largely of Belgian descent, who lived in the coastal area of Izabal Department.

Initial Proposals for Highway and Port Construction

In 1951, an Economic Survey Mission of the International Bank for Reconstruction and Development (IBRD) visited Guatemala to assist in the formulation of a program of economic development.

In its investigation of the single-track railway the Mission concluded that IRCA was nearing the point of saturation in its traffic and could satisfactorily meet future demands for rail freight movement only through the use of equipment with greater capacity or by expensive double-tracking. Furthermore, the Mission found that average freight rates per ton-mile exceeded those of many other countries and were possibly higher than

[4] IRCA memo to the Brookings Institution (August 1963).

they should have been. Among the causes cited for the higher ton-mile rates in Guatemala was the absence of effective competition. The Mission observed that even after the provision of competition, transport rate regulation should be implemented.

The Mission described the lack of a highway connection between the northern terminus of the Atlantic Highway (Los Amates) and Puerto Barrios as "the weakest link in transport facilities." It assigned a very high priority to the creation of a heavy duty highway between Guatemala City and Puerto Barrios as well as to the construction of a second pier at Puerto Barrios. The Survey Mission estimated the total costs of the project at $19.5 million, of which $17 million was for the road and $2.5 million for an additional pier at Puerto Barrios. The Mission's cost estimates were based on data provided by the Guatemalan government and were acknowledged to be at best rough approximations. The Mission did not attempt to develop its own cost data.

Construction of the Atlantic Highway

Between 1951 and 1954, some $5 million was spent from Guatemalan government funds for the construction of the new port of Matías de Gálvez.[5] During the same period over $15 million in Guatemalan government funds were spent on the construction of the Atlantic Highway. During the fiscal year 1955 (July 1, 1954-June 30, 1955), while negotiations were in progress with the IBRD and the International Cooperation Administration (ICA), an additional $3.1 million was spent on highway construction.[6]

International Assistance

INTERNATIONAL BANK FOR RECONSTRUCTION AND DEVELOPMENT. In 1955, the government of Guatemala applied for, and received, a loan of $18.2 million from the IBRD to finance part of the con-

[5] Source: IBRD.
[6] Source: Dirección General de Caminos, Guatemala City.

struction of the Atlantic Highway and the Pacific Highway and to finance an improved highway maintenance program for the country as a whole.

In its appraisal of the proposed highway loan in 1955, the IBRD justified the project on the following grounds:

1. It was needed to support and supplement the single-track railroad which was nearing the point of saturation. The primary function of the highway was seen as providing an alternative link between Guatemala City and Puerto Barrios and connecting Guatemala City with Matías de Gálvez.

2. An alternative mode of transport was said to be required because the capacity of the railroad was inherently limited by its single track and steep grades. The Survey Mission's report had concluded that raising the capacity of the railroad would require large investments for new equipment, lengthening of sidings, or the construction of a second track.

3. Officials of the IBRD felt that incremental funds would help to raise the economic potential of the large investment which the Guatemalan government had already made in the highway.

4. The economic advantage of the Atlantic Highway was said to be its ability to alleviate the delays which occurred on the railroad due to (a) the priority given to banana traffic, and (b) landslide and other damage. Also, the Atlantic Highway was seen as the mechanism for handling development traffic in the future although it was not visualized as primarily a development road.

UNITED STATES INTERNATIONAL COOPERATION ADMINISTRATION. In September 1955, the International Cooperation Administration undertook to provide financial assistance "in an amount not to exceed $2,805,000" (not counting $500,000 made available by ICA earlier that month). This sum was, however, only the beginning of United States assistance. During the next three years, ICA made nine additional grants to the Guatemalan government, totaling over $13.5 million.

The Cost Overrun

At the end of the first four years of work on the highway, expenditures on the highway and port had reached approximately the total initial estimated cost of the highway. The IBRD now estimates that during the first—Guatemalan financed—phase of the project the Guatemalan government spent $18 million to complete 20 percent of the work, while during the second—internationally financed—phase the remaining 80 percent was completed for some $29 million.

Causes of the cost overrun were several: inaccuracy of cost projections, an engineering design which created slides that had to be removed, and the necessity of more subbase material than was originally expected.[7] But, regardless of the cost overrun, by 1959 the project was completed. The Atlantic Highway and the port of Matías de Gálvez had cost almost $53 million, and transportation between Guatemala City and the Caribbean coast assumed the design shown in Figure III-1. For the first time in the nation's history it was possible for shippers to choose between alternate routes and modes of surface transportation connecting the country's largest city and its major port complex.

Highway Tolls

When the highway was officially opened on November 28, 1959, a scale of tolls was established for traffic on the road, over the strong protests of the IBRD, which felt that the imposition of tolls might discourage maximum use of the road and that in any case the revenue collected would not constitute a significant contribution to the cost of the highway's construction or maintenance. The scale of toll charges and the amount of tolls paid on the Atlantic Highway are shown in Table III-2.

[7] A prime cause of the overrun was the lack of time to make detailed estimates based on appropriate field work (such as surveys and borings). This, in a sense, was the "price of haste." Also, slopes were deliberately designed steeply with the intention to "let nature show" where flatter slopes were needed when slides occurred. Such design reduced initial cost, through savings on quantities of material moved. However, due to construction delays and the failure of the government to take over maintenance responsibilities, some slides occurred during construction, were removed by the contractors, and were charged to "construction."

TABLE III-2. *Tolls on the Atlantic Highway, 1960-63*
(1 quetzal = 1 U. S. dollar)

Scale of Toll Charges in Quetzals			
Section	Motorcycles	Autos	Others (per axle)
Guatemala-Zacapa turnoff or vice versa (km. 16–17)	.25	.40	.20
Zacapa-Puerto Barrios or Matías de Gálvez turnoff or vice versa	.35	.50	.30

Tolls Paid 1960–63	
Fiscal Year	Totals in thousands of quetzals
1960 (February–June)	43.2
1961	112.8
1962	118.9
1963	133.8
Total	408.7

Source: From the records of the Contador General de la Nación, provided by Lic. Ing. Victor Manuel Rosales

Effects of the Highway

Before going on to a discussion of the rapid and dramatic effects of the opening of the highway, we might first take a brief look at Guatemalan highway transportation.

The Trucking Industry

Most locally owned trucking firms are small. A few large trucking companies exist, several of which seem to have significant foreign ownership. A trucker, once licensed, may transport goods between any points in the country at any time and on such terms as he can get. The law governing truck licensing, however, is so complex in form, so cumbersome in administration, and so inadequate in enforcement that it serves, in effect, to encourage violation.

It is extremely difficult to obtain operating data on transportation companies. Most of the smaller firms fail to keep reliable data, and the larger ones are not anxious to release it. The trucking industry is generally described, however, as being in a chaotic financial state. Bankruptcies are said to be widespread but are difficult to confirm because when a trucker goes out of business he usually does not do so in any formal way or in any bankruptcy proceeding involving the courts. Instead, he simply sells his equipment to anyone who will buy it. Unlicensed operators contribute to a chronic overcapacity in the industry.

Road-Rail Price Competition

As soon as the paved highway was completed, trucking interests began operating to and from the port without published tariffs. They engaged in rate-cutting until trucking rates had been forced down to less than a third, in some cases less than a quarter, of those that IRCA had been charging. Beginning in late 1959 the price war intensified steadily, indicating marked overcapacity in the trucking industry. The Guatemalan government invested in a fleet of twenty large trucks, organized its own trucking firm (Atlantida) and led in the drive for lower rates.

The railroad generally met competitive rates. The major changes (see Table III-3) included reductions from $0.98 to $0.35 (later raised to $0.50) per hundredweight for the transportation of coffee from Guatemala City to Puerto Barrios, from $0.93 to $0.60 for the transportation of heavy machinery in the reverse direction, and from $1.98 to $0.40 for the haulage of general merchandise in local transportation. In general, rates on import and export haulage over the route fell from about $1.00 per hundredweight to less than $0.50. Table III-4 shows the changes that occurred in the railroad's operations between 1958 and 1962.

THREAT OF GOVERNMENT INTERVENTION. During the first years following completion of the highway, a combination of overloaded vehicles and inadequate maintenance kept the road in an almost constant state of disrepair.[8] In spite of its interest in the government-owned trucking line, Atlantida, the Guatemalan government appears to have considered novel measures to stop disintegration of the highway. The action considered, in collaboration

---

[8] As of September 1963, the maintenance situation had improved markedly. In contrast with the Ydígoras government, which lost interest in the highway during its last years in office, the current military government has evinced concern for both economic and military reasons.

TABLE III-3. *Reductions in Railroad Tariffs after Completion of the Atlantic Highway, Guatemala, 1957-63*
(In quetzals; 1 quetzal = 1 U.S. dollar)

Commodity	1957	1958	1959	1960	1961	1962	1963
Local freight (per hundredweight)							
Beans	.595	—	—	—	—	—	.40
Corn	.595	—	—	—	—	—	.40
Rice	.710	—	—	—	—	—	.40
Fruits and vegetables	.990	—	—	—	—	—	.40
Lumber	.515	—	—	—	—	—	.40
General merchandise	1.980	—	—	—	—	—	.40
Guatemala-Puerto Barrios export freight (per hundredweight)							
Sugar	—	.43	—	—	—	.30	.40
Logs	—	.36	—	—	—	.30	—
Coffee	—	.98	—	—	—	.35	.50
Puerto Barrios-Guatemala import freight							
Bulk Petroleum Products (per gallon)	—	.02¼	.02	.01¾	.01¾	.01¾	—
Wheat (per 100 lbs.)	—	.40	.40	.25	.25	.25	—
Fertilizer (per 100 lbs.)	—	.40	.32	.32	.32	.32	—
Iron and Steel (per 100 lbs.) bars, sheets, tubes, wire	—	.43	.43	.30	.30	.30	—
Tallow (per 100 lbs.)	—	.47	.32	.32	.30	.30	—
Automobiles and trucks (per unit up to 4500 ft.)	—	60.00	40.00	40.00	40.00	40.00	—
(per unit over 4500 ft.)	—	71.80	71.80	71.80	71.80	71.80	—
Bottles, glass (per 100 lbs.)	—	.60	.32	.32	.32	.32	—
Insecticide, agr. (per 100 lbs.)	—	.60	.32	.32	.32	.32	—
Groceries (per 100 lbs.)	—	.60	.45	.32	.32	.32	—
Machinery, not over 14,000 lbs. piece (per 100 lbs.)	—	.60	.60	.60	.35	.35	—
Machinery, over 14,000 lbs. piece (per 100 lbs.)	—	.93	.93	.93	.60	.60	—
Paraffine and stearine (per 100 lbs.)	—	.50	.32	.32	.32	.32	—
Chemicals, Industrial NOS (per 100 lbs.)	—	.60	.60	.35	.35	.26¼	—
Wines and Liquors (per 100 lbs.)	—	.75	.75	.35	.35	.35	—
Paper, Newsprint and Wrapping (per 100 lbs.)	—	.60	.45	.35	.30	.30	—

Source: International Railways of Central America.

TABLE III-4. *Change in Guatemalan Railway Freight Traffic, Revenues, and Expenses, 1958-62*

Operating Sector	Percentage Change 1958–62
Tons of freight handled	
Export bananas	−15
Export coffee	+27
Other exports	+20
Imports	− 8
Local	−46
Operating revenues	
Export banana freight	−24
Export coffee freight	−21
Other export freight	+33
Import freight	−22
Local freight	−29
Passenger revenue	56
Express and miscellaneous	−22
Port revenues	−18
Total operating revenues	−27
Operating expenses	
Maintenance of way and structures	−19
Maintenance of equipment	−22
Traffic	−13
Transportation	−12
Port expenses	no change
General expenses	−20
Total operating expenses	−16

Source: International Railways of Central America.

with railroad officials, would have driven the major truckers out of business on all roads serving communities that were also served by rail and ultimately might have *raised* the cost of rail transport to the users.

Among the measures proposed were: (a) additional tolls for trucks, (b) increased license plate taxes on trucks and buses in intercity traffic, (c) a 5-cents-a-gallon tax on diesel fuel, and (d) collection of tolls by municipalities. The tolls and taxes were to be so established as to force the truckers to raise their rates to the point at which the traffic would logically pass to the railroad.

These measures were never implemented. The press, traditionally free and unrestrained, learned of the proposals and raised a hue and cry which aroused public opinion and legislative debate. It is beyond the scope of this study to analyze the motives of the parties involved, but it may be noted that discouraging traffic seems a rather drastic weapon for solving maintenance problems. During the period 1955-60 the government seems to have vacillated from one extreme to another in its transport policy—from a policy of creating intense competition for the railroad to one of maintaining the railroad in its preeminent position in the transportation of goods over routes served by its tracks.

AGREEMENT AMONG TRUCKERS AND IRCA. In 1962 the price war took its toll, and all parties to the battle sought peace. In November of that year the trucking companies proposed that the rates to and from the ports of Matías de Gálvez and Puerto Barrios be increased to a level that would permit the truck lines to operate without an out-of-pocket loss. The truckers were practically bankrupt and would have had to cease operations unless the railroad joined them in increasing rates. The railway had approached the truck lines on several earlier occasions in an attempt to secure an adequate rate structure that would have permitted both the railway and the trucking interests to operate without actual losses. It welcomed such an arrangement.

Rates were restored to a "more sensible" level on February 1, 1963, but they were still much below that which would permit both railway and truck operators to make a reasonable profit.[9] There is no formal written rate agreement between the trucking interests and the railroad although one exists among the major trucking firms.

LOCAL TRAFFIC. The agreement among the truckers does not apply to local traffic, for which an entirely different set of ground rules is currently in effect. Railroad rates are generally about $0.10 per hundredweight less than trucking rates for similar distances in order to offset the cost of pickup at one end of the line and delivery at the other. Many shippers continue to use the railroad for carload lots, but since the opening of the highway, trucks have captured much of the traffic because of their greater flexibility of service. As

---

[9] IRCA memorandum (August 9, 1963).

is indicated in Table III-4, local tonnage handled by IRCA on its Atlantic route had declined by 46 percent between 1958 and 1962. Flexibility in the local movement of freight is so important that truckers have been able to set their rates without considering those of the railroad. At times truck rates have been as much as 50 percent higher than railroad rates for comparable local hauls.

Some of the marked advantages of trucks in local traffic apply also to short-haul export traffic. For example, most export cotton is grown near the Pacific coast and shipped via Pacific ports to customers in the Orient. Within Guatemala it is transported by truck.

Import and export haulage rates are fixed by the explicit agreement among truckers to which the railroad has tacitly consented. However, some undercover price-cutting has been taking place, and the truckers are somewhat dissatisfied with the agreement. The situation is in a state of flux, and it is not now known whether price-cutting will become so widespread as to destroy the agreement or whether the railroad and the truckers will maintain a solid front in their relations with shippers, thus facilitating future rate increases.

Influences on Choice of Transport Mode

The following factors influence the shipper's choice of inland transport mode:

PORT USE. The Atlantic port through which cargo is to enter or leave Guatemala effectively determines the mode of inland transport that will be used. Virtually all goods passing through Puerto Barrios move inland by rail, and trucks deliver and receive all goods moving through Matías de Gálvez. The railroad has not been able to negotiate terms with the government for construction of a railroad spur from Puerto Barrios to Matías de Gálvez to enable goods to move to and from the latter by both road and rail. Furthermore the government has a set of regulations designed to encourage use of Matías de Gálvez. The following are examples of such government regulations now in effect:

1. All commodities imported via the East Coast for the account of the national government or for municipalities must enter the country through Matías de Gálvez. This regulation also applies to material imported by firms operating under government contracts.

2. All East Coast imports consigned to persons or firms enjoying the tax and customs benefits of "pioneer industry" status under the Law of Industrial Promotion must be imported through Matías de Gálvez. This regulation, however, is not strictly enforced.

3. All exports of sugar under the quota granted to Guatemala by the United States must be shipped through Matías de Gálvez.

4. The Guatemalan government has established its own steamship line,[10] the "Gran Flota Centro-Americana" (Flomerca). The line has only two cargo vessels in service, but charters additional space in ships of other lines. When Flomerca was established, a decree was issued to the effect that all exports from Guatemala to the United States East Coast ports and to Europe must be handled in Flomerca vessels, unless the exporter obtained an exemption certificate from Flomerca. Flomerca vessels use Matías de Gálvez exclusively. In practice, the limited capacity of the line has resulted in the frequent issuance of exemption certificates. On the import side a unique situation exists with respect to imports of British origin. Officially, there is a surcharge of 100 percent of the duty on imports from Great Britain and Northern Ireland, but the surcharge is not collected if the imports are handled by Flomerca (through Matías de Gálvez). To date, Flomerca has not offered service from Great Britain or Europe, but has chartered space in other ships to handle such imports.

On the other hand, the railroad has been very reluctant to permit trucks to pick up and deliver goods at Puerto Barrios, which is physically unsuitable for large-scale loading and unloading of trucks.

TIMING. Export crops are generally sold, with the delivery date specified, to a particular ship at a particular port. The flexibility of

[10] Against the strong advice of the IBRD Survey Mission. Since the author's field trip was made, the line has been transferred to private ownership.

trucks has been an important factor influencing their use by producers of coffee and cotton. To date the banana producers have continued their exclusive use of the railroad. United Fruit, however, is considering using trucks for boxed bananas.

NATURE OF THE CARGO. Truckers prefer not to handle certain kinds of "dirty cargo" (such as carbon black) which may make the trailer unfit for hauling other goods. In other cases, the trucking industry has provided special facilities (for example, refrigerated trailers for frozen cargo).

SPECIAL SERVICES. The railroad is more flexible than the truckers in the use of equipment. Some manufacturing firms near Guatemala City prefer to import raw materials by rail because IRCA is willing to leave a sealed car at a factory's siding until a customs inspector can come out from Guatemala City to inspect the cargo and until the factory can spare labor to unload the car.

On the other hand, the railroad cannot compete effectively with trucks for the cotton export trade because the hauls are short and gins do not have labor available for loading railway cars. Truckmen select, weigh, and load bales for their account. Railway rates are generally only two-thirds of going truck rates, but cotton exporters will not use railway service. The oil companies still ship some petroleum products by rail, even though it is generally agreed that road transportation rates are lower. Some of the oil companies consider IRCA a major customer and have therefore continued to give some petroleum haulage business to the railroad.

Passenger Transportation

In Guatemala, as elsewhere in Central and South America, the distinction between passenger and cargo transport is frequently hard to establish, especially in the case of highway transport. For example, many of the buses operating on the Atlantic Highway carry impressive amounts of cargo on their roofs. Trucks, on the other hand, are frequently used to transport passengers. While the extent of this practice is hard to determine, the majority of trucks on the Atlantic Highway carry people as well as cargo. The passengers apparently negotiate their own financial arrangements with the truck drivers.

The Atlantic Highway has made possible increased speed and flexibility in the movement of people. The railroad has traditionally operated only two passenger trains a day between Guatemala City and Puerto Barrios. Rail passenger traffic is mostly local in nature, the average trip being about thirty miles. Similarly, until 1961, AVIATECA, Guatemala's national airline, maintained a DC-3 passenger service of one or two flights daily between Guatemala City and Puerto Barrios. Now, because of the highway, road transport has replaced air transport as the principal first-class mode of passenger travel. The Atlantic Highway must be one of very few highways to have the distinction of driving aircraft from the sky.

The air service required about one hour for the trip. It is now possible to drive the length of the highway in reasonable comfort in about five hours, and the express buses regularly adhere to a five-hour schedule. The trip by rail takes about twelve hours. The air fare was formerly $11. After the highway was opened, it was reduced to $7, but the airlines could not compete with the bus companies which began their services charging $4 and soon lowered this, because of intense competition, to $3 for the express service and $2.95 for the local. Railroad fares were, and are, $2.95 second class and $5.90 first class.

The current state of the bus transport industry can only be described as chaotic, with vehicles of every description operating along the Atlantic Highway. Some eighteen companies operate over the entire length of the highway, while at least eighty-nine others are licensed to operate over routes which entail the use of portions of the highway. Long-haul charges are generally fixed by the competitive situation, but local charges are determined by "what the market will bear." In some cases local fares are higher per kilometer than through fares, and in many instances they are appreciably lower.

Many passengers, of course, are transported in private cars and pickup trucks. The passenger traffic lost by the railroad has been

TABLE III-5. *Traffic Count at Garita No. 7 on the Atlantic Highway, 1960's*[a]

Year	Total[b]	Autos	Buses	Trucks
1960 (Jan.–Nov.)	183,352	84,658	43,996	54,698
1962 (Jan.–Nov.)	173,956	73,308	52,132	48,516
Average Number of Vehicles Per Day				
1960 (Jan.–Nov.)	556	257	133	166
1962 (Jan.–Nov.)	527	222	158	147

[a] The data are based on the traffic counts made by the Traffic Police at Garrita No. 7, which is located some 6 kilometers from Guatemala City. This point is between Guatemala City and the Toll Station at Kilometer 17.
[b] Does not include the following traffic:

	Bicycles	Motorcycles	Tractors	Wagons	Cattle
1960	17,274	15,051	1,916	752	13,875
1962	19,939	16,574	929	574	26,288

captured by a combination of private vehicles, buses, and formalized hitchhiking on trucks.

Such data as are available suggest, however, that there has been no dramatic growth of passenger transportation since the opening of the highway. Tables III-5 and III-6 contain all of the available data on the volume of traffic on the highway since its opening.

As shown in Table III-5, the average number of vehicles per

TABLE III-6. *Number of Vehicles on the Atlantic Highway, Guatemala, October 9-15, 1962*[a]

Type of Vehicle	Guatemala Km. 17	El Rancho Km. 81	Garita Peaje Km. 127	Puerto Barrios Km. 292
Passenger cars	2,416	1,589	1,684	1,137
Trucks	1,956	1,507	1,302	1,211
Buses	715	380	155	295
Total	5,087	3,476	3,141	2,643
Average Number of Vehicles Per Day				
Passenger Cars	345	227	240	162
Trucks	279	215	186	173
Buses	102	54	22	42
Total	726	496	448	377

[a] The data are based on a special traffic survey conducted by highway engineers of the Dirección General de Caminos, Guatemala, during the week of October 9-15, 1962.

day in 1960 did not differ very much from the traffic registered in 1962. Data on tolls collected (see Table III-2) also tend to support the conclusion that there has been no substantial traffic growth, although it should be noted that toll data do not include Guatemalan government or foreign diplomatic vehicles.

Entrepreneurship and the Movement of Capital and Labor

CAPITAL. The most significant *new* type of entrepreneurial activity within the transport sector has been refrigerated trailer service for frozen cargo. One major firm, owned by an American corporation, is currently operating this service between Central American points and Miami. Goods are hauled by road from as far away as Costa Rica, and the freezer trailers, each carrying 20 tons of cargo, are placed aboard ferry boats at Matías de Gálvez. Such exports, including meat, vegetables, shrimp, garlic, tomatoes, and pineapples, were valued at slightly more than $3.5 million in a recent twelve-month period. The company also carries substantial imports on the return trip and has recently secured an exclusive contract for delivery of United States surface mail to Central American points at a considerable time-saving.

There seems to have been little visible movement of capital as a result of the highway. Some commercial farming of garden crops (mainly tomatoes) has been started in the Teculután area to supply produce to a few canneries and bottling plants near Guatemala City. Other ventures include small-scale hog and chicken raising, rubber planting, and corn growing. Two efforts at resettlement failed because of the unhealthy conditions in the coastal area, indicating the need for investment in supporting development services such as public health, drainage, irrigation, and education.

LABOR. The road was not designed primarily to encourage specific labor flows and has not done so. It has neither tapped new sources of labor for the cities nor encouraged significant resettlement of agricultural workers. The resettlement schemes that have been started along the highway seem to have floundered because of a lack of supporting programs such as those mentioned above.

Land Use

RURAL LAND. In general, there have not been dramatic changes in land use along the highway. While it is extremely difficult to ascertain the price at which land changes hands in Guatemala, there is reason to believe that land along the highway, formerly valued at about $5 an acre, is now selling at $15 an acre, which implies some investor confidence in future changes in the use to which the land will be put.

URBAN LAND. The Atlantic Highway begins in the northeast corner of Guatemala City. With no formal approaches, it is reached by narrow streets, many of them unpaved and in very unsatisfactory repair. There has been only light industrial development along the part of the highway near the city. A few companies have purchased land and constructed factories, but many of the industrial sites are off the highway proper near the railroad tracks. Although there are some small-scale housing developments, no significant suburbia has developed. This may be due somewhat to natural limitations since extremely rugged terrain inhibits major expansion of the city toward the northeast.

Similarly Zacapa, which is located among small farms and grazing lands and is the largest town between Guatemala City and Puerto Barrios, has not changed much since the highway was opened.

Matías de Gálvez has evolved as a permanent settlement since 1955, when the new port was built on the site of the former settlement of Santo Tomás. It is linked to Puerto Barrios and the interior by the Atlantic Highway. Substantial development has occurred along the road to Puerto Barrios, and some minor roads have been constructed between the highway and the sea. The area inland from the highway, however, has remained virtually untouched.

Measurement of the Effects of the Highway

In this section we will attempt to measure the reductions which have occurred since 1958 in the rates paid by shippers for transportation services between Guatemala City and the Caribbean ports. It should be noted that such savings are not necessarily benefits to the Guatemalan economy, but are simply reductions in expenditure on transportation. While the second and third order effects of reductions in transportation expenditures are beyond the scope of this study, their existence should be noted. The extent to which reduction in such expenditures may fail to benefit the economy may be indicated by the fact that the IRCA is the largest employer of labor in Guatemala. In order to calculate *benefits* in such a situation, it would be necessary to know the use to which savings on transport expenditure were put.

Savings to Users of Transportation

A series of computations on savings to shippers indicates the following results:

(1) In 1962, the shipper savings on the transportation of goods between Guatemala City and the Atlantic ports for imports and exports amounted to some $4.6 million, relative to former railroad rates on the same tonnage. This figure is based on the rates in effect in 1962 when rates were at their lowest point in the price war. Shipper savings on local transport in 1962 are not included in the estimate since rate data for that year are not available.

(2) In 1963, the shipper savings on the same quantity of imports and exports were reduced to $3.5 million. The decline of $1.1 million over the savings realized in 1962 stems from the higher rates agreed upon among the truckers in February 1963.

(3) In 1963, shipper savings on local traffic amounted to some $2.9 million, relative to average railroad rates prior to 1962. Thus total 1963 shipper savings on 1962 traffic volume amounted to about $6.4 million.

The 1963 shipper savings were computed from the total 1962

volume of exports, imports, and local cargo, using the 1963 rates. Shipper savings on imports and exports were computed from data on selected commodities as well as from statistics on other imports and exports considered in the aggregate.

Data on the composition of exports by commodity and by port had not been available in Guatemala prior to this study. They were prepared by the Dirección General de Estadísticas in Guatemala City. Rail tariffs in 1958 and 1962 were available only for selected commodities.

These selected commodities[11] accounted for some 57 percent of imports and some 61 percent of exports (by volume). Shipper savings on coffee amounted to nearly 50 percent of the total savings on exports. On the other hand, the savings on specific imports which could be computed comprised only 8 percent of savings on total imports. Three factors explain the small proportion of the savings on the selected import commodities: for some commodities there was no change between the railroad rates in 1958 and rail/truck rates in 1963; for some others there were only small rate reductions in 1963 compared to the 1958 rates; and for still others the 1963 rail/truck rates increased over the rail rates prevailing in 1958. The bulk of shipper savings on imports and half of the savings on exports were realized from the rate reduction in unspecified "general cargo."

The traffic rate data on these unspecified general imports and exports are based on a series of assumptions as to the volume of such traffic moving over the Atlantic route and an estimate of average reduction in rates derived from local sources other than IRCA. Based on these sources a rate reduction of 50 percent from $1.00 per hundredweight in 1958 to $.50 per hundredweight in 1963 was assumed to be reasonable. It should be noted that bananas were omitted from the export calculations because the changes which have occurred in the user charge for banana shipments resulted from litigation and were unrelated to the changes in the transportation system.

The railroad furnished specific local traffic rates for only a small group of commodities and "general merchandise." It was as-

[11] Wheat, petroleum, fertilizers, paper, iron and steel, machinery, autos and trucks for imports; coffee and sugar for exports.

TABLE III-7. *Volume of Cargo Handled at Guatemala's Atlantic Ports, 1953-62*
(In thousands of hundredweight)

Year	Imports	Puerto Barrios Exports	Total	Imports	Matías de Gálvez Exports	Total	Total Both Ports	Matías de Gálvez Traffic as Percentage of Total
1953	4,182	5,248	9,480	—	—	—	9,480	—
1954	4,197	4,434	8,631	—	—	—	8,631	—
1955	5,883	4,392	10,275	—	—	—	10,275	—
1956	6,845	3,933	10,778	368	603	971	11,749	8.3
1957	6,666	3,930	10,596	208	680	888	11,484	7.7
1958	5,407	3,826	9,233	174	397	571	9,804	5.8
1959	5,953	4,434	10,387	772	285	1,057	11,444	9.2
1960	6,196	5,874	12,070	1,291	501	1,792	13,862	12.9
1961	5,914	4,833	10,747	1,435	578	2,013	12,760	15.8
1962	6,444	3,177	9,621	1,734	1,484	3,218	12,839	25.1

Source: Based on data collected by the Ministry of Statistics, Government of Guatemala.

sumed that a weighted average calculation of local traffic savings to shippers would show a reduction of $1.10 per hundredweight. Applying a set of assumptions regarding the Atlantic Division's share of IRCA's total local traffic indicates that local traffic on the Atlantic Division in 1958 was about 1,436,365 hundredweight. We have also assumed that traffic lost by the railroad since 1958 is now carried by truck and that no significant general increase has occurred in local cargo transportation. Local transportation savings will be overstated to the extent that we have overstated the saving to rail users—that is, to the extent that truckers may now be charging more than the $.40 per hundredweight charged by IRCA.

Although shippers have made some significant changes in transport mode since the highway was opened, rail remains the most significant means for transporting bulk commodities. Table III-7 presents data on the volume of exports passing through Guatemala's Atlantic ports since 1953. Since the opening of the highway in 1959, the percentage of goods moving by truck to Matías de Gálvez has increased from 9.2 percent of total exports through the Atlantic ports to 25.1 percent in 1962. Total traffic volume during the same interval has increased by 12.2 percent, but it should be noted that the total traffic is subject to some cyclical swings unrelated to available modes of transport. For example, the peak year for the Atlantic ports was 1960—a year of exceptionally high banana production.

It should also be noted that rail traffic moving through Puerto Barrios exceeded its 1958 volume in each succeeding year. The highway's major effect upon the railroad has been to diminish its revenue. In the process of adjusting its rates, however, IRCA seems to have succeeded in retaining its absolute volume of traffic, although its share of total traffic has diminished. Puerto Barrios remains the major Atlantic port, despite government efforts to encourage the use of Matías de Gálvez.

Effects Other Than Shipper Savings

As previously mentioned, the refrigerated trucking service handled some $3.5 million in exports during a recent twelve-month period. It is estimated that some $2 million of such exports were of Guatemalan origin and that this service, which is a direct result of the completion of the highway, constitutes a significant new source of foreign exchange for Guatemala.

It is difficult to quantify precisely the value of new crops now grown along the Atlantic Highway. Using only the tomato crop grown in the Teculután area for shipment to the canneries near Guatemala City would give a value of $250,000. No estimates are available for the value of the pineapples, melons, chickens, hogs, cattle, and sugar which are also grown along the road.

In addition, virtually all of the tomatoes and melons sold in the Central Market in Guatemala City originate in the Zacapa-Teculután area. Irrigated areas near Zacapa, north of the Motagua River, have converted from subsistence to commercial agriculture since the construction of the highway. After the highway was built, the south bank of the Motagua was linked to the highway by means of the bridge at Mármol. In this area, the added convenience of truck transportation, which is more closely tailored to the needs of individual farmers than was the railroad service, has spurred commercial agricultural development on both sides of the Motagua.[12]

Effects of the Highway on Passenger Travel

In a country such as Guatemala, it is difficult to measure the value to passengers of speed or flexibility of travel. In most instances, it seems unlikely that time saved is put to productive use. It is possible, however, that the availability of fast and frequent transport creates some travel not previously in existence, such as increased travel by farmers to urban markets. It is difficult to tell whether the Atlantic Highway has decreased the cost of passenger traffic. The cost of first-class travel for the complete trip from Puerto Barrios to Guatemala City has declined for passengers now using the bus; from $5.90 on the railroad to $3.00

[12] For the data contained in the preceding paragraph, the author is indebted to Lt. Col. Charles G. Markham of the Air Science Division, Colorado State College, who conducted research in the Teculután area under the supervision of Professor C. W. Minkel, after the author's departure from Guatemala.

for the express bus. First-class rail travel is virtually a thing of the past, and most of the passengers who formerly used it may be presumed to travel today in private vehicles which may be more expensive than bus travel.

In the case of second-class travel, the bus fare is $0.45 lower than the rail fare for the through journey. Through trips, however, constitute but a minor share of total travel, and it is not possible to determine whether a net saving has been realized on local traffic, for which precise fare data are not available.

Costs and Effects

Costs

The total cost of the Atlantic Highway and the port of Matías de Gálvez approached $53 million. It is estimated that annual maintenance expenditures of approximately $240 thousand will be required if the utility and life of the road are not to be significantly impaired. Estimates of annual cost of construction and maintenance of the road vary with assumptions concerning its life and an appropriate discount rate. The range of reasonable annual cost assumptions probably lies between about $3.6 million (a 40-year life and a 6 percent interest rate) and $7.0 million (a 25-year life and a 12 percent interest rate).

Effects

The major quantifiable effect has come in the form of cost reductions to users of transportation. Without further evidence of the uses to which the savings were put, it is not possible to characterize such cost reductions as positive benefits to the economy, but it seems clear that the highway initially achieved one of its major goals: reduction of transport rates through the provision of an alternative mode of transportation. In 1962, the users of transportation saved a minimum of $7.5 million compared to prior rates. In 1963, as noted earlier, the magnitude of the saving was reduced by some $1.1 million to approximately $6.4 million.

FIGURE III-2. *Proposed Guatemalan Highway Program*

Relationship of Costs and Effects

The dynamics of this case make hazardous any attempt to estimate a benefit-cost ratio. It may be that the effects will not prove to be real benefits to the economy. The shipper savings may be dissipated in the coming years if, in the absence of transport rate regulation, joint action by road and rail interests continues to raise transport charges. The first round of such increases in 1963 reduced the aggregate annual shipper savings to $6.4 million, a point well within the range of reasonable annual cost assumptions. It is conceivable that future rate increases may result in an escalation of rates to or beyond the level of monopoly rates formerly enjoyed by the railroad. While calculations based exclusively upon shipper savings do not take account of such indirect benefits as stimulation of agricultural production, encouragement of expanded regional travel, and creation of new exports (through the freezer trailer service, for example), it seems clear that from a benefit-cost viewpoint, the Atlantic Highway project as a whole was a marginal investment. From a conservative viewpoint, it is possible that the benefit-cost ratio in 1963 or any future year may fall below 1. A liberal calculation, taking account of indirect and scarcely quantifiable effects, suggests a ratio of 1.5, which is low by project evaluation standards currently in use. Thus there are reasonable grounds for classifying the highway as a relative failure. The future role of the highway as a strategic link in a broader regional transport network may, however, extend the reach of the Atlantic Highway and render this judgment premature.

Future Role of the Highway

Beyond the direct effects just discussed, the Atlantic Highway may play a key role in the development of the rest of Guatemala's internal highway network and in the development of the Central American highway system which has been approved in principle by the governments of the five Central American nations.

The Guatemalan Highway Plan

Figure III-2 shows the routes of proposed new links in the Guatemalan highway system. First priority is being given to the El Rancho-Coban link. Coban is the capital of Alta Verapaz Department, which Guatemalan planners see as a future "breadbasket" of the country. The road would open up for the produce of the area domestic markets in Guatemala City and export markets through the Atlantic and Pacific ports. A second step would extend the El Rancho-Coban road to El Ceibal and Flores, facilitating new settlement and making possible the efficient shipment of the timber, cattle, and produce of Guatemala's vast untapped North. Another link in the system would carry the road west from Coban to the desperately poor Indian settlements of Huehuetenango Department and from Coban to El Estor on Lake Izabal. There are immense practical difficulties in such an undertaking, which might make possible resettlement of the Indians of the West in the more fertile North and East—a favorite dream of Guatemalan planners. Another link planned for the region north of the highway would connect El Ceibal and Puerto Modesto Méndez with the Atlantic Highway and the ports, thus tying the central area of Izabal Department to the sea and to the interior. A final link in the highway system would be a road between Río Hondo and Esquípulas. This road would be important domestically in its encouragement of tourist travel to Esquípulas, an important destination of religious pilgrimages. It would also have international significance since it would form an important link in the Central American highway system.

Whatever the economic merits of the Guatemalan highway program, however, it seems clear from the Atlantic Highway experience that its purpose cannot be achieved without large and basic investments in such projects as irrigation, drainage, electricity, education, and public health. A carefully planned program of resettlement is desperately needed. None of these ancillary programs nor the highway program itself appears to be likely in the foreseeable future without substantial external assistance.

Conclusion

The Atlantic Highway cost almost three times as much as the original rough estimate. In the construction of the road, haste fostered errors of design and engineering which in turn increased costs. After the highway was completed, maintenance was inadequate, tolls were levied (against the advice of the World Bank), and the Guatemalan government became involved in a scheme designed to impede or destroy the utility of the highway. The immediate effect of the opening of the highway was to plunge the transport industry into a major rate war. The Guatemalan government failed to respond to suggestions that an independent regulatory body be established. Finally, the truckers agreed, with the railroad's encouragement and tacit consent, to establish a fixed schedule of identical tariffs over the Atlantic route.

Initially, the alternate transport mode reduced significantly the cost to shippers of moving Guatemala's imports, exports, and internal freight. Clearly, however, the duration and future significance of such savings will depend upon the degree to which the transport industry restricts competition in the setting of rates. While the highway has caused a significant increase in the transportation of goods by road, the railroad remains the dominant mode of inland transport of goods in foreign trade, and Puerto Barrios still handles three times the volume of cargo shipped through Matías de Gálvez.

In terms of true development effects, no magic has occurred nor was any expected. It seems fair to conclude that such development potential as the road may have is latent and may be realized only through the provision of supporting investments in other sectors of the Guatemalan economy: irrigation, drainage, public health, power, education, and guided resettlement. With the injustice of hindsight, we may note that had construction costs been significantly lower, some of these programs might have been financed.

Alternative uses of funds in other sectors might have resulted in a higher development "payoff." A retrospective examination of such alternatives is almost impossible, however, and it is reasonable to assume that other *transport* investments would have been no more effective, given a similar lack of supporting investments.

Some Lessons of the Atlantic Highway

While there is danger in attempting to apply morals from a unique situation to other cases, there are some lessons that emerge from the story of the Atlantic Highway.

First, it is surprisingly easy for a developing country to obtain foreign financial help and then go its own way in spending the funds. It seems clear that foreign assistance in this case was provided largely on the recipient's terms. Guatemala received a great deal of help from two major external sources of development finance, without finding it necessary to accept their suggestions concerning tolls, rate regulation, maintenance policy, or highway approaches.

Second, it seems clear that there may be widely differing motivations among the planners of a project. In the case of the Atlantic Highway, the prime impetus was the recommendation of a highly reputable IBRD survey team. Initial sponsorship of the proposed project, however, was the responsibility of a Guatemalan government motivated by internal political considerations and the desire to obtain redress of grievances against an unpopular United States firm. For example, it seems doubtful that the recommendation of the IBRD would have been adopted so readily if the railroad had been Guatemalan-owned. It is possible that the variance in the motives of the planners may have contributed to subsequent disagreements over such matters as tolls, maintenance, and rate regulation.

Third, in a developing country, neither the motivation behind a project nor the effects of the project should be considered as static. In Guatemala, the character of the government shifted significantly while the project was under construction, and the policies of subsequent governments have vacillated between an anti-railroad bias and an anti-truck bias. Current policy appears to be stabilizing at a point of moderation, and the railroad may actually be linked to the port built for the truckers. Similarly it is impossible to predict the ultimate savings to users of the Guatemala City-Puerto Barrios "corridor" as a result of the highway, because the future level of transport charges is not known. It will probably continue to be affected by agreements among the truckers and the railroad. The character of such agreements will in turn depend on such factors as whether the railroad is linked to Matías de Gálvez.

Finally, it is clear that transportation development should not be considered a remedy for other national ills. Transportation improvement may serve as an effective catalyst for development in other sectors, but if it is to perform this function, other elements must also be present.

CHAPTER IV

The Littoral Highway in El Salvador

LEON V. HIRSCH*

E<small>L</small> S<small>ALVADOR</small>, <small>THE SMALLEST</small> of the Latin American countries, has an area of somewhat more than 8,000 square miles—about the size of Massachusetts. (See Figure IV-1.) In 1954, the start of the period on which we shall focus, its population was 2.2 million, about 15 percent of which was urban. With its 275 inhabitants per square mile, it was then, as it is today, the most densely populated country in Latin America. El Salvador's present annual 3.6 percent rate of population increase is one of the highest in the world.

The economy is primarily based on agriculture, and coffee is traditionally the major crop. In 1954, over 37 percent of Gross Domestic Product was derived from agriculture, and two-thirds of the economically active population was employed in agriculture. In this same year, per capita income amounted to approximately $180. Distribution of income has been uneven, with 90 percent of the population receiving less than 50 percent of national income. Between 1939 and 1954, national income had risen by almost 5 percent annually, and with a rate of population growth slightly over 2 percent in this period, per capita income rose by between 2 and 3 percent per year.

Unfortunately, almost half of this rise in income was a result not of increased production but of enhanced prices for coffee, which in 1954 accounted for 88 percent of El Salvador's export earnings. Such improvement in the terms of trade—the relationship of export to import prices—does not usually continue indefinitely and, on the basis of history, a reversal was likely. In

* United Research Incorporated.

FIGURE IV-1. *El Salvador: Transportation Network*

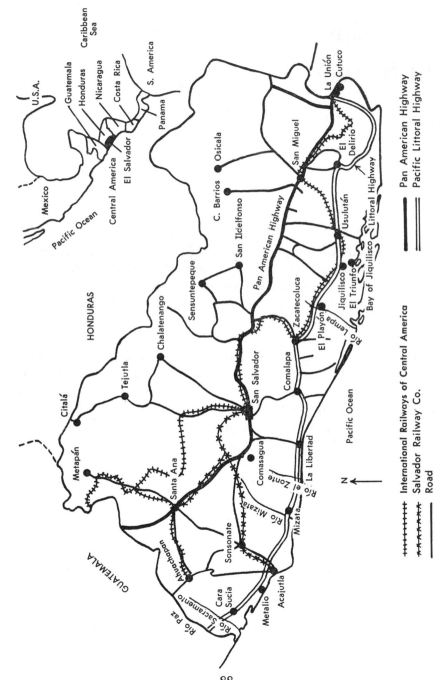

+++++ International Railways of Central America
✕✕✕✕✕ Salvador Railway Co.
——— Road

━━━ Pan American Highway
═══ Pacific Littoral Highway

88

fact, this came in 1957-58. To help insure its growth, El Salvador clearly needed to increase its income not only through price changes but more importantly through increased production and an expanded base for the economy which would lessen dependence on coffee. El Salvador had and continues to have a problem of unemployment and underemployment, and one of its major problems has been how to employ its growing population.

Introduction

In 1954, there was only one major geographic region in El Salvador which was clearly underutilized, the Pacific coastal plain, the littoral. One of the key problems of developing the coastal region was its inaccessibility. Some roads and one railroad served a portion of the area, but large parts of the littoral had almost no transportation facilities. In some areas squatters grew the staple foods of the country, corn and beans, for their own consumption, but much of the land was unused and unoccupied. A road along the littoral would open up this area to more intensive development.

The road which was eventually built, the El Salvador Littoral Highway, is most properly designated a developmental highway because it provided a necessary condition for development along almost its entire length. Furthermore, the vast bulk of its effects did not depend on its being a complete unit. That is, various segments of the highway could and did have development effects independent of other segments. Until 1961, the Littoral Highway ended in a virtual dead end at the Río Paz, which marks the El Salvador-Guatemala boundary. A large part of the road, particularly in the western part of the country, was not built until a number of years after earlier segments were constructed. Despite these facts, development took place on completed segments almost from the day the road was built.

This study seeks to answer some related questions about the El Salvador Littoral Highway: first, what happened, and why, in the region served by the highway; and second, what lessons can be learned concerning the development of the littoral which may be applicable to countries similar to El Salvador?

Background of the Littoral Highway

In 1954 El Salvador had one of Central America's best transportation systems, but there were obvious inadequacies. Of the country's three major regions—the northern, the central, and the coastal—only the central coffee-growing highlands were well served by highways. In addition, roads connected the coffee-growing region with the ports of Acajutla, La Libertad, and La Unión/ Cutuco. There were also two railroad systems in the country, the Salvador Railway Company, Limited, operating domestically, and the International Railways of Central America (IRCA), connecting the country with Guatemala. (See Figure IV-1.)

Around this time there was talk of enlarging and improving the country's highway system. Two major trunk roads were said to have been under consideration, one north from the capital to Honduras and the other east and west, the "Littoral Highway" along the Pacific coast. The former was later described as a "socio-political" road, the latter an "economic" road. Shorter roads were also being considered either as alternatives or substitutes for trunk roads. John H. T. Clarke, in a 1952 United Nations Report, *Inland Transport in El Salvador*, did not doubt the ultimate need for the Littoral Highway. However, he thought it might be less expensive and equally beneficial to construct a series of branch roads to the Pan American Highway instead of a lateral road running east and west. The 318-kilometer coastal highway was ultimately favored, however, over other possibilities.

Prior to 1954, transportation facilities were poor in El Salvador's littoral. In some sections there were no roads at all; in other sections, just oxcart trails. During low tide, the Acajutla-La Libertad beach could be driven on. Other parts of the region could be traversed during the dry season if one were willing to roll rocks out of undeveloped trails. There was a paved road from

Comalapa to El Playón and a passable dirt road from there to Usulután built between 1934 and 1940.

The El Salvador branch of the International Railways of Central America paralleled this road for much of its distance, connecting Zacatecoluca, east of Comalapa, and Usulután. The railway also connected Usulután with La Unión/Cutuco via San Miguel, a route to the north of the to-be-constructed Littoral Highway.

Plans for the Littoral Highway

It was originally estimated that the highway would cost slightly less than $16 million to complete, of which $11.1 million represented foreign currency costs. Implicit in the cost estimate was the decision to build the highway to primary standards.[1] This decision was based on the fact that in El Salvador the Pan American Highway was built to lower than primary standards, and its traffic density was heavy. It was felt that the country should have at least one major primary road traversing it east to west and forming a link in an international highway system. In October 1954, the World Bank extended a loan of $11.1 million to El Salvador for the foreign currency requirements of the road. The term of the loan was fifteen years and the interest rate 5¾ percent, with amortization to begin four and a half years later in April 1959.

The final cost of the construction which was originally estimated at $16 million amounted to approximately $24.4 million. Part of the additional cost was due to the inclusion of certain expenses which had not been contemplated when the original estimate was prepared. Furthermore, some complementary projects were added to the Littoral Highway program at a cost of approximately $1.1 million. Approximately $3 million of construction had been undertaken by the government before the loan was granted.

[1] Road standards refer to geometrical standards—the maximum degree of grade and curvature involved and the width of the highway; and also to the surface treatment of the road, whether it is paved or not, and its exact type of surface. As a rough comparison with U.S. roads, a primary class road in Central America is equivalent to a first-class, two-lane state highway; a secondary road to a good farm-to-market road; and a tertiary road to a good unpaved road.

TABLE IV-1. *Summary of Littoral Highway Costs*
(In thousands of U. S. dollars)

	Estimated by TAMS[a]	Original Bid Price	Actual Price
Preliminary construction prior to 1954 World Bank Loan	—	—	$ 3,021
Original project (not including cost of preliminary studies)			
Construction and contingencies	$14,262[b]	$18,552[c]	20,822
Right-of-way	40	—	negligible[d]
Local administration	750	—	2,244
Engineering	924	—	1,316
Total	$15,976		$24,382
Complementary projects			
Paving: La Libertad-Comalapa	—	593	635
Río Sacramento-Río Paz extension	—	—	400 (est.)
Río Paz Bridge (El Salvador's 50 percent share)	—	—	80
Total			$ 1,115
Grand total			$28,518

[a] Based on Tippetts-Abbett-McCarthy-Stratton (TAMS) reports.
[b] Estimate based on assumption that contractors would be exempt from duties and taxes.
[c] Reflects the government decision that contractors would not be exempt from duties and taxes as originally contemplated.
[d] No money was paid for right-of-way. The government provided only barbed wire (no posts) since the increased land values were considered to be more than ample compensation.

Therefore, the total ultimate cost of the completed Littoral Highway amounted to $28.5 million. Table IV-1 presents a summary of Littoral Highway costs. Foreign currency supplied by the World Bank for construction of the highway amounted to approximately $11.7 million, including approximately $0.6 million supplied in 1959 for the complementary projects mentioned above. Total foreign currency costs are estimated to have amounted to $18 million. Fortunately, during this period the government had reasonable resources of both foreign and local currency available for funding the additional costs of the road.

The original timetable called for completing the road in less than four years by mid-1958. In fact, the final segment of the road was not completed until January 1962, three and a half years after the estimated date. Fortunately, most of the delay took place on the extreme western end of the highway which ended in a near dead end at the Guatemalan border and so presented fewer problems than a more important link in the highway would have.

Anticipated Benefits

The primary purpose of the highway was to open up new areas of cultivation, making increased agricultural production possible. Previous transport costs were high because of poor access to markets, and transport in the sections remote from the railway was at a standstill during the rainy season. The result was that operators of large farms restricted output to those cash crops that were sufficiently valuable to support high transport costs. The small farmer was forced to survive on a subsistence basis.

The new highway, with feeder roads to be built by the government, was expected to alleviate this situation. With year-round access, the World Bank anticipated that production in the coastal zone would increase in value by the equivalent of about $10 million a year. Food crops and cattle were considered to be the items whose production was most likely to expand since these were the major products of the area.[2] In fact, however, production of these goods *fell* as a result of the construction of the Littoral Highway while agricultural output as a whole increased by several times $10 million because of the vast expansion of the growth of an unanticipated product, cotton.

The Bank also expected some subsidiary benefits from the road. Developing the littoral was expected to relieve population pressure elsewhere in El Salvador, particularly in the North. Along with migration, an independent peasantry might develop. The Bank also felt that the road might become an important international link between El Salvador and Guatemala and Honduras.

[2] International Bank for Reconstruction and Development, *Press Release No. 376,* October 12, 1954.

It was noted from the outset that more than the road would be necessary to realize the hoped-for benefits (or, in other words, that costs additional to that of the road would be required). The World Bank pointed out that the government would have to continue its efforts to improve health conditions in the coastal plain, to promote better land use, soil conservation, and production methods through enlarged agricultural extension services, and to facilitate the establishment of more adequate processing, storage, and credit facilities. As it turned out, little was done in these areas, although the private cotton cooperative did perform some of these important functions.

Changes in the Littoral Region

This section will discuss the changes which have taken place in the littoral region since the construction of the highway. This does not imply that the highway was the sole or, in some cases, even a major contributing cause of these changes. Other inputs, both material and human, were required. The costs of these inputs must be added to the costs of the road in order to obtain *total* costs. In the section "Evaluation and Conclusions," benefits will be related to the cost of the highway, its maintenance, and other inputs.

There is no official demarcation of the littoral region generally, or specifically of the area directly affected by the highway. An attempt was therefore made to define the region affected by the

TABLE IV-2. *El Salvador, Population Increases, 1950 and 1961*
(Population in thousands)

Area	Total Population			Urban Population			Rural Population		
	1950	1961	*percentage change*	1950	1961	*percentage change*	1950	1961	*percentage change*
Littoral Region Total—	395	578	*146.5*	138	196	*142.3*	257	383	*148.7*
El Salvador	1,856	2,511	*135.3*	677	967	*142.8*	1,179	1,544	*131.0*

Source: Census of Population.

highway through discussions with a number of people. From these discussions the following areas were included as being affected: (1) all municipalities south of the highway, (2) those through which the highway passes, and (3) those municipalities north of the highway which investigation indicated are probably primarily dependent on the Littoral Highway for road transportation. Only the Littoral Highway per se is considered here; its feeder roads are not. The reason is that this study is retrospective, and at the time it was conducted (early 1964), there were probably only very limited effects from the newly completed or to-be-completed feeder roads. A redefinition of the area to include the territory affected by subsidiary roads would be necessary should someone undertake a study of the littoral *system* in the future.

Population Increases in the Littoral

Although yearly population estimates by municipalities are made, these estimates diverge somewhat from actual periodic census figures. For this reason, it was decided to compare actual census figures, although they are available for only two relevant years, 1950 and 1961. (See Table IV-2.)

While urban population in the littoral grew at about the same rate as urban population in the country generally, rural population in the area grew at an annual rate approximately 50 percent greater than it did in El Salvador as a whole. The over-all growth of rural population increase was 148.7 percent for the littoral as compared with a national increase in rural population of 131 percent.

It is reasonable to assume that rural population in the littoral would have grown at about the same rate as it did in the rest of the country had the highway not been built. A not unrealistic estimate is that the total additional population in the littoral which the highway (not including feeder roads) has made possible is 75,000, since the highway was not fully complete in 1961 and since there is probably a lag in migration in response to new opportunities. The figure of 75,000 is equal to between 2½ and 3 percent of the entire population of the country.

Because the census was conducted in the month of May, it gives a good indication of the *net* population of the area, since seasonal labor requirements are comparatively low during that time of year. In contrast, around the turn of the year, there is a dramatic influx of agricultural workers into the littoral. Many come from the north of El Salvador and others, on ninety-day permits, from Guatemala and Honduras. It is not possible to estimate the total number of these seasonal workers, but there is no doubt that the seasonal influx has increased markedly since construction of the Littoral Highway.

Agricultural Changes in the Littoral

MEASUREMENT: IDEAL AND POSSIBLE. Ideally, to measure the agricultural changes that have taken place after the building of the Littoral Highway, present cultivated area and output should be compared with an estimate of what would probably have been the case had the road not been constructed.

Unfortunately, no comparative agricultural data by municipalities were available at the time of the study. When available, figures for the 1961 agricultural census could be compared with those of the 1950 census. Even had these figures been available, however, they would have left something to be desired since early segments of the road were not completed until 1958 and the final segment was finished only in 1962. There was probably a delay in response to the road, and therefore the 1961 census would not have recorded all of the effects of the road even in areas where it had been completed.

There are some comparative agricultural data by departments, but because departments run south and north, that is, from the coast inland, the available data are of little help in determining what happened along the east-west zone of highway influence. Also, there is some doubt as to the accuracy of the data, since different sources, such as the Department of Statistics of the Ministry of Economy, the Central Bank, and the Cotton Cooperative disagree.

This discussion of the available information should not be

viewed as critical of data generation in El Salvador. Although processing tends to be somewhat slow, the general level of data generated is relatively good. The purpose of these remarks is simply intended to give the reader some idea of the limitations of the information available.

DEVELOPMENT OF COTTON. Before the building of the highway, the main crops in the littoral were corn and beans, the primary food crops of the country and the typical products of subsistence or near-subsistence farming. These crops are often grown in conjunction with each other, beans frequently planted between rows of corn. Cattle used for beef and milk were also raised. Sorghum, cotton, sugarcane, and rice were other crops; rice was grown dry and mainly sold abroad for seed. Much of the land was not utilized or was underutilized and devoted to woods or pasture.

With the building of the Littoral Highway, there has been a striking and dramatic increase in the cotton grown in the region, particularly in the section from Comalapa to La Unión. Part of this region (Comalapa-Usulután) was served by a passable dirt road before the highway was built, and some cotton was grown here. The major increase in output took place, however, after the completion of the new highway. This eastern region is also well suited to corn production, but with the shift to cotton the amount of land devoted to corn has dropped sharply. In the littoral as a whole, it was estimated that the area devoted to corn dropped by half, although total output probably has not decreased significantly owing to improved yields from the increased use of fertilizer and hybrid seed.

Bean production in the littoral is estimated to have decreased only slightly or to have remained about the same since the construction of the highway. The main reason is that there was little dual cropping in the present cotton-producing eastern area where bean plants grow tall but produce few beans and that beans are still the major crop in the Acajutla-Sonsonate region.

Cattle production in the littoral has dropped markedly, as more intensive use has been made of the land previously devoted to pasturage. Output of the minor crops, rice and sorghum, has remained about the same. Sugarcane production has increased, but only a small proportion of the country's total output is produced in this region. The output of "Balsam of Peru," so named because the Spaniards wanted to keep the country of origin of this medicinal product confidential, increased somewhat after the mid-1959 completion of the Littoral Highway segment affecting it. Balsam grows wild in the coastal region east of Acajutla to La Libertad, an area too steep for crop cultivation. Almost the entire output of this crop is exported. Export figures from the *Anuario Estadístico,* 1955-63, follow:

Year	Quantity (Metric tons)	Value (Thousands of U.S. dollars)
1955	74.7	$142.6
1956	57.9	109.5
1957	96.8	198.7
1958	99.6	210.5
1959	116.4	251.1
1960	123.7	243.8
1961	106.1	198.6
1962	102.0	178.2
1963	109.5	185.9

In summary, the main agricultural change in the area has been a dramatic increase in cotton output, almost 90 percent of which is exported, realizing world market prices. Fortunately, from the point of view of this study, the vast bulk of El Salvador's cotton is grown in the littoral. Since national figures are available, it is possible to use these to make some quantitative judgments as to the increase in cotton production which the highway made possible.

Table IV-3 shows the growth in the area devoted to cotton and its output in El Salvador. Growth has been dramatic. Between 1953-54 and 1959-60 the area devoted to cotton doubled from 52,000 acres to 106,000, and production increased by 2½ times, from 13,000 to 31,000 metric tons. There was even a greater rate of increase after 1959-60, the crop year in which the Usulután-La Unión segment of the Littoral Highway, traversing land of high cotton potential, was completed. Between that crop year and 1964-65, the area devoted to cotton almost tripled to 302,000 acres, and output increased by more than two-and-one-half times to 80,000 metric tons. As can be seen from Table IV-3, the average price realized drifted downward starting in 1954-55. In 1959-60 it began to rise slowly, only to turn downward again in 1963-64. In

TABLE IV-3. *El Salvador Cotton Production, Area, Quantity, and Price, 1953-54 to 1963-64*

Crop Year	Area (Thousands of acres)	Quantity of Lint (Thousands of metric tons)	Average Price (U. S. dollars per metric ton)
1953–54	52.2	12.9	761.9
1954–55	73.1	20.5	734.1
1955–56	113.0	30.8	634.2
1956–57	94.8	32.4	617.5
1957–58	98.7	36.0	593.0
1958–59	132.4	39.7	517.9
1959–60	106.3	31.1	571.9
1960–61	140.1	41.9	584.3
1961–62	202.5	58.7	585.7
1962–63	231.4	72.4	584.3
1963–64	294.3	75.1	573.9
1964–65	302.1	80.0	561.3
1965–66	241.0 (est.)	67.0 (est.)	—

Source: Salvadorean Cotton Cooperative, Ltd., *Memoria* for 1962–63 harvest. Data subsequent to 1962–63 from the Cotton Division, Foreign Agricultural Service, U. S. Department of Agriculture.

1964-65, it was less than 75 percent of the 1953-54 price. Because of an even lower anticipated world price for the 1965-66 season, both area and output were expected to drop.

Most of the land south of the highway was and is owned by a few nonresidents in parcels of hundreds or thousands of acres. North of the highway the concentration is less pronounced although the land is still held by relatively few people. One estimate is that about two-thirds of the land in the entire littoral was held by large private holders, about one-quarter by the government and the remainder by small holders. Before the highway, squatters occupied some of the land, but for the most part it remained undeveloped. The highway, however, has not changed the pattern of ownership. What it has changed, as already noted, is the intensity and efficiency of land use, due, not to the owners of the land, but to independent investors.

The principal agents of this change were "agricultural entrepreneurs," professional or business people most of whom live in San Salvador, who rent land from the large owners and use it for productive purposes. Their activities have been described as "speculative farming by absentee investors." Recognizing the profit potential from cotton, these people began renting land in the littoral. Many of them are members of the growing middle class who supplement their incomes through investment of their relatively moderate savings. They have been described as sophisticated and willing to take risks and to spend some time managing their investments. Investments in cotton growing proved to be an ideal outlet for them, especially after the highway was completed.

However, there was some cotton development before the highway was constructed. Indeed, it has been suggested that interest in cotton caused the highway to be built rather than the other way around. But, as was the case in Nicaragua, the highway greatly facilitated this kind of nonresident investment and control by permitting easy access to the land. Part-time farm management became practical on a large scale for nonresidents only when people could drive in a few hours from San Salvador to the areas of production. There are many variations to this pattern, but the dynamism of the area must be attributed mainly to the agricultural entrepreneur who actively seized the economic opportunity opened up by the highway.

In all this the role of the cotton cooperative was also significant. The Cooperativa Algodonera Salvadoreña, Limitada, was established in 1940 as a private, nonprofit institution which by law has statutory authority to license cotton growers. It has a monopoly on the purchase, ginning, and sale of cotton. Licenses are freely issued. The organization pays for cotton on the basis of world market prices; lends money for seed, fertilizer, and insecticides; and gins, stores, and arranges for the sale of cotton. These activities greatly simplify the job of the potential agricultural entrepreneur and allow him to concentrate attention on one aspect of the business, namely, growing the cotton. Without being spared the problems of marketing, many small-scale entrepreneurs would probably not have the time, money, or ability to enter the business. This is true especially of men who participate in the business as a sideline.

The dramatic developments in agriculture since the highway, and to a lesser extent before it, have been spontaneous in nature rather than planned or organized. Various schemes of land redistribution and resettlement, provision of credit to small farmers, grain price stabilization, extension services, and irrigation have made little impact in the area although attempts along these lines have been made for some years back and are still continuing. The existence of agricultural entrepreneurs with some capital available, assisted by the Cotton Cooperative, represent the key to the dynamism of the region. However, the direction of development and the resulting distribution of benefits was different from that originally contemplated when the loan for the highway was made.

It is a matter of judgment as to what cotton output would have been, had the Littoral Highway not been constructed. However, a crude projection of the trends in cotton output from the beginning of the sharp rises after 1953-54 (see Table IV-3) to 1959-60, the year that those sectors of the highway passing through the most productive cotton land were completed, suggests that had this trend continued, output in 1964-65 would have been no more than 50,000 to 60,000 metric tons. Even the higher figure is 25 percent less than the actual output for 1964-65. It is therefore reasonable to attribute at least that much of the total output for 1964-65 to the highway.

In order to make an accurate benefit-cost calculation of production, it is necessary to take account of the capital and operating costs involved in its production. Furthermore, an indeterminate amount might be deducted for the decrease in the output of alternative crops. The calculations are based on a very conservative estimate of the increase in value of cotton production attributed to the highway. Therefore, this latter factor can be assumed to be implicitly taken into account.

Deforestation, clearing, and drainage are necessary to prepare land for cotton cultivation. This cost was estimated by the Ministry of Agriculture to amount to an average of $70 per acre. Presumably some areas did not require extensive clearing; however, to keep our estimates conservative, the full amount of $70 will be used in our computations. Where there is significant ground slope, a further expense for protection against erosion is involved. The Ministry of Agriculture encourages the building of levees, charging $7.20 per hour for bulldozer rental. It is estimated that protection against erosion costs an additional $12 per acre. Further investment is needed for physical construction—fencing, private farm roads, storage facilities, and other buildings—at an estimated cost of an additional $12 per acre. An indeterminate investment in tractors and other machinery is also required. Total capital costs to prepare the additional acreage that has been planted in cotton since construction of the Littoral Highway are estimated at about $15 to $16 million. Capital costs applicable to new production made possible by the Littoral Highway would therefore amount to about $4 million on the estimate that 25 percent of the recent output is properly attributable to the highway.

At the time of the study there were varying estimates of the operating costs of growing cotton. The estimate used here is based on average realized sales of $150 per acre with an average profit net of all costs of $25. A value-added figure per acre may be assumed to lie considerably above $25 since the opportunity costs of the land and labor would be below the costs actually incurred. Rent should be deducted from gross costs, since it is the actual or potential output of the land itself which gives it its sale and rental value. Because there is an oversupply of agricultural labor in El Salvador except during harvest seasons, it is reasonable to assume that had not labor been used for cotton growing, much of it would have been redundant. Therefore, on an opportunity basis, relatively little alternative output was lost by employing men in cotton production. For this reason, the cost to the economy of Salvadorean labor (as opposed to that of foreign migrants) should be calculated at considerably less than its market value. Adjusting for these differences the value-added figure is estimated at $100 per acre. On this basis the net contribution of cotton to the El Salvador economy can be put (in the 1964-65 year) at $30 million. Again, if 25 percent of this is attributed to the highway, the net value added (on the conservative basis of no further increases in future years) will be $7.5 million per annum. This figure is also approximated by taking half of the gross value ($15 million) of the output attributed to the road in the preceding calculations.

COMPARISON OF COTTON WITH ALTERNATE USES OF LAND. It was generally agreed in El Salvador that cotton, from the point of view of immediate economic return, is the most profitable alternative crop in areas agriculturally suited to it. As a rough estimate, its net return is 150 percent that of corn. It was stated by some individuals that in almost all cases it would be preferable to plant cotton and use the returns to buy corn from Guatemala where it sells for $40 or $50 per metric ton as opposed to $70 per metric ton in San Salvador. Furthermore, cotton has additional advantages over corn in that it is more difficult to steal, easier to store, and has a more stable market.

The opinion was expressed that the only reason that corn is grown at all in preference to cotton in some areas of the littoral is that it is a matter of custom for the small farmer to grow corn for his own needs. Furthermore, when areas of less than approximately 170 acres are involved, the economies of cotton production are not fully realizable. Very large cotton growers may also plant some corn and other food crops to feed their farm workers.

Despite the immediate economic advantages of growing cotton, there were some serious questions raised as to its ultimate value in some areas. A few agricultural experts, mainly from the United States, claimed that current high yields could not continue, at least not with present methods of cultivation. Current yields were said to be the result of bringing rich underutilized land into cultivation. With the deep plowing and deforestation necessary for cotton production, there was a strong possibility of erosion, and insufficient land was protected. Another expert felt that, while more land could profitably be protected against erosion, most of the susceptible land was in fact protected.

It should be noted that the problem of erosion is not unique to cotton farming, although because of cultivation methods, this crop is more susceptible than corn. Between La Libertad and Acajutla some hill areas are planted in corn, as are some areas of shallow, stony soil between Acajutla and the Guatemalan border. This land is said to be very susceptible to erosion, and according to U.S. agricultural advisors, it should be planted in pasture or timber and tree crops. Yields in this area are said to be marginal because of the difficulty of tending the land and the impracticality of applying pesticide to the sharply sloping fields.

Another problem of cotton cultivation is that lack of crop rotation is said to be depleting the land, thus requiring the provision of constantly greater amounts of fertilizer. Continuous cotton cultivation on the same land encourages the growth of insect pests and fungi, which ultimately might not be controllable, even with the liberal application of pesticides. One individual claimed that cotton output would start to drop noticeably after five years of intensive cultivation.

The large cotton growers interviewed are concerned with the problem of rotation. Much land had previously been rotated between corn and grass crops, but with the decrease in cattle raising in the area, grass crops, formerly fed to cattle, were no longer an economic alternative. There was some feeling among agricultural experts that corn could become an economic alternative to cotton if cotton yields started to drop since it was anticipated that there would be increasing yields from corn, because of the better use of fertilizer and the introduction of hybrids.

There are alternatives to corn as a rotation crop. Sugarcane appears to be especially attractive. In fact, it is said to be possible to realize a net return per acre in cane of as much as $115. However, cane can only be grown in areas close to the mills where it is to be crushed. A mill at Sonsonate, with a capacity of 92,000 metric tons per year, based on 24-hour operation for six months, was being planned at the time of this study. The mill will require that 1,730 acres in the region, much of it in the littoral, be devoted to cane. Over the next few years, cane could become a major crop in the area.

The raising of cattle in the littoral may again become economically practical. One individual who formerly raised cattle and who is now growing cotton stated that he felt that 300-400 head could be raised on 500-700 acres with the use of feed. There are also a number of other agricultural products which appear to have potential in the littoral. Melons appear to be especially attractive if certain problems can be solved. The cantaloupes grown in El Salvador are of particularly high quality and mature during that time of year when they are not in season in the United States.

Marketing problems with products such as melons are considerably more difficult than with staple products such as cotton or corn with established grades and an international market. Furthermore, to make melons economically competitive, the United States duty will have to be lowered or eliminated. Some entrepreneurs have already investigated the possibilities of the commercial growing of melons, but it is still too early to estimate the probable results. Other possible crops for the littoral are tomatoes, pineapples, safflower, castor beans, and cashews.

Shrimp Fishing

There has been a dramatic increase in shrimp output in the littoral since the construction of the highway. From virtually nothing before 1957, shrimp exports increased to almost 4,300 metric tons worth more than $5.8 million in 1961. In 1962, exports amounted to over 3,600 metric tons worth $4.5 million.

The shrimp was first put on ice and now is dry frozen. The leading producer of shrimp stated that the industry could not have developed without the construction of the Littoral Highway and that previous attempts to develop the industry had failed. The shrimp ports are not of the size or nature to permit large-scale shipment. Shrimp is shipped out of the country by three main routes: the most important is by refrigerated truck from Jiquilisco and El Triunfo to the Guatemalan port of Matías de Gálvez on the Caribbean Sea; shipment in refrigerated ships from the El Salvador deep-water port of Acajutla, and to a lesser extent from other ports, such as La Libertad, is growing in importance; some shrimp is also flown out of the country from Ilopango Airport near San Salvador.

It is not possible to determine the investment necessary and the operating costs involved in the industry, but a conservative estimate of the net contribution of the industry to the economy in 1963 was half of its total earnings of $4.5 million, or $2.3 million. This should be considered a net benefit of the road which acted here as a "bottleneck breaker." The shrimp industry also provides direct revenue to the central government which imposes a $.06 a pound export tax. Also there is a tax for local improvements of $.01 per pound, yielding total governmental revenues of approximately $500,000 annually at 1962 production rates.

An investigation is being made of the possibility of canning tuna and other fish, now practicable with the building of the highway.

Industrial and Commercial Development in the Littoral

With the exception of cotton-ginning facilities, there has been little industrial growth along the littoral. A major industrial development is presently underway in the Acajutla area to complement the construction of a deep-water port. According to the head of the port commission, however, most port traffic passes over the Acajutla-Sonsonate-San Salvador road and only a small amount over the Littoral Highway.

There has been a good deal of petty commercial development along the length of the highway. Almost every crossroad boasts of several small shops, generally selling food. According to observers, these grew up almost immediately after completion of the road. In some cases, as in that of Mizata and Cara Sucia, the shops are established in abandoned construction shacks.

The largest of these new commercial developments is near the Río Paz border with Guatemala. It has thirty shops and a gasoline station. There was little similar development on the Guatemalan side of the road across the Río Paz, but there has been some commercial growth around the customs house several miles from the river.

Recreational Development Along the Littoral

The region from the Río Mizata to just west of La Libertad consists of a narrow area of glorious black sand beaches and steep wooded foothills. Although there are small isolated patches of corn grown in the area, it is generally too steep for anything except the production of "Balsam of Peru."

The Río Mizata-La Libertad land was virtually worthless until the Littoral Highway provided access to it. One source indicated that before construction of the highway it was possible to buy an acre for little more than $5. With access provided by the Littoral Highway, land values have shot up astronomically. Land has changed hands at anywhere between $7,000 and $23,000 an acre, with most land being sold at $11,500 to $16,000 per acre.

There has been similar development in other areas served by the highway. It was said that some choice land along the Bay of Jiquilisco has sold for as much as $3.20 a square foot. In the Metalio area, small lots have sold for between $400 and $800.

There is no information available on the amount of resort-potential land which has been enhanced in value by the construction of the Littoral Highway. It does appear, however, that between 30 and 50 kilometers of good ocean-front land have been made accessible. The total area of resort-potential land probably amounts to between 7 and 10 square kilometers, somewhat less than half of which is in the Río Mizata-La Libertad area. In total, land values for recreational purposes have increased by approximately $20 to $30 million, as a result of access provided by the construction of the highway. If this very rough estimate is, in fact, correct, the increased value of the resort land *alone* has equalled the total cost of the highway!

The government has realized virtually no direct revenue from the enhanced value of the land. In late 1963 a very moderate capital gains law was enacted which would affect subsequent land transfers. There are no land taxes in El Salvador. There is, however, a very moderate net worth tax on the total value of an individual's holdings. Only 24,000 returns are submitted annually although it has been estimated that 75,000 individuals are actually subject to the tax.

Foreign Tourism

The highway should help to increase the number of foreign tourists to El Salvador and the length of time they stay in the country. Areas of tourist interest, such as the exceptionally fine Pacific beaches, are more accessible for one thing, and for another the Río Paz bridge completion has provided an alternate Central American road link constructed to higher standards than the Pan American Highway.

On the other hand, one somewhat negative factor is that border facilities are rather primitive for tourists. However, probably only a small number of tourists make the trip to El Salvador by road. The Littoral Highway will continue to act cumulatively with the other attractions of the country, and future tourist growth is likely, particularly if the Central American countries act as a group to promote it.

Education

Intensive investigation disclosed no stated or apparent changes either in educational facilities or in educational measures, such as literacy training, in the littoral. In recent years, the rate of literacy has grown most rapidly *outside* the littoral. There is no reliable comparative information on actual school enrollment, as a proportion of the total potential, by municipalities. The enhanced opportunity for movement concurrent with construction of the highway might be presumed to act to broaden the outlook of the population and contribute to the dispersion of ideas, but evidence of such changes were not found.

Health

In the area of health the highway has helped increase the effectiveness of an antimalarial program and the provision of health services to isolated communities.

Areas of El Salvador below the 100- to 200-meter level, which include most of the littoral, are subject to malaria. As an indication of the endemic nature of this disease, at one time 70 percent of the inhabitants of Acajutla had malaria. The settlement of El Delirio (The Delirious) received its name from the effects the disease has on its victims.

In 1949 a malaria control program was started with international help. In 1956 it was extended to cover all susceptible regions of the country. Control of malaria helped make the job of building the Littoral Highway easier and was an important factor in making development of the region practicable.

Conversely, the building of the road made possible a change from a malarial *control* program to one of *eradication,* and in 1957 such an expansion in the antimalarial program was undertaken. In fact, the first vehicle to travel over the Acajutla-Río Paz segment of the Littoral Highway was a UNICEF DDT truck. Although most malaria mobile units can travel over poor roads, road improvement has contributed greatly to the effectiveness of the antimalarial operation.

At present, less than 3 percent of the population in the previously endemic malarial areas are affected by the disease, and this figure includes those who have had relapses after contracting the disease many years ago. In other malaria-susceptible areas along the highway, less than 1 percent are affected. A total of approximately 15,000 Salvadoreans are estimated to be affected by the disease at present. In the late 1940's, approximately 3,000 people a year died of malaria; in 1953, 1,000; and at present, only 450. An interesting sidelight of cotton development in the littoral is that the insecticides used in cotton cultivation also kill the anopheles mosquitos which carry the malaria parasite.

Foreign Exchange

Up until the present time, El Salvador's foreign exchange position has always reflected the vagaries of one or a limited number of agricultural crops. El Salvador, at least until recently, has been a country characterized by monoculture. The country was originally a leading exporter of indigo, and its economy was based on this crop until demand for it was replaced by synthetic dyes developed during the first World War. At that time the coffee plant had been introduced from Brazil, and in 1926 this product began to be the dominant element in the country's export trade; it continues to maintain this position. When the coffee market was good, things were very good for El Salvador. However, in 1957-58, world prices for coffee dropped. Coffee exports as a percentage value of all exports fell from 79 percent in 1957 to 48 percent in 1963. Had cotton production not increased at about this same time to become the country's second largest foreign exchange earner, El Salvador would have been in a very weak financial position. Cotton exports rose from 11 percent to 24 percent during this same period, thus helping to redress the unfavorable foreign exchange balance. In addition to cotton, shrimp has also become an important source of foreign exchange. Development of other crops in the littoral, such as sugar, will mean that the region will continue to contribute to El Salvador's balance of payments. It is difficult to quantify the favorable foreign exchange effect of the Littoral Highway, but there is no doubt as to its importance.

Traffic on the Littoral Highway

Traffic is, of course, related to the character and amount of population and economic changes in the region. The mistake should not be made, as has been done by some individuals in El Salvador, of assuming that the Littoral Highway is "no good" because traffic on it is light, particularly over the newer segments of the road. A *development* highway should be judged by the development it has helped cause in the region it serves, not by the traffic passing over it per se. As an extreme example, a road may have to be built to give access to a gold mine. Even if only one truckload of gold passes over the road each month, the road may still have been more than justified.

Traffic Counts

There have been very few traffic counts made in El Salvador. This, as well as limited cost data, make it impossible to calculate user benefits even for that part of the littoral which had transportation facilities prior to the highway's construction. Traffic counts were made during the last five months of 1959 and again in 1962. The average daily and Sunday traffic in 1959 traveling over various segments of the highway between Comalapa and La Unión was as follows: traffic through Zacatecoluca averaged 653 vehicles on weekdays and 698 on Sundays; through Usulután, 390 on weekdays, 408 on Sundays; and into La Unión, 298 on weekdays and 291 on Sundays. Not all the traffic into La Unión came from the Littoral Highway; an undetermined part came from the Pan American Highway.

The 1962 count is not directly comparable to the first because the checkpoints differed and because the counting was done by machine rather than by hand tally. As far as can be estimated from the noncomparable data, traffic on the Littoral Highway in the Zacatecoluca area increased by about one-third; that through Usulután, by approximately three times; and that to La Unión, by about 60 percent, a considerably greater percentage increase than appears to have taken place on the Pan American Highway. Despite this traffic growth, volume to date has not been great enough to justify primary design standards on the El Delirio-La Unión or possibly on the Acajutla-La Libertad and the La Libertad-Comalapa sections.

Future traffic growth is difficult to predict, but it is estimated in the feasibility report for the El Salvador National Highway Program that it will increase at an annual rate of 9 percent.

Composition of the Traffic

The traffic counts do not break down traffic in terms of its composition, and insufficient data are available from which to estimate the vehicle miles traveled for each component. It is generally estimated that 20 percent of all traffic is heavy buses and trucks.

BUSES. The Transport Department of the Ministry of Economy regulates the bus system of El Salvador by franchising routes and fixing prices. To determine whether a route over a new or existing road is practical, the Department makes an economic investigation of the number of people who will be served, the general demand for trips, and the demand for school trips. The financial requirements for servicing a route can be relatively small, and there has been no shortage of applicants for franchises. Most operators serve only a single route, although there are some very significant large operators.

Bus service on the littoral appears to be excellent. Service was instituted as soon as sections of the road were completed and has grown with demand. It is estimated that service has increased by 50 percent since the segments of the highway were built.

According to the Transport Department, the maximum prices which it sets are not based on an exact formula but are established in comparison with long-standing established rates on other routes.

For large buses that hold from thirty to sixty passengers, rates per 100 passenger-kilometers ranged from approximately $.50 for ordinary buses making many stops, to $.70 for buses making limited stops. Smaller vehicles, such as station wagons of eight-ten passenger capacity, charged between $.80 and $1.20 per 100 passenger-kilometers, depending on the number of stops they made and whether they provided door-to-door service. These rates are all for transit over paved roads. There is also some small-vehicle service over poorer class unpaved roads, at rates about double those over paved roads. All these rates appear quite low when compared with estimates of the cost of providing service.

TRUCKS. In contrast to buses, there is no government regulation of trucks (although there are rumors that it may be initiated), and information on operations is difficult to obtain. In El Salvador, there are only four or five medium or large operators and a host of small entrepreneurs who usually own only one or a small number of trucks. These small operators are often combination haulers and entrepreneurs, buying and selling for their own account the products they carry.

One large trucker serves the International Railways of Central America, and the others are mainly capital-to-port operators. As such, they use the Littoral Highway only incidentally. The only major trucker which appears to make significant use of the Littoral Highway is Tragua. This international line transports shrimp from the El Triunfo—Bay of Jiquilisco area along the Littoral Highway into Guatemala, where it is shipped out through the Caribbean port of Matías de Gálvez.

Truck charges appear to vary widely, depending on the nature of the operator, the type and amount of goods hauled, the distance traveled, and the quality of the road. Some small operators may at times price on the basis of their variable costs only. Over good roads, they may charge as little as $0.022 per metric ton-kilometer and go bankrupt in the process. Low rates are charged primarily during the months of April to October (the season known as "winter" in Central America). At this time, as opposed to the summer, there is no heavy demand for the shipment of harvested crops. More usual charges over good roads are between $0.032 and $0.06 per ton-kilometer, the variation due to the type of goods carried and the distance traveled.

Rates over poorer roads vary. For mediocre but paved roads, rates average about 30 percent higher than those charged over good paved roads. Charges for transport over unpaved roads amount to about $0.11 per ton-kilometer, about double that over good paved roads. For Central America as a whole, it was said that tariffs as high as $0.25 per ton-kilometer were charged for transport over roads passable only by jeep or truck.

The Central American Research Institute for Industry (ICAITI) has made a detailed study of costs and tariffs for all types of transport in the various countries of Central America, but the information has not been made public.

Other Modes of Transportation

Oxcarts are frequently seen on the Littoral Highway. Operator costs, including imputed costs, of haulage by oxcart are said to range between $0.13 and $0.24 per ton-kilometer, considerably higher than the costs of truck operation.

There has been little intercoastal shipping among El Salvador's three ports or with the Pacific ports of other Central American countries.

The International Railways of Central America connects San Salvador with Zacatecoluca and then runs parallel to the Littoral Highway to Usulután. It connects Usulután and La Unión/Cutuco; however, it passes through San Miguel rather than running along the coast as does the highway.

An official of the railway stated that competition with road transportation began, not when the highway was completed, but in 1939, when the Río Lempa between Zacatecoluca and Usulután was bridged. He claimed that the Littoral Highway actually has helped the railroad over-all, rather than, as happened with Guatemala's Atlantic Highway, significantly hurting it.

The official stated that railroad passenger traffic over the entire length of the El Salvador line has dropped by 22 percent in recent years, mainly because of competition with bus lines operating on the Littoral Highway. The officials' statement would, of course, mean that the loss was significantly greater over those areas directly competitive with the highway.

The railroad now carries about 2 million passengers a year, only 2,000 of whom travel first class. Rates are $0.75 per 100 passenger-kilometers for second class and double that for first class. Passenger tariffs on the railroad have been the same for the past decade. Rates for buses are set by the Transport Department on the basis of railroad fares. Buses have the advantage of much quicker running times and center-to-center travel, but the railroad offers good and reliable service and is seldom late.

Although passenger traffic on IRCA has dropped, freight and, as a consequence, profits seem to have held up very well. Freight is carried both by second-class trains and by extras. Although rail data were not divulged, figures of rail traffic in thousands of ton-kilometers developed by Salzgitter Industriebau GMBH for the Port of Acajutla Commission, as shown below, appear to bear out unofficial reports:

Year	Local Service	Exports	Imports	Total
1957	23,375	14,780	39,226	77,381
1958	21,516	18,364	43,079	84,158
1959	19,394	20,131	42,271	81,796
1960	16,242	24,308	46,632	87,182
1961	11,217	22,133	43,449	76,799
1962	13,171	30,640	39,646	83,458

The reason the Littoral Highway was said to have helped, or at least not to have hurt, the railroad is related to the expansion of the cotton crop. Before the completion of the highway, both raw and bulk cotton was transported to and from gins by the railroad. Now, almost all raw cotton moves by truck to the gins which are almost all located both on a highway and on rail lines. Virtually all baled cotton, however, is shipped out by railroad through the port of La Unión/Cutuco. The great expansion in cotton production means that, although the railroad's share of the cotton traffic has dropped by about half, the actual amount carried has risen. Futhermore, fertilizer imports have increased markedly; because most is shipped by rail, the railroad has benefited.

Because of limited information and the wide variety of different tariffs, it was not possible to compare truck and railroad rates. The railroad appears to have an advantage only for relatively large, long-distance line-haul shipments. Like passenger rates, freight rates have not changed significantly in the past decade.

Foreign Trade over the Highway

The Littoral Highway should not be considered merely in its national context, but, equally important, as part of a Central

American regional road network. There is no doubt as to the value of economic integration to Central America because small national markets do not permit economies of scale in many industries and because integration allows each country to produce the goods for which it is best suited. Highways contribute to such integration by their very existence, but no quantitative measure has been made of such a contribution. This section will discuss what is known about trade between El Salvador and its nearest neighbors, Guatemala and Honduras.

With the completion of the Río Paz link in 1962 there was a dramatic shift in both import and export trade to Guatemala from the Pan American Highway to the Littoral Highway as shown in Table IV-4.

TABLE IV-4. *Goods Traffic by Road Between El Salvador and Guatemala*

(In thousands of metric tons)

Year	To El Salvador	From El Salvador	Total
1960[a]	35.8	10.3	46.1
1961[a]	52.9	13.4	66.3
1962	44.5 { 11.5 Pan American / 33.0 Littoral[b]	13.8 { 1.3 Pan American / 12.5 Littoral[b]	58.3 { 12.8 Pan American / 45.5 Littoral[b]
1963	77.5 { 13.1 Pan American / 64.4 Littoral	21.1 { 1.5 Pan American / 19.6 Littoral	98.6 { 14.6 Pan American / 84.0 Littoral

Source: *Anuario Estadístico*, 1963, Vol. 1, pp. 8–9.
[a] All traffic in 1960 and 1961 was on the Pan American Highway.
[b] The Littoral link was open only for the last eight months of 1962.

During its first full year of operation, the Littoral Highway attracted 85 percent of the Guatemalan traffic. While the distance from San Salvador to Guatemala City over the new highway is 22 kilometers longer than the old route, it is preferred to the Pan American Highway because of its higher standards. This trend to use the Littoral in preference to the Pan American Highway will be maintained at least until the standards of the Pan American Highway are improved to conform to those of the Littoral Highway.

There has been a dramatic increase in *total* traffic between El Salvador and Guatemala, part of which is no doubt due to the new highway.

At its eastern end, the Littoral Highway connects with an extension of the Pan American Highway near La Unión. Cutuco, the port of La Unión, is a railroad port—goods arriving by truck have to be loaded on railroad cars to be taken onto the pier because there is no direct road access. Therefore, it is not surprising that the Littoral Highway has had no discernible effect on imports and exports through this port.

Because all traffic on the Littoral Highway bound for Honduras would have to make the last part of its journey over the Pan American Highway, it is not possible to estimate the amount of

TABLE IV-5. *Goods Traffic by Road Between El Salvador and Honduras*[a]

(In thousands of metric tons)

Year	To El Salvador	From El Salvador	Total
1953	12.4	5.0	17.4
1954	21.6	9.0	30.6
1955	10.2	11.2	21.4
1956	28.0	10.2	38.2
1957	25.5	15.7	41.2
1958	30.2	24.3	54.5
1959	52.4	28.4	80.8
1960	49.7	24.4	74.1
1961	47.4	29.5	76.9
1962	82.5	37.3	119.8
1963	75.5	39.3	114.8

Source: *Anuario Estadístico*, 1963, Vol. 1, pp. 8–9.
[a] Amatillo checkpoint on the Pan American Highway.

traffic that might have been diverted to the newer highway from the older. No comparable information over a given time period is available from the traffic counts discussed earlier. In total, traffic to Honduras increased as various segments of the eastern part of the highway were completed in 1957 through 1959, as shown in Table IV-5. Since this trend started before the eastern part of the Littoral Highway was fully completed, it is difficult to ascribe a specific effect to this highway in encouraging traffic to and from Honduras. The doubling of traffic between 1958 and 1962, however, suggests that the impact was substantial.

Maintenance of the Littoral Highway

In the early years after construction of the Littoral Highway, maintenance expenditures were less than they should have been. As a result the road deteriorated. The following table shows the amount spent on maintenance of the Littoral Highway, according to the General Administration of Roads of the Ministry of Public Works, from 1959, the first year when a significant fraction of the highway had been built, until 1962. At the end of 1962, as will be described later, the maintenance program was reorganized.

Year	Total Spent on Littoral Highway Maintenance (Thousands of U. S. dollars)	Approximate Amount per Completed Kilometer
1959	$69.8	$600
1960	46.7	170
1961	57.1	192
1962	52.4	164

It is generally agreed that the ideal amount for maintenance on the highway should have averaged approximately $800 per kilometer annually. This would total about $240,000 annually for the full length of the Littoral Highway. Except for 1959, the amount allocated for maintenance amounted to only 20 or 25 percent of the ideal. Furthermore, the bulk of these expenditures was for hand labor, which it has been estimated costs approximately 50 percent more than does comparable machine labor at El Salvador prices. The problem of poor maintenance is not unique to El Salvador in Latin America. In fact, El Salvador has probably been better than average. Poor maintenance is said to result mainly from lack of know-how, equipment, and funds; furthermore, sometimes funds earmarked for maintenance are devoted to road improvement.

By 1962, the results of several years of undermaintenance became obvious. Although the Littoral Highway was still in relatively good condition, there had been a considerable amount of visible pavement breakup such as potholes. Undergrowth intrusion had taken place on the sides of the road. There were other examples of neglect. In areas which consist of cuts—approximately

50 percent of the road—it is necessary to insure good drainage; otherwise the road will deteriorate. Engineers estimated that approximately 15,000 cubic meters of dirt slough off into the drainage ditches annually; to insure long life, the ditches must be continually cleaned. This task had not been adequately done. In three sections, each of approximately 150 meters in length, one-third to one-half of the width of the road had been washed out because of plugged up culverts. (The six-foot culverts were plugged because trees, chopped down by farmers who were clearing land, washed into the mouths of the culverts during an extremely heavy storm.) The road also suffered from another problem which caused the Minister of Public Works to state that "Many people have been afraid to travel on the Littoral Highway." As a cost saving measure, it was decided not to line the many tunnels in the Río Mizata-Río El Zonte segment with reinforcing steel and concrete or asphalt. Therefore, periodic rock fall, mainly at the end of the rainy season, covered a total distance of a maximum of a half kilometer. The falls interferred with traffic, and required clearing the road and meeting the associated expenses. An additional half kilometer had problems of passability because of landslides. (These will tend to decrease over time, however, with the process of land stabilization.) A number of laymen criticized the standards to which the Littoral Highway had been built, not realizing that the road was constructed to primary standards and the problems were due to poor maintenance.

The World Bank and its affiliate, the International Development Association (IDA), recognized that poor maintenance was threatening the investment in the Littoral Highway. In November 1962 the IDA decided on a bold course of action, granting a development credit to set up over a four-year period a complete maintenance program for the Littoral Highway, probably the first time such a comprehensive plan had been adopted by the IDA. The development credit formed part of a much larger loan for a national highway program. It had not been incorporated in El Salvador's original development credit application and was included only near the end of contract discussions between IDA and the government.

Of the total foreign exchange credit of $8 million, somewhat less than $0.6 million was directed toward the Littoral maintenance program: $285,000 for equipment, $40,000 for spare parts, and $250,000 for the foreign exchange costs of the operations. The credit is for fifty years with repayments to start after ten years. One percent of the principal is to be paid annually from the tenth to the twentieth years and 3 percent thereafter. A service charge of three-quarters of 1 percent, but no interest, is payable on the amount withdrawn and outstanding. In addition to foreign exchange requirements, the Salvadorean government was to provide the local currency equivalent of $5.5 million for the over-all program, of which $0.7 million was to be allocated to the maintenance plan. The total amount, therefore, directed to the Littoral maintenance program was $1.3 million. Work on the program started in March 1963.

Although the imported equipment was to be amortized over the four-year period of the program, it would probably have an additional life of three to five years. The Salvadorean maintenance program would thereby gain a head start in building up its stock of needed equipment.

Taking all these factors into account, it appears that the amount devoted to the Littoral Highway maintenance program is realistic, and that if the El Salvador government continues the program at its present level, the Littoral Highway can be maintained in satisfactory condition.

Evaluation and Conclusions

The Relationship of Benefits and Costs

The benefits realized from the development of El Salvador's littoral are a result both of investment in the Littoral Highway and of other capital investment, primarily that required for incremental cotton production. Because these are joint costs, any attempt to develop a benefit-cost relationship for the highway by itself would be artificial. For this reason, the following discussion will relate the over-all benefits derived from the investment made to the costs of such investment.

The cost of the highway has been estimated as $28.5 million.

Additional investments applicable to the increment in cotton production in the areas served by the highway may be estimated at some $4.0 million. Thus, the total capital investment may be assumed to be $32.5 million. The annual increase in net value added due to increased cotton production which is assumed would not have been realized in the absence of the $32.5 million investment, has been conservatively estimated at $7.5 million. Annual net value added from shrimp fishing was put at $2.3 million for a minimum of $9.8 million annual benefits. From this must be deducted the annual cost of necessary maintenance of the highway, previously assumed to be $240,000. Thus, annual net benefits will run to about $9.6 million. Even if the highway's economic life is only twenty years, rather than a more likely forty years, this implies a benefit-cost ratio of about 3 to 1, assuming an 8 percent discount rate.[3] These computations omit the potential for tourism and other industries, assume a discount rate higher than the interest rate prevailing for prime loans in El Salvador (8 percent vs. 6 percent), assume no further growth in cotton or shrimp output, and neglect the health benefits from stimulating the malaria eradication program. Furthermore, no account is taken of the increased value of recreational land. As such, the computations are extremely conservative. In short, taking as narrow a viewpoint as possible, the investment in the Littoral Highway must be judged to have already realized a very significant payoff.

One simplifying assumption in this discussion has been that "a benefit is a benefit"; all benefits are weighted equally no matter who receives them or how the increased product is allocated between consumption and investment. The limitations of such an assumption are most apparent in evaluating the dramatically increased value of resort-potential land. The distribution and uses of benefits are complex matters, and they involve economic, social, and political considerations. While definitive measurements of these considerations are probably not possible, it is important to recognize that they exist.

[3] The benefit-cost ratio technique of relating benefits and costs was used here to make this case comparable with others in this book. The author actually prefers the calculation of an internal rate of return, a method which takes full account of time dimensions. It involves computing the annual discount rate which equates the total stream of benefits with the total stream of costs.

As already pointed out, the Littoral Highway is made up of a series of segments which are, to some extent, independent of each other. A further question, then, is whether it would have been advisable to have built only some segments of the road, deferring the construction of other segments.

Making a benefit-cost calculation for each section would in fact be possible, *if* comparative agricultural information were available by municipalities; however, this is not the case. In any calculation by section, of course, it would be necessary to take account of the value of the link to any group of sections or to the system as a whole; then the problem of project interdependence would have to be faced.

The Acajutla-La Libertad link has come in for particularly strong criticism, because of its low traffic volume and the lack of agricultural development in the area. One individual stated that while the people in Acajutla may eventually have to communicate with those in La Libertad, there was no present need for such communication. A reasonable argument might have been made for delaying or eliminating construction of the Acajutla-La Libertad sector if the increased value of the seashore land were not taken into account.

Assuming a road across the complete length of El Salvador were merited, alternative routes would have been possible in certain sectors. The Ministry of Agriculture thought that there had not been sufficient planning of the route of the road from the point of view of its potential effects on development. Individuals in the Ministry stated that the route was selected on the basis of minimum construction costs necessary to join certain population areas and to give competition to the railroad. They believed that the Ministry should have been consulted on the routing of the road. Other sources stated, in contrast, that the Littoral Highway and its associated feeder roads were well planned in relation to agricultural potential.

Some people have contended that the road should have been built through the good coffee land further north instead of along the coast between Acajutla and La Libertad. However, it was explicitly stated by Tippetts-Abbett-McCarthy-Stratton (TAMS), the engineering firm which planned the highway, that any major change in the Acajutla-La Liberated routing would have been impractical, owing to engineering considerations. With the construction of feeder roads in the Comasagua area, the littoral will be increasingly tied into the coffee hinterland, and complaints against the Acajutla-La Libertad sector of the road by coffee growers will probably decrease.

Granting that a road completely traversing El Salvador and following the present alignment should have been built, could the road or segments of it have been built to lower standards? From our previous examination of traffic counts made in 1962, it is clear that traffic has not been sufficient to justify primary standards on the El Delirio-La Unión segment, and possibly on the Acajutla-La Libertad and the La Libertad-Comalapa sectors. Had these segments been built to lower standards, traffic on connecting segments would probably not have been much affected.

In Central America the viewpoint has been growing that because of capital scarcity, roads should not be overbuilt, and that it is preferable to use what money is available to build more roads to lower standards rather than fewer roads to higher standards. An evaluation of this question must be made on the basis of the specific circumstances surrounding each route. Probably the best technique for such an evaluation would involve comparisons of the costs and benefits resulting from building the road to alternative standards, taking into account such factors as the probable earlier economic obsolescence of the lower-class sections. Such calculations for the relevant segments of the Littoral Highway are beyond the scope of this study.

The Relationship of Direct Government Revenue to Littoral Highway Cost

User taxes on vehicle operation provide direct revenue to the government. This revenue is of the nature of a transfer payment and should not be looked upon as a benefit to the economy as such. While it is not normally expected that the income from user taxes will completely pay for the amortization of a highway, it is one means by which the government recovers its investment. A comparison of direct government revenue to highway cost is valuable because it gives a picture of government cash flow related to the highway and indicates to what extent carrying charges and amortization can be paid for out of current revenues. In addition to direct revenue realized from road user charges, El Salvador also realizes direct revenue from the shrimp export tax described earlier. Road user taxes are not normally segregated in the national budget, nor are they earmarked for specific highway purposes. With El Salvador's extensive road program, it is likely that the expenditures on highways exceed receipts from user taxes.

Direct government revenue per vehicle-kilometer is estimated in the feasibility study for the National Highway Program of the Ministry of Public Works. Estimates are derived from computations for passenger cars only, since refinement for other vehicles was not judged necessary. (Heavy vehicles pay more of certain taxes per kilometer and less of others.) The computations are based on the existing 26 percent tax on vehicle import, a tax on fuels and lubricants at $0.26 per gallon, a tax on tires and spare parts, estimated at $24.00 for each 50,000 kilometers of travel and a fixed annual license fee of $18.00 per vehicle per 12,000 kilometers travel. The average vehicle is considered to cost $3,000 and have an estimated life of 125,000 kilometers. Fuel consumption is estimated to be 20 kilometers per gallon. So the total can be figured in this manner:

Tax from new vehicles
 (26 percent × $3,000 = $780)
     $780 ÷ 125,000 km = $0.0062

Tax from fuels and
 lubricants   0.26 ÷ 20 = 0.0130

Tax from tires and
 spare parts   24.00 ÷ 50,000 = 0.0005

Licenses at $18.00 per year
or 12,000 km. travel 18.00 ÷ 12,000 = 0.0015

              ————

  Total estimated $0.0212 per vehicle-
                 kilometer

On the basis of the 1962 traffic counts presented previously, a daily rate of vehicle-kilometers was calculated for each section of the highway:

Section	Daily Vehicle-Kilometers
Guatemalan Border—Sonsonate-Acajutla Road	15,795
Sonsonate-Acajutla Road—La Libertad	16,863
La Libertad—Comalapa	7,028
Comalapa—Zacatecoluca	23,638
Zacatecoluca—Usulután	56,484
Usulután—El Delirio	19,665
El Delirio—Eastern terminus of the highway	8,586
Total	148,059

Multiplying total yearly vehicle kilometers by revenue per kilometer yields, in 1962, total gross direct government revenue from the Littoral Highway amounting to $1,124,000. Net revenue amounts to $900,000 after subtracting 20 percent for administration and collection (the percentage deduction used in the feasibility study for the National Highway Program). From this figure, annual ideal maintenance charges of $240,000 should be deducted leaving a result of $660,000. This amounts to approximately 2.3 percent of the $28.5 million total cost of the road, not including interest. Therefore, direct revenues in 1962 paid for less than half of actual or imputed interest on the cost of the highway. Looked at in another way, over the anticipated forty-year life of the highway, government revenues at 1962 rates will almost cover the cost of the highway (without allowing for interest). It is expected that traffic volume will expand at a rate of 9 percent a year (equivalent to doubling every eight years). Should such expectations be realized, direct government revenue from the Littoral Highway will increase accordingly.

Future Development of the Littoral Highway System

The World Bank realized that the Littoral Highway would require subsidiary roads in order to develop its full potential. In 1954, it was estimated that these subsidiary projects would cost the equivalent of $3-$4 million. In 1959, as part of a $5 million loan, the World Bank supplied El Salvador with $4.6 million toward an estimated total cost of $8.9 million for the construction of 21 feeder roads, 18 of which were to connect with the Littoral Highway. The total length of the feeder roads was 230 miles. It was expected to take four years to complete the projects.

The loan was for a term of fifteen years and bears interest at 5¾ percent including the 1 percent commission allocated to the Bank's special reserves. Amortization was to begin in April 1963, when it was expected that the program would have been completed.

The program, as finally executed, involved some changes in the location of the feeder roads and a reduction from eighteen to fifteen of the roads connecting with the Littoral. The program was substantially complete by mid-1963 and involved a cost of almost $12 million, 20 percent more than estimated.

In November 1962, the International Development Association extended an $8 million development credit toward an estimated total cost of $13.5 million for improvement and extension of the El Salvador Highway system. As discussed earlier, part of the program involves modernization of maintenance operations on the Littoral Highway. The credit also covers construction or improvement of four roads directly connecting with the Littoral system, and other roads which might be expected to have some effect on the system.

The development and improvement of subsidiary roads for the Littoral Highway and for the country's highway network generally would appear to have more than met the expectations of the World Bank when it extended its first loan for the development of the highway. While it is too early to calculate the realized benefits of even the first feeder road project, it is reasonable to expect a further increase in benefits and traffic on the Littoral as a result of continued improvement of the total highway network.

The Littoral Highway has been constructed to higher standards than the Pan American Highway, and it offers an important alternative to this route. The completion of contemplated improvements in the El Salvador link of the Pan American Highway may, in the short run, work to decrease the regional role of the Littoral Highway. On the other hand, the improvement of the Escuintla-Taxisco segment of Guatemala's Littoral Highway should have an impact on the Salvadorean segment of this road. Construction of a road between Choluteca in Honduras and Puente Rela in Nicaragua, where presently there is only a dry weather road covering part of the distance, will work to increase traffic both on the Littoral Highway and the Pan American Highway in El Salvador. Improvements in the port of Acajutla will probably attract some additional regional traffic to the Littoral Highway. The road should draw increasing numbers of tourists; some will be part of the through traffic, and others will come to enjoy the scenic and recreational features of the Río Mizata-La Libertad segment, which was described earlier.

In short, although the main traffic and benefits of the Littoral Highway will be local in nature over the foreseeable future, its role in a Central American network can be expected to increase in importance.

CHAPTER V

Additional Cases of Highway Impact

GEORGE W. WILSON

ADDITIONAL CASE STUDIES of transport investments assembled from a variety of sources provide further evidence of the economic impact of improved transport standards in developing countries. Among the cases selected are road projects in Thailand, India, North Borneo, Nicaragua, Peru, Venezuela, and Uganda.

The Friendship Highway in Thailand [1]

The Friendship Highway, completed in 1958, connects the towns of Saraburi and Korat. (See Figure V-1.) It is a paved, high-standard highway throughout its 166 kilometers, and it connects with another highway which is passable but still under construction. The latter highway links Saraburi to Bangkok. Formerly, Saraburi and Korat were connected by an unpaved, circuitous route some 340 kilometers in length. It was not usable during the rainy season, and during the dry season its surface was dusty and corrugated. A railroad constructed in the 1890's linked Bangkok to Korat and beyond via Saraburi, thereby providing a direct transport connection between the two ends of the Friendship Highway.

[1] Based on "Economic Effects of the Friendship Highway," by Wisit Kasiraksa. (Unpublished Master's thesis, Bangkok, SEATO Graduate School of Engineering, 1963.)

FIGURE V-1. *Map of Thailand*

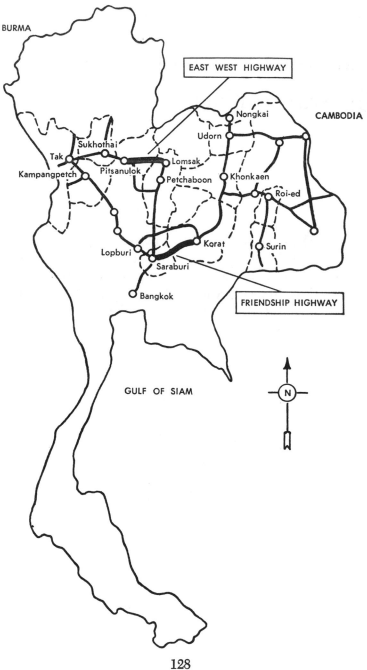

Effects of the Friendship Highway

The fact that this study examines the effects of a new, high-standard highway paralleling a railroad makes it, in this sense at least, analogous to the Guatemalan case already presented and to the Nicaraguan study to be discussed later.

TRAFFIC. Traffic studies in 1959, only a year and a half after the completion of the highway, are summarized below:[2]

> The volume of traffic at the west end of the Friendship Highway is of the order of 1,000 vehicles per day, of which trucks constitute 50 percent, and buses and passenger cars account for about 25 percent each. Traffic is about equally divided by direction. The westbound[3] vehicles largely originate from Korat and areas along the Friendship Highway; about 60 percent are destined for Bangkok, and most of the remainder for the vicinity of the Saraburi-Lopburi road. The eastbound traffic derives about 60 percent from Bangkok and 40 percent from the area between Saraburi and Lopburi; it terminates largely along the Friendship Highway (40 percent) and in Korat itself (45 percent).
>
> Eastbound traffic diminishes gradually along the Friendship Highway, falling off rapidly after Korat. Only 15 percent of the eastbound traffic entering the Friendship Highway continues beyond Korat. North of Korat, passenger cars represent only 10 to 15 percent of the total traffic volume.
>
> North of Jorhor Junction, 7 kilometers north of Korat, traffic mainly consists of short local trips. The volume depends upon the size of the community and the dispersion of the population in relation to the traffic-counting station.
>
> Between 1957 and 1959, sharp increases in highway traffic were recorded at counting stations to and including Banphai.

The relatively high volume of traffic along the Friendship Highway suggests that from the user's point of view, there are important time and cost savings as compared with both the old road and the railroad.

[2] *Ibid.*, pp. 20-21.
[3] The orientation of the Friendship Highway is more correctly described as NE-SW.

It took eleven hours to travel between Saraburi and Korat on the 340-kilometer old road, while it now takes only three hours between the same points on the direct 166-kilometer new highway. At the same time, passenger fares have been reduced from $3 on the old road to $0.50 on the new road.

As a result of these significant advantages and despite the absence of information regarding freight rates and costs, it is estimated that about half the total traffic on the old road, in terms of vehicles per day, was diverted to the Friendship Highway. The railroad reported a loss of about 70 tons a day and 50 passengers a day since the new highway was completed. This means about 20 vehicles a day using an average truck payload of 4 tons and an average bus load of 29 passengers. Total diverted traffic, however, amounts to only 12 percent of the average daily traffic presently estimated for the Friendship Highway, the remainder being new traffic induced by expanding production.

AGRICULTURAL PRODUCTION. Evidence of sharp increases in agricultural output in the area served by the Friendship Highway is given in Figure V-2, and a comparison is made with two other regions described as having "transportation facilities roughly comparable to those existing in the study region prior to the construction of the Friendship Highway."[4] The sharp increase in production of upland crops and vegetables following the opening of the highway is evident. In addition, the momentum appears to have continued at least through 1961. This contrasts sharply with the two control areas where production and acreage harvested exhibited a steady but nonspectacular growth in output of upland crops and vegetables over the same period. The changes in output are not related to rainfall variation, the only other variable considered in this study. Rainfall trends are similar in all three areas. Thus the author concludes that "the remarkable increase in production of upland crops and vegetables in Saraburi and Korat [provinces] has been a direct result of the existence of the Friend-

[4] Kasiraksa, op. cit., p. 14.

FIGURE V-2. *Production of Upland Crops and Vegetables*

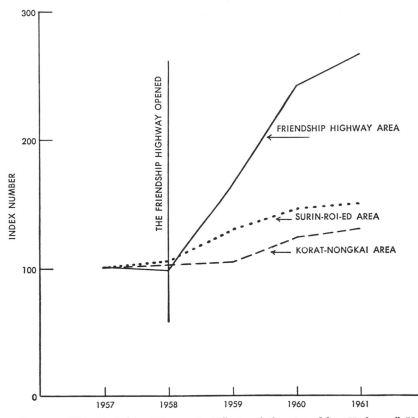

Source: Wisit Kasiraksa, "Economic Effects of the Friendship Highway," Unpublished Master's thesis (SEATO Graduate School of Engineering, Bangkok, 1963), p. 48.

ship Highway."[5] Comparable conclusions are reached with respect to poultry and swine.

Conclusions

The general conclusion emerging from this study, as well as the analysis of the East-West Highway in Thailand, has been succinctly stated as follows:

The chief inference to be drawn from this research is that development roads do more than reduce the cost of transport. By open-

[5] *Ibid.*, p. 47.

ing up new areas, they encourage industry to expand and disperse; in large measure, augmented vehicular traffic is induced by activity which is external to the highway itself. In general, development roads act as a catalyst to accelerate the rate of economic progress of a region.[6]

The East-West Highway in Thailand [7]

The East-West Highway links the towns of Pitsanulok and Lomsak in North-Central Thailand, passing through a dense forest area. (See Figure V-1.) The 131-kilometer facility was built at a cost of $17.2 million (or $131,000 per kilometer), including right-of-way acquisition and construction. It was completed in 1959, when the final 45-kilometer section connecting Lomsak to the branch extending eastward from Pitsanulok was opened for traffic.

Effects of the Road

This is the only direct link between the two towns. Prior to the East-West Highway the towns were connected by a circuitous gravel road, impassable during the wet season and dusty and corrugated during the dry season. The old route involved a journey of 217 kilometers compared with the 131 kilometers by the new road. Even more important, however, is the fact that prior to 1959 the Pasak valley, which supports the main cities of Wichianburi, Petchaboon, and Lomsak, was linked to the rest of Thailand mainly by water transport and inadequate roads. Furthermore, there was no direct access from the valley to the rail connection at Pitsanulok. In other words, the valley which reportedly had

[6] John Hugh Jones, "Economic Benefits from Development Roads in Thailand," Technical Note No. 15, SEATO Graduate School of Engineering (Bangkok, April 15, 1964), p. 31. Professor Jones supervised the preparation of the thesis summarized here and the thesis dealing with the East-West Highway.

[7] Summarized from "Economic Effects of the East-West Highway," by Tasana Patanapanich. (Unpublished Master's thesis, Bangkok, SEATO Graduate School of Engineering, 1963.)

substantial economic potential was relatively isolated. Penetration into a region of substantial potential justifies the East-West Highway even more than does linking the towns of Pitsanulok and Lomsak.

TRAFFIC. Estimates of average daily traffic along the East-West Highway during 1963 suggest that about 470 vehicles a day used the highway near Pitsanulok, with the volume declining to 96 near the midway point and 37 near Lomsak. The low level at the eastern end reflects the relative inaccessibility and underdevelopment of Lomsak. Studies are now under way on a connection between the East-West and Friendship Highways. The author speculates that if the road from Saraburi to Lomsak were improved ". . . the traffic volume along the eastern portion of the East-West Highway would increase to a level at least comparable to that observed at the western end."[8]

Trucks and buses comprise the bulk of the vehicles. In the section studied, they accounted for 83 percent of the average daily traffic in 1963 (excluding buffalo carts and motorized cycles), and over the rest of the highway for about 70 percent.

Although the traffic volumes are not especially high as yet, the considerable time and cost savings involved in moving between Pitsanulok and Lomsak should serve to stimulate movement and possibly orient Lomsak more toward the railroad at Pitsanulok. The only evidence on costs presented is the bus fare, which over the old highway was $2.00 between these towns, while over the new connection the fare is only 75 cents. The average travel time has been reduced from 11 hours to 2½ hours.

The impact upon the railroad has been favorable, as would be expected in view of the fact that the East-West Highway serves primarily as a feeder to the railroad. In 1960, the year in which the East-West Highway was completed, metric tons of goods dispatched from the town of Pitsanulok were almost twice the level of 1959. The number of cattle and buffalo dispatched from Pitsanulok increased by about one-third from 1959 to 1960 and by

[8] *Ibid.*, p. 11.

40 percent from 1959 to 1962. This contrasts sharply with the rail experience in the Friendship Highway area.

AGRICULTURE. As in the Friendship Highway study, data on the major items of agricultural output were compiled showing the situation before and after opening of the East-West Highway. The most dramatic increase after 1959 was in poultry production (over seven times), and this higher level of output has been sustained. In every other case, too, the growth since either 1957 or 1959 has been greater in the East-West Highway area than in the area studied for control purposes, although the trend has not been steady over the six-year period. As far as crops are concerned, data on rainfall do not indicate any relationship to production, and this variable is ruled out as not having much influence. However, the variation in paddy production is accredited to ". . . alternating drought and flood, resulting from inadequate control of river conditions upstream from the farm lands."[9] As was found in the Friendship case, some substitution of upland crops and vegetables for paddy crops has taken place, although the extent of this is not indicated.

FOREST PRODUCTION. Since the East-West Highway traverses a dense forest area, it would be expected that providing access to such a region would stimulate lumber production as well as open up new possibilities for agriculture. As far as forests are concerned, lack of easy access may be an absolute barrier to exploitation. In the Western Montaña in Peru, lumber production proved to be closely tied to the presence of roads. In the provinces which are served by the highway, there were substantial increases in lumber production, other than teak, in 1960 and 1961. This contrasts with declines or negligible increases in the control area.

Since the opening of the highway, two other wood products—fuel wood and charcoal—have exhibited dramatic increases that did not occur in the control area. The rise in fuel wood output is attributed to the demand for it by the railway for use in steam locomotives. The increase in charcoal production has helped to satisfy the demand in nearby provinces.

[9] Patanapanich, *op. cit.*, p. 27.

The Ramnad Road in Southeastern India[10]

In September 1955, the Ramnad-Mandapam Road, almost 21 miles in length, was completed as part of National Highway No. 49 in southeastern India. It is a paved highway, of asphaltic concrete, 12 feet wide, and was constructed at a cost of approximately $300,000. Before the road was built, a narrow path, unusable even as a cart track, and a railway joined the towns of Ramnad and Mandapam.

Effects of the Road

The region involved, approximately 100 square miles, produces agricultural products and has some industry—fishing, mat-making, and woodchopping. There are 47 inhabited villages in the region, which has an overall population density of about 510 per square mile. The study involves an examination of the impact of a short, all-weather road paralleling a railroad and constituting one small link in a more extensive highway network.

TRAFFIC. Average daily traffic along the whole road has been estimated as follows for 1959:[11]

Ton-miles	1,040
Passenger-miles	11,100
Cycle-miles	840
Cart-miles	960
Car-miles	510
Bus-miles	700
Truck-miles	340

Cart and cycle traffic prevail especially around the Ramnad area, while average daily traffic by motorized vehicles is very low —less than 100 vehicles per day during the busiest day of the

[10] Based on *Economic Benefits of Ramnad-Mandapam Road, 1959-60,* by India, Ministry of Transport and Communications, Department of Transport, Road Wing (1961).

[11] *Ibid.,* p. 13.

week. The prevalence of passenger traffic is attributable to the large number of tourists and pilgrims who visit Rameswaram, "a famous place of pilgrimage."

The study indicates that there has been no net loss of business by the railroad since the road was completed. Between 1954 and 1959 rail traffic within the stretch has increased from roughly 4,000 tons in 1954 to about 5,000 tons in 1959. Since there was no good road connection prior to September 1955, the bulk of the traffic now moving by road may be taken as a net increase. Thus the study suggests that the ". . . increase in agricultural and industrial production which was due to the road facility has tended to benefit railways also because some of the finished products go long distances by rail."[12]

GROWTH OF AGRICULTURE. For almost every agricultural product previously produced rather substantial increases in output were recorded between 1954-55 and 1958-59. The study also investigated the change in agricultural area and output in sample villages located at varying distances from the highway. As far as cultivated acreage is concerned, the substantial increase in the area is said to be due to the fact that ". . . the construction of the road has made it profitable to bring under plow the lands which were hitherto marginal or inframarginal."[13]

However, despite an almost 60 percent increase in acreage under cultivation, the output of cereals and other crops did not rise by anywhere near this amount. Indeed, cereal production increased by only 16 percent. Generally, except for paddy production, output increased at all recorded distances from the road. No clear-cut pattern of differences in output at varying distances is discernible except that generally the biggest relative increases have occurred in villages 3 to 4 miles from the road.

INDUSTRY. There has been increased output of the principal products in the area, such as baskets, pottery, cloth, firewood and fish, ranging from 11 percent to 108 percent. The increase was interpreted as being ". . . due mainly to the construction of the new road."[14]

[12] *Ibid.*, p. 19.
[13] *Ibid.*, p. 20.
[14] *Ibid.*, p. 31.

OTHER EFFECTS. In a sample of twenty-eight villages, the value of agricultural land in twenty-five of them increased between 1954 and 1959. The exceptions were three villages which apparently were still waterlogged from the 1955 floods. The value of land for house construction also increased in about 70 percent of the sample villages.

The total number of shops has risen since the road was completed, and a far greater number of villages now have one or more shops. Furthermore, there has been an increase in the number of elementary schools and student enrollment. In 1958-59 there were six post offices compared with three in 1954-55; a number of dispensaries have been opened; and the Marine Fishing Research Institute has begun to provide advice beyond the coastal region on fish culture and improvement. In general, the area now receives a greater variety of goods and services in more convenient locations.

Finally, the trend in prices of selected items for which data were collected indicates a steady decrease in the differences among prices in three centers. A network of feeder roads, induced partly by the highway itself, has helped bring prices in many villages more closely in line with those prevailing at the Ramnad market.

North Borneo[15]

North Borneo (now Sabah), with a population of about 454,000, produces mainly agricultural products. The most important product is rubber, although the largest single export at the time of this study was timber. Other important crops are coconuts, hemp, and cocoa. Since there is virtually no industry, the transport facilities are almost entirely concerned with moving agricultural exports and imports of manufactured products and rice. The most exten-

[15] Summarized from R. S. P. Bonney, *The Place of Transport, Particularly Road Transport in the Economic and Social Development in North Borneo* (United Nations Conference on the Application of Science and Technology for the Benefit of the Less Developed Areas, E/Conf. 39/E/37, 15 Oct. 1962).

FIGURE V-3. *Map of North Borneo*

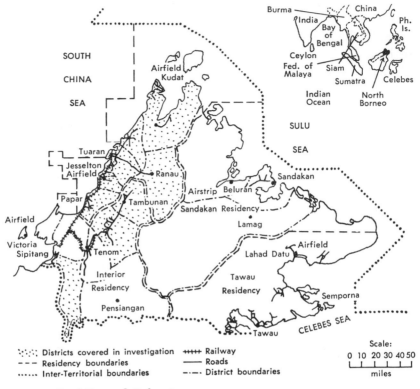

Districts covered in investigation ++++ Railway
--- Residency boundaries —— Roads
...... Inter-Territorial boundaries —·—· District boundaries

Scale:
0 10 20 30 40 50
miles

Source: Road Research Laboratory.

sive transport facilities are roads, and until recently there were
only about 500 miles of isolated networks within the total land
area of North Borneo, about 29,000 square miles. These networks
are being linked together and improved by expenditures totaling
28 percent of the outlays under the development plan. (For location and detail of the transport networks, see Figure V-3.)

Effects of Improved Transport

LAND. The effective demand for land, as measured by the number
of applications, is assumed to depend upon three main factors—
population growth, prices of major crops, and improvements in
accessibility by road.

Since the amount of land held per capita was roughly the same in 1947 as in 1960 and since population grew steadily at roughly 2.5 percent a year, it is believed that there is a long-term correlation between "natural demand" and population growth. Fluctuations in effective demand around this long-term trend are occasioned by price changes and road construction. Nevertheless, land taken up because of improved access has more stable and lasting benefits than land taken up because of high prices that may later decline.

VALUE OF OUTPUT. The standard of the road has a direct influence on the value of output at varying distances from the market. The evidence suggests that all-weather roads lead to development up to 25 miles from the market, while the impact of the earth road falls off sharply between 5 and 10 miles from the market in terms of value of output. Bonney suggests that ". . . small holders are deterred from development when they have the prospect of transporting cash crops over more than about 8 miles of roads which are frequently difficult to traverse and may well be closed in periods of bad weather."[16] A close relationship was observed between the extent of cash crop production compared with subsistence farming and the type of road surface. This is all the more significant in countries where evenly distributed rainfall permits the growing of crops that are harvested the year round or crops that are perishable. In other situations, the standard of the road surface may be of little consequence. (See the Uganda case for a contrasting set of circumstances.)

The location of the road is of significance in hilly terrain. Bonney points out that a road built along a steep ridge is unlikely to stimulate much development beyond a narrow strip of poorer roadside land. This in turn requires more extensive feeder roads to tap additional land remote from the highway. Again, should traffic develop, it is more costly to upgrade a ridge road than a road in the valley.

POPULATION. If there is population pressure in one area, roads are obviously important to induce or permit easier movement to alternative locations. But in North Borneo, Bonney finds that ". . . there is no general desire to move for economic reasons, except perhaps to move nearer the larger towns, despite considerable

[16] *Ibid.*, p. 5.

pressure on land." Even when people are assisted in various ways, the results are not encouraging. He concludes less pessimistically, however, that when a road is constructed between an overpopulated area and another area suitable for development, ". . . a natural movement often occurs and this type of movement does have a much more stable basis and produces more satisfactory results."[17]

ETHNIC DIFFERENCES. The report concludes with a brief illustration of how social considerations can modify the expected economic results of road construction. Arguing that the inhabitants of North Borneo do not appear any less hard-working than people in more temperate climates, the author nonetheless notes that certain ethnic groups ". . . within a country respond to a lesser extent than others to the opportunities of development which road access brings."[18] Furthermore, a poor response is not due solely to lack of education. The following illustration is offered:

In the Kota Belud district, the variation in response to development is clearly shown where the two races of Dusuns and Bajaus occupy adjacent areas. The area in which the Dusuns are settled is hilly country and is served by one road. The Bajau area is served by a small network of roads and is much easier country. Nearly 100 percent of rubber planted in the Kota Belud district is in the Dusun area, and the road is well used. The Bajaus, however, have continued to cultivate padi fields and to rear buffaloes, the return from these being lower than that from rubber, and the work only occupies about four months of the year, the roads barely being used. In fact, it is doubtful if road access in the Bajau area has led to any increased local development at all. Certainly, although there may be sound administrative reasons for these roads, there is little economic justification for them. In such areas, which are generally indicated by a fundamental lack of initiative, other measures together with road access must be employed to institute development, and unless such an area is particularly required for development it will have low priority for investment.[19]

[17] *Ibid.*, p. 6.
[18] *Ibid.*
[19] *Ibid.*

A comparable situation was found by the author of this book near the village of Raub near Kuala Lumpur, Malaysia, where two penetration roads in similar territory led to vastly different economic results. The apparent reason was that one area was taken over by immigrant Chinese, while the other area, served by a far superior road, went through territory occupied by Malays. In the case of the Western Montaña in Central Peru, ethnic or cultural differences again proved significant, especially when the Pozuzo area is compared with Satipo.

Conclusions

The implications of the study, aside from the empirical relationships deduced, are that more than accessibility is frequently required to stimulate economic growth. Aside from the different effects of varying road standards in the North Borneo climate, Bonney specifically mentions a survey taken among families with small children. It shows that in areas not served by roads few ever travel to the larger towns; crops are poorer; there is little appreciation of the benefits from planting higher-yield crops; the provision of schooling on a more fragmented basis virtually doubled the cost per class unit; and the benefits of centralized, well-organized agricultural training centers were lost.[20]

The Pacific Littoral Highway in Nicaragua[21]

Construction of the Pacific Littoral Highway connecting the cities of Managua, León, Chinandega and Corinto (see Figure V-4), was completed in 1961. The 141-kilometer paved highway was built at a cost of $8.8 million, or about $62,000 per kilometer. When the cost of various feeder roads is added to that of the main road, the total investment amounts to $12.5 million.

[20] *Ibid.*, p. 7.
[21] Based on an unpublished study by John F. McCamant.

FIGURE V-4. *Map of Nicaragua*

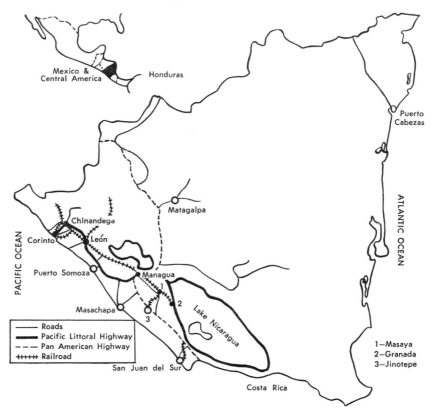

Nicaragua and Its Economy

Nicaragua is the largest of the Central American countries with an area of almost 60,000 square miles. The overall population density is low, about twenty-five people per square mile. Since the population is heavily concentrated in the western plains and central highlands, this understates the extent of crowding. The small area bounded by Lakes Managua and Nicaragua and the Pacific Ocean has a density of almost 350 inhabitants per square mile.

TERRAIN. Four main regions are usually distinguished: (1) the Western Plains along the Pacific coast—containing extremely fertile volcanic ash soils, where cotton, sugar, corn, rice, and beans are grown; (2) the Managua-Carazo uplands—a small sierra plateau especially suited for coffee production; (3) the Central Montane—rugged, with small lowland valleys and plateaus, also suited for coffee but with substantial stands of pine trees; and (4) the Eastern Plains—covering over half the land area with a prevailing vegetation of tropical evergreen hardwood forest.

CLIMATE. The climate is generally hot and humid, depending upon the elevation, with a marked wet and dry season except in the Central Montane region.

ECONOMY. The economy is chiefly agricultural. The main export crops are coffee, cotton, sesame, rice, and sugar. Corn, sorghum and beans are the basic domestic crops. There is an important livestock and forestry industry and a small manufacturing sector specializing mainly in processing, textiles, beverages, apparel, and shoes. Gold and silver are mined. There are known deposits of such materials as copper, iron, and bauxite, but they are not effectively exploited at present.

Imports are predominantly manufactured commodities.

Previous Transportation Facilities

Until the early 1950's the country's only railroad, the government-owned Ferrocarril del Pacífico de Nicaragua (FCPN) monopolized the surface transportation of export and import freight passing through the Pacific port of Corinto. The volume of freight traffic gradually increased in the early fifties as a result of expanded trade and a cotton boom on the Pacific coast. Then the railroad became heavily burdened, and it was totally unable to handle the traffic during the harvest season. Rail capacity suffered from antiquated equipment, a narrow gauge, and the inefficiencies inherent in handling small shipments. Furthermore, delays and high costs of the railway were aggravated by the many intermediate stops made along the line.

The anticipated further growth of the Western Plains region required an increase in transport capacity, either by modernizing the railroad through large investments or by building a parallel highway. An IBRD mission concluded that construction of a highway would be better than a large-scale expansion of the railroad. Trucks would provide a considerable saving on short hauls and were especially needed to replace oxcarts for hauling cotton to the ginning mills. Distances involved were short, and goods were moved in small quantities—two factors that make rail transportation uneconomical.

The rough and disconnected roads in the Pacific region led to high vehicle operating costs. Most local agricultural products were carried on mules or in oxcarts from the growing areas to the railway stops. In short, the relative inaccessibility of ports in the fertile western plains area, especially toward Corinto, meant that little of the agricultural potential was being realized. Much of the land was used for grazing or subsistence production of corn and beans. Much was left uncultivated. Improved access was considered essential to facilitate the expansion of cotton and sugarcane production, which was already underway in response to rising prices during the early fifties. The Pacific Littoral Highway was believed to be the most appropriate way to achieve additional access.

Effects of the Highway

RAIL FREIGHT. The railroad had already been affected by the construction of a few other roads in the western part of the country before the highway was completed in 1961. Completion of these roads and partial completion of the Pacific Littoral Highway undermined the railroad's monopoly of surface transportation. The railroad's revenues gradually declined through loss of traffic, and for the first time in its history it was operating at a deficit in 1957. Until 1955 it had managed to maintain profits of up to $850,000 a year by virtue of its monopoly.

RAILWAY RATE REDUCTION. In 1958 the anticipated opening of the highway to Corinto, coupled with competition from other roads, forced the railroad to reduce its rates. The major changes included a reduction of tariffs on imported goods. Rates on the shipment of iron and steel goods were reduced from 11 cents a ton-kilometer to 4.4 cents for less-than-carload lots and from 8 cents to 3.3 cents for carload lots. On textiles the reduction was from 13 cents a ton-kilometer to 5.3 cents for less-than-carload lots. In general it is estimated that shippers of imported goods saved about 6 cents a ton-kilometer as a result of the reductions.

By comparison, savings on the transport of export products were very small. The reduction for cotton was from 3.7 cents a ton-kilometer to 3.3 cents, and for coffee from 3.7 cents to 3 cents.

The smaller reductions in the rates for export goods can easily be explained. Under the old rate system (based on value) export cargo consisted of relatively low-value bulk commodities, such as coffee and cotton, while import cargo was composed largely of small shipments of high-value manufactured goods. With the introduction of truck transport, competition for the import traffic was especially severe since trucks are better suited to the movement of high-value, small-package commodities.

LOCAL TRAFFIC. Although the highway attracted much of the railroad traffic, the principal advantages of truck transport were found in local hauling of small shipments. Trucks have replaced oxcarts in delivering seed cotton from the growing fields to the gins along the highway. Moreover, the short highway distances between the gins in areas near the Port of Corinto have enabled trucks to deliver processed cotton directly to the port without transshipment on the railroad.

The impact of the new highway has been even greater on the delivery of local consumer goods. Local manufacturers and distributors of bottled beverages in some areas can now deliver their goods directly to stores in company-owned trucks. This direct delivery service has eliminated the difficulties and expense involved in arranging shipment on the railroad with pickup service at the destination.

PASSENGER TRAVEL. In Nicaragua, as elsewhere in Central America, it is hard to distinguish between passenger and cargo transport, especially on the highways. Many buses (including microbuses, station wagons, and converted pickup trucks) carry impressive amounts of cargo on their roofs, while some trucks carry passengers with cargo.

Passenger travel appears to have been greatly stimulated by

the availability of buses and private vehicles. A rough estimate suggests that in 1963 total passenger-kilometers on the highway in the north Pacific region were from three to four times greater than the total rail passenger-kilometers in 1954 and 1955. In 1963 buses and private vehicles accounted for over 300 million passenger-kilometers, while the railway accounted for only 50 million passenger-kilometers, substantially less than in 1954 and 1955. The volume of highway passenger traffic by private vehicles between León and Chinandega was about twice that between Managua and León, indicating that there was considerable short-distance travel over the highway.

This spectacular increase in highway passenger traffic has come about despite low passenger rates on the railway. Second-class railroad coaches are still the cheapest means of travel. Many people prefer to travel by bus since buses provide a smoother ride and more frequent departures. Moreover, the buses leave from the center of town, usually from a market rather than from the edge of town where the railroad stations are located.

In 1955 the railroad introduced self-propelled diesel passenger wagons, which cut travel time by one-third. However, the regular buses provide just as fast service as the diesel train, and express buses and private vehicles offer even greater speed. Since those who travel by private motor vehicle generally belong to an important economic group—businessmen or government officials—time is an important factor influencing the type of transportation chosen.

Agricultural Production

The north Pacific region of the country is completely dependent on agricultural production and, in recent years, on the export of cotton.

COTTON. Although the production of cotton increased sharply during the decade after highway construction began, the increase is not wholly attributable to the new road. In Nicaragua, expansion of cotton production had a momentum of its own in the early 1950's. The León and Chinandega areas are ideally suited for cotton, but production was uneconomical until after World War II because of the pests and diseases that accompany the region's rainy season. However, with the introduction of modern insecticides and with the encouragement of rising world prices in the early 1950's, farmers began to cultivate cotton on Nicaragua's Pacific plains.

In a single decade the area devoted to cotton cultivation in the State of Chinandega expanded five times, and cotton production increased more than ten fold. The impact of the highway on cotton production can best be assessed by examining the major factors that are necessary in the production process.

Constant inspection of growing crops is necessary, especially during the rainy season. Since the growing season coincides with the rainy season and the rain washes away insecticides, farmers must apply insecticides at least two or three times a week during October and early November. Many of the cotton growers live in the cities at some distance from the fields and without improved transportation, frequent travel to the cotton fields would be almost impossible.

Cultivation of cotton calls for shipment of a large volume of fertilizers, seeds, and insecticides. Gasoline and spare parts have to be transported for tractors. Paved roads are essential if uninterrupted delivery of these supplies is to be made.

Mention has already been made that mechanized highway transport replaced oxcarts and mule packs in the local hauling of cotton to the gin. The secondary, all weather, farm-to-market roads which connect the highway and the railroad played a large role in making this possible. The previous farm-to-market roads were mere trails and were impassable during the rainy season.

It should be noted, however, that increased cotton production results not only from successful use of the highway but also from a number of other factors. The improved road facilitated travel of cotton growers, local hauling of cotton, and the opening of new fertile land. Cotton production was greatly stimulated also by high profits stemming from the rise in cotton prices in the early fifties, introduction of effective insecticides, use of improved fertilizers, and liberal farm credits.

OTHER CROPS. Much of the land now used for cotton production was previously devoted to pasture and the production of other crops, such as rice, beans, corn, sesame, and sorghum. Consequently, with the advent of the highway, production of these crops declined.

Conclusions

In 1940 Nicaragua had only 27 kilometers of paved road in a total of 461 kilometers of roads of all kinds. By 1962 the country had 761 kilometers of paved road in a total of 6,151 kilometers covering the whole Pacific and central regions. Now only the vast and sparsely populated Atlantic region remains outside the system. Until 1956 the government-owned railroad had a virtual monopoly of internal transportation through the most populous and productive part of the country.

Construction of the Pacific Littoral Highway and other roads put an end to the monopoly and turned its substantial profits to losses.

Most of the cargo carried over the highway goes to or from the port of Corinto. A lesser amount of cargo and a great many passengers are carried between towns. Since the highway runs parallel to a large stretch of fertile land, it also serves as a farm-to-market road for both cargo and passengers. These three uses make the highway exceptional and result in considerable benefits to the country.

Introduction of an alternative mode of transportation and the consequent attempt of the railroad to meet the competition by cutting freight rates saved shippers of imported goods about 6 cents a ton-kilometer.

Since the reduction there is little difference between railroad and truck rates. However, the trucks have captured a large amount of cargo traffic from the railroad because of the advantage the former have in the local hauling of small shipments.

The availability of bus and private vehicle transportation on paved highways has led to greatly increased passenger travel. Speed, flexibility, frequent departures, and cost have all been important factors in inducing passengers to use highway rather than rail travel.

A final benefit resulting from highway construction was the acceleration provided to the substitution of cash crops for subsistence cultivation. The Nicaraguan economy is changing from one of subsistence and export agriculture, which could not support industry, to an economy with a much enlarged domestic market and an even more important Central American market which makes diversification through manufacturing possible. The production of the Pacific region is having an important effect on the Nicaraguan economy for two reasons. It is now connected with the rest of the Nicaraguan market, and increasingly with the total Central American market, not only by the railroad but by the expanding network of highways. And the foreign exchange from new export earnings permits importation of needed capital equipment. Although the Pacific Littoral Highway cannot be considered to have caused these changes, it has obviously facilitated them and, in this sense, made an important contribution to the further development of the economy of Nicaragua.

The Western Montaña in Central Peru[22]

The intent of this study was to examine the influence of transportation on stable settlement in the Montaña and on the rate of economic growth. The approach, however, is unlike the one used in the preceding cases.

Drewes examined four areas in the Western Montaña of Central Peru that are all physiographically similar and oriented to the major market in Lima. Because each area differs greatly in the nature of its transportation facilities, each differs in the degree of accessibility to Lima. The author then analyzes the extent to which present and past characteristics of each area, with respect to population, levels of living, patterns of production, imports, and exports, are related to the differences in transportation facilities.

[22] Based on material drawn from Wolfram U. Drewes, "The Economic Development of the Western Montaña of Central Peru as Related to Transportation: A Comparison of Four Areas of Settlement," published by the *Peruvian Times* (Lima, 1958).

FIGURE V-5. *Map of Peru*

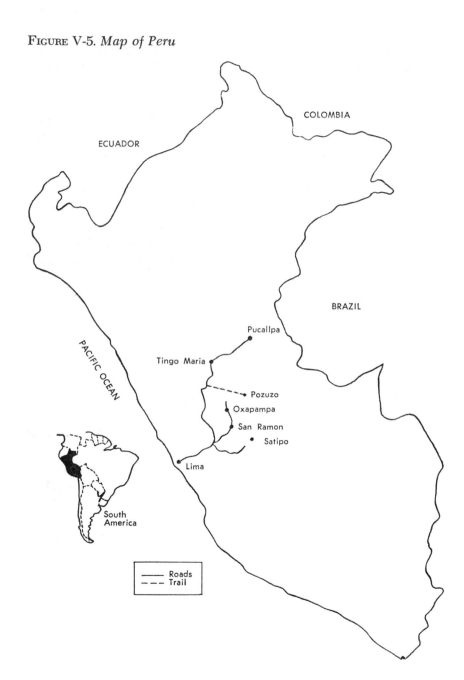

Relative Accessibility of the Four Areas

The four areas of settlement and their transportation routes are shown in Figure V-5. Pozuzo, the most poorly served in terms of transportation, is virtually isolated. Only a jungle trail suitable for mule trains links Pozuzo to the road head some 48 miles distant. Satipo was served by a road between 1940 and 1947, but an earthquake in 1947 destroyed the road, and it had not been rebuilt at the time of Drewes's analysis. Therefore, Satipo has been virtually isolated since 1947. In this respect Satipo resembles Pozuzo except that it has an airport which is used to send produce to San Ramón for transshipment to Lima. The San Ramón-Oxapampa area is well served by what are called "major" roads and has the advantage of proximity to Lima. Tingo Maria-Pucallpa also possesses good highway facilities but is much further from the Lima market. Water transport is available in some areas, but is most important for the Tingo Maria-Pucallpa area.[23] The relative accessibility of the major centers in each region is reflected in costs and time involved. The cost of shipping one metric ton of coffee from San Ramón to Lima is about $6.80 while the comparable figure is over $50 when it is shipped from Pozuzo. On the basis of the evidence shown in the study, Pozuzo and Satipo are at a distinct transportation disadvantage compared to the Tingo Maria-Pucallpa and San Ramón-Oxapampa areas.

Having established the relative accessibility of the four areas in terms of cost, time, and distance, Drewes then examines three other factors that might influence the economic development of each area. These are referred to as: (1) attitudes, objectives, and technical abilities, (2) age of settlement, and (3) governmental policies.

Attitudes, Objectives, and Technical Abilities

The settlers of Pozuzo originally came from Germany. They are described as hard working, skillful, and resourceful, with a strong

[23] Drewes, *op. cit.*, p. 34.

community spirit but with no interest whatever in affairs beyond their small settlement.

The settlers in the Satipo area are Peruvian farmers who moved in when the area was accessible. Since the destruction of the road, the area has virtually stagnated partly because of what Drewes refers to as the inability of the people to adapt plus their lethargy and lack of initiative.

The people in the San Ramón-Oxapampa area are described as being more energetic than the Satipo residents but less resourceful than the Pozuzinos. Settlers in the valley came with the intention of growing cash crops for Lima and the highlands. Drewes suggests, however, that ". . . the greater part of his profits leaves the valley. The settler does not intend to make the valley his home and spends the proceeds from his investment in Lima."[24] In the section surrounding Oxapampa, the settlers have shifted from farming to lumbering and have reinvested the profits from timber in trucks and large concessions.

The typical colonist in the Tingo Maria-Pucallpa area is viewed as somewhat ". . . unsure of his purpose," but he is also described as ". . . energetic and interested in the development of his area."[25]

Age of Settlement and Government Policies

The Satipo and Tingo Maria-Pucallpa areas were settled mainly within the last two or three decades, while settlement of the other areas began in the nineteenth century. Government policies regarding settlement and immigration have varied greatly over the past century, and because the areas were settled at different times, the extent of governmental assistance provided has likewise varied among the areas. Generally the colonist of the Tingo Maria-Pucallpa area has been treated generously. From the beginning, he received land free or at a nominal price, as well as seeds, implements, and money through the first harvest season. He also received advice and assistance in the event of a plant disease and had access to credit facilities at an agricultural bank.

[24] Ibid., p. 35.
[25] Ibid.

Schools and hospitals were also provided. None of the other areas have received much in the way of government assistance.

Economic Characteristics

Drewes seeks to explain the differing economic characteristics of each area as it existed in the mid-1950's, in terms of accessibility, cultural differences, and government policies, although primary attention is paid to the first two factors. The influence of age of the settlement is ruled out.

POPULATION. The data suggest a close correlation, especially in Satipo, between accessibility and the rate of population growth.

INDUSTRIES AND AGRICULTURE. Manufacturing in all four areas takes the form of small-scale processing of local raw materials. But the number and variety of such activities differ sharply. At the time of writing (1955), Drewes reports that Pozuzo had only one small brick factory while Satipo had only a small furniture plant. The Oxapampa area had only one cola beverage plant, one wood-flooring plant, and one ore concentration plant at the Pachita Caluga mine (lead-zinc) near San Ramón. By contrast, Tingo Maria-Pucallpa had an oil refinery, ". . . three rosewood oil factories, five rice mills, a banana dehydration plant, two tea factories, an ice plant, a brick factory, and a cola bottling plant."[26]

Of the extractive industries, lumbering is the most important and is concentrated along transport routes. It is not surprising, therefore, that Tingo Maria-Pucallpa, with relatively extensive transport facilities, has substantial lumbering activities and an estimated thirty-four sawmills. For similar reasons the Oxapampa section of the Oxapampa-San Ramón area supports more than a dozen sawmills. Satipo lost its lumber industry after the road was destroyed, and Pozuzo never had one that catered to anything beyond local needs for which one sawmill is adequate.

There are substantial variations in the quantity and variety of exports and imports among the four areas. Although no figures on value of imports and exports are given, some estimates in terms of weight were made. The Tingo Maria-Pucallpa area is outstanding

[26] *Ibid.*, p. 37.

in terms of the comparatively large volume of its trade, accounting for over 63,000 metric tons of exports and 20,000 metric tons of imports in 1954. By way of contrast, the volume of trade in the Pozuzo area is negligible, accounting for only 60 metric tons of imports and exports combined. As would be expected, agriculture and lumbering predominate in the export sector.

Conclusions

Drewes concludes that transportation exerts a direct influence on population growth, as well as on the amount and variety of cash crop production which in turn generates exportable surpluses and the ability to import a greater amount and variety of goods. "The final conclusion reached . . . is that modern transportation is indispensable to the economic development and successful settlement of the Western Montaña of central Peru. But other factors are just as indispensable. Without colonists with favorable attitudes and technical abilities, or without favorable government policies that provide public services as well as the incentive for private services, the development of the Western Montaña is severely hindered."[27]

West Nile Area in Uganda[28]

The West Nile district of Uganda has a population density of less than 150 inhabitants per square mile, abundant rainfall (40-60 inches a year), and a distinct wet and dry season. It is considered to be a good cotton growing area. Three territories within this district—Terego, Madi and Jonam—differed during this period primarily in terms of feeder road construction. Between 1948 and 1952 a series of feeder roads were built in Madi and Jonam. They were all dirt roads, generally unusable during the rainy season beginning in April. However, the main crop, cotton, is har-

[27] *Ibid.*, p. 43.
[28] Summarized from N. D. S. Smith, "A Pilot Study in Uganda of the Effects Upon Economic Development of the Construction of Feeder Roads," Research Note No. RN/3408/NDSS, Department of Scientific and Industrial Research. (Road Research Laboratory, Hammondsworth, England, 1959). (mimeo.)

vested between December and February and is not perishable, so dirt roads are adequate to get the cotton out. Terego had no new roads built until 1956.

The study examines the changes in population, in cotton acreage per capita, and in incomes from cotton for each of the three areas. During the period of the study the main difference between Madi and Jonam on the one hand and Terego on the other was the feeder road construction in the first two. The results are summarized in Table V-1.

TABLE V-1. *Uganda, Percentage Increase in Road Mileage, Population, and Cotton Production in the Three Regions, 1946-56*

Area	Road Mileage (1946–56)	Population (1948–55)	Cotton Acreage Per Capita (1946–56)	Income From Cotton (1948–56)
Jonam	400%	70%	380%	525%
Madi	200	22	364	373
Terego	0	12	−38	230

Source: N. D. S. Smith, "A Pilot Study in Uganda of the Effects upon Economic Development of the Construction of Feeder Roads," Research Note No. RN/3408/NDSS, Department of Scientific and Industrial Research. (Road Research Laboratory, Hammondsworth, England, 1959). (mimeographed).

Each of the three variables showed relative rates of increase according to the rate of growth of road mileage. The increase in income from cotton was due partly to a sharp rise in cotton prices which virtually doubled between 1948-49 and 1955-56, but this does not change the general consistency of the rates of change with road investments. The price rise does explain the increase in income from cotton in Terego despite a 38 percent reduction per capita in acreage with only a 12 percent rise in population.

The Tejerías-Valencia Highway in Venezuela[29]

In 1958 Venezuela completed its second major *autopista,* a high-grade, limited-access highway which parallels the Pan American Highway as well as the Central Railway of Venezuela.

[29] Based on a field report by Charles J. Stokes.

The 62-mile road which was opened to traffic in 1958 cost about $98 million with an additional $7.5 million spent to bring the road up to traffic demands in 1962.

The new superhighway serves a region located mainly in the Venezuelan states of Aragua and Carabobo. It connects their capital cities of Maracay and Valencia with Tejerías and with Caracas, the national capital, via a continuation of the Pan American Highway. (See Figure V-6.)

Venezuela and Its Economy

Venezuela, the wealthiest country in Latin America by most indicators, had a population of close to 8 million in 1962 and an area of 352,150 square miles for an average population density of 22.4 persons per square mile. Four-fifths of the people live in the highly urbanized northwestern section of the country, from San Cristóbal through the Lake Maracaibo region to Caracas.

Petroleum is the most important product in the Venezuelan economy, accounting for 90 percent of the total value of exports in 1959. Iron is the second most important mineral product. Gold, copper, coal, salt, tin, manganese, asbestos, diamonds, and mica are some of the other mineral products that are exploited in Venezuela.

Coffee is the most important agricultural product and second only to petroleum in terms of export value. Corn, bananas, yucca, sugarcane, cocoa, tonka beans, and rubber are also produced. Cattle raising is of special importance to the region traversed by the new superhighway. Most of Venezuela's output of cotton, rice, and citrus fruit comes from this area as well.

Venezuela is now rapidly industrializing, particularly in the fields of steel, petro-chemicals, plate glass, flour milling, and bagasse fiber.

Previous Transport Facilities

In 1954 the route between Valencia and the gateway to the Caracas valley at Tejerías was served by a single-track, narrow-gauge railway and the Pan American Highway—a two-lane paved

FIGURE V-6. *Map of Venezuela*

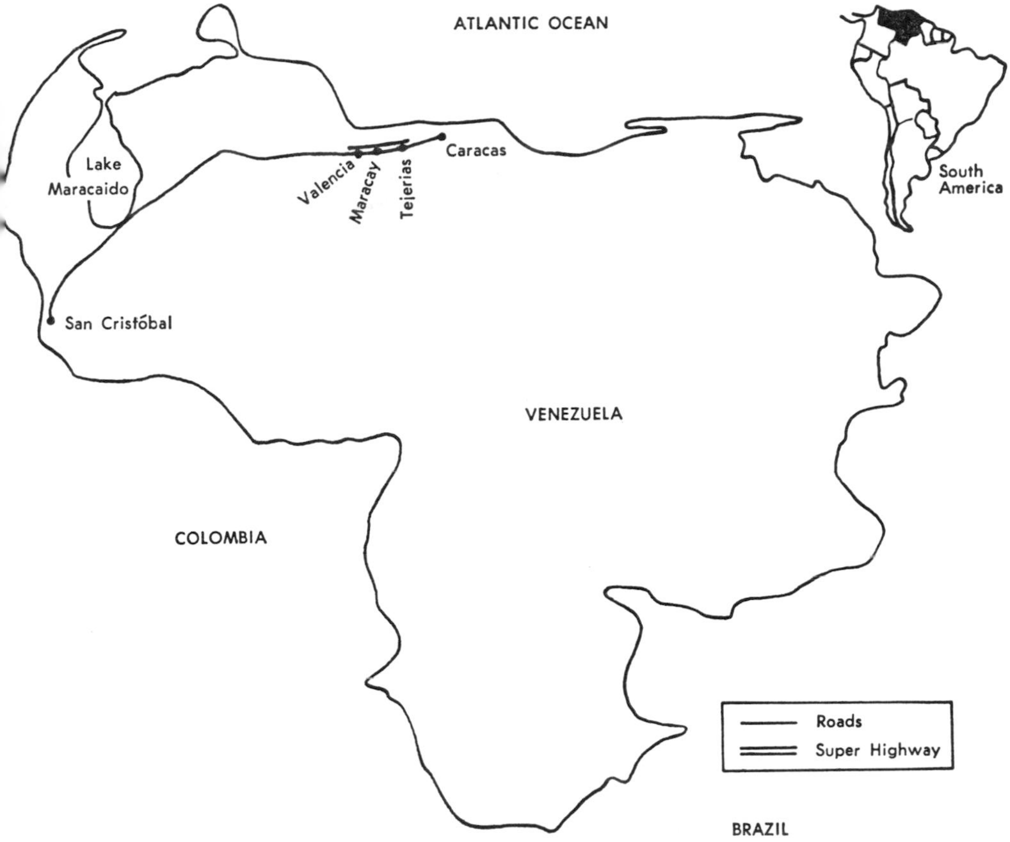

road, running through the principal valley towns.

The Central Railway of Venezuela had reached maximum use in 1944, when some 179,000 tons of freight and 507,000 passengers were moved over the route between Valencia and Caracas. At this time, the railway began to suffer from antiquated design and equipment. Moreover, the tortuous route from Valencia to Caracas takes more than four hours.

By 1954 rail freight tonnage had fallen to 39 percent of its 1944 freight peak level, and passenger traffic was only 19 percent of its 1944 peak. The Pan American Highway had attracted freight formerly carried by the railroad and in addition had captured much of the increased tonnage.

NEED FOR FURTHER CAPACITY. By 1954 existing rail and highway facilities were incapable of handling the growing traffic between Tejerías and Valencia. There was an urgent need to increase transportation capacity in the area if future growth prospects were to be realized.

There were two alternatives to the highway: (1) improving the Pan American Highway and (2) expanding rail capacity. The former was rejected because the very high and growing traffic densities called for a limited access highway to supplement the present highway.

The railroad option, on the other hand, appeared to be excessively costly. Cost estimates ranged from about $60-$130 million, including rolling stock, while the original estimate for the highway was only $45 million.

On these grounds, the decision to build the highway seemed clearly preferable to the other alternatives.

Effects of the Tejerías-Valencia Highway

SAVINGS IN TIME AND OPERATING COSTS. Because of a lower traffic density and higher possible speeds on the highway with its superior design, travel time was reduced by one hour and ten minutes for trucks and fifty minutes for cars, compared with the travel time required on the Pan American Highway.

Shipper savings, calculated by subtracting the weighted average rate per ton imposed on freight passing over the new highway from the rate charged by truckers on the Pan American Highway, amounted to $4.65 per ton on the new highway. Truckers were able to lower rates because of a reduction in operating costs of $0.20 per vehicle kilometer occasioned by the new facility.

The traffic taking advantage of these shipper and carrier savings came largely from the spillover dynamism centered on Caracas, the growth center of the Venezuelan economy in the 1940's. The narrowness of its valley limited the supply of land and forced up costs. This encouraged spillover into other regions—the movement of labor, capital, and entrepreneurial ability away from Caracas.

LAND. The opening of alternative and cheaper highway routes into the adjacent Aragua valley and the Lake Valencia region permitted new lands to be occupied. The spillover of the Caracas industrial growth, as well as the growth of the demand for agricultural products, resulted in a definite reshuffling of land-use patterns in the Aragua valley. Any industry which could not produce enough through the sale of its products to cover the rising cost of land had to locate outside Caracas.

LABOR. As new industries were established along the highway in the vicinity of Valencia and Maracay, new jobs were created. There were no problems in filling them since not only did the Aragua-Valencia region itself have available a labor force at least equal in ability and training to that in the Caracas valley, but workers from outside the area were also attracted to the new industries. In addition, from the industry owners' standpoint, there was the advantage of lower wages outside of Caracas for comparable positions.

CAPITAL. The outflow of investment capital from Caracas permitted the exploitation of the geographical advantages of the Aragua valley. As these new areas are growing rapidly, it is reasonable to expect that they will provide a large market, establish a base for sustained economic growth somewhat independent of Caracas, attract labor, and perhaps ultimately export capital.

A migration of entrepreneurs from the city of Caracas was a natural part of the spillover process which accompanied the outflow of capital. Entrepreneurial opportunities in Caracas had apparently reached the saturation point, and investment opportunities elsewhere were welcomed.

In short, spillover readiness was high in Caracas, and the very rapid industrialization of the Aragua valley following the construction of the highway was an obvious result. The direction of development spreading from a growth center is largely dependent upon the availability of efficient transport facilities. Thus the *autopista* served to channel the spillover of dynamism toward the west rather than in another direction.

The tangible results of this process are evident when the behavior of certain demographic and production data is examined.

Population increased more rapidly in Aragua and Carabobo states than in the nation as a whole from 1950 to 1961, while the cities of Valencia and Maracay grew even more rapidly than the states. Total manufacturing output in Aragua and Carabobo similarly grew faster than in the Caracas area or in the nearby states of Miranda, Zulia, and Lara. The share of total manufacturing output originating in Aragua and Carabobo has risen from less than 8 percent of the national level in 1955 to around 14 percent in 1962.

AGRICULTURE. The impact of the highway is also apparent in agriculture. Packing and slaughtering activities, which depend heavily upon transport, became even more important to the economic base of the Lake Valencia region than before completion of the highway.

As far as crops are concerned, the picture is mixed. Coffee and cacao output declined by greater percentages in Aragua and Carabobo than in the nation as a whole, while the increase in output of black beans, rice, and corn was below the national average. On the other hand, sugarcane, coconuts, and papaya recorded increases in physical output in these two states well above those for the nation as a whole. The number of hectares cultivated doubled in Carabobo but declined slightly in Aragua between 1950 and 1961.[30]

Such figures as have been presented can give only an impression of the nature of the change. There was deconcentration of economic activity in Caracas and much of it favored these states. The growth of new industrial areas accelerated the process of import substitution. The import structure changed to more raw materials and parts assemblies but fewer foods and finished goods. At the same time a widening and upgrading of the remaining finished goods imports took place, and domestic production as a proportion of total consumption rose from 65 percent in 1959 to 82 percent in 1962.

[30] Data from Venezuela, Ministerio de Fomento, *Memoria y Cuenta* (Caracas, 1963).

Conclusions

The Tejerías-Valencia Highway illustrates the spillover effects of a transport facility upon a region adjacent to a growth center. The Caracas valley and the Lake Valencia region are adjacent but were separted by geographical barriers which made transport between them expensive. Spillover growth from Caracas (the growth center) to the Maracay-Valencia region was impeded by the congestion of existing transport facilities. However, once a superhighway was built connecting these two regions, rapid industrial growth took place. The superhighway substantially lowered vehicle operating costs and thereby facilitated the development of nascent economic forces. The rapidity of this spillover was due partly to the relatively low-cost land and labor in the Lake Valencia region and partly to the many industries in Caracas seeking expansion to a place where the expected rate of return was substantially higher. The highway served mainly to channel this spillover from Caracas into the Lake Valencia area. As such it cannot be viewed as a generator of economic growth. Rather it conditioned the geographical distribution of a well-established overall dynamism.

CHAPTER VI

Concepts and Approaches: A Critique

GEORGE W. WILSON

AN EXAMINATION OF THE CONCEPTUAL, statistical, and methodological aspects of the cases will clarify certain points before the more detailed analysis and general interpretation. Although it is directly related to the cases, much of what is said here has relevance to the entire field of the economics of growth applied to underdeveloped countries.

Conceptual Ambiguity

The purpose of the case studies was to record and interpret the events following the construction of additional transport capacity in order to shed some light on the relationship of transport to economic development. In general, a functional relationship between these variables, and others, is presumed of which more will be said later. But the variables themselves are not free from ambiguity. The notion of additional or improved transportation capacity is capable of a wide variety of interpretations. Since the cases deal mainly with roads, this narrows somewhat the extent of variation. Yet the roads are of different kinds with different physical and economic capacity. The notion of capacity depends not only on the highway itself but also on the types of vehicles available to utilize it as well as the prospects of acquiring and using vehicles of different qualities. This is especially important in underdeveloped economies suffering from balance-of-payments difficulties. While all of these considerations will be reflected to some degree in relative transport costs, rates, and services, the extent to which this is true will depend upon the degree of competitiveness that actually emerges. This in turn will depend upon the response of producers to improved access, rates, and service. Both the vehicles and the right-of-way determine the amount and kind of capacity created, as do storage facilities, managerial quality, and so on. Depending upon these and other factors, the actual capacity generated (in terms of both vehicles and right-of-way) is itself a variable item and, as is shown below, is not closely related to the cost of the highway.

But of more importance is the meaning of the much-abused term "economic development." Even if it is equated with rising per capita output, an overly simplified definition of a complex notion, there are related problems of income remission from the nation or region. Furthermore, there are all the difficulties involving the distinction between incomes from productive activity accruing to normal residents and output within the confines of a geographical area, which are especially vexing when dealing with segments of a single nation. All of these problems are in addition to the lack of reliable statistics. Even in the narrow sense of rising income or output per capita the concept of economic development abstracts from income distribution effects and other criteria of economic welfare, to say nothing of the noneconomic aspects of development.

The intent of the cases to throw some light on the relationship between transport and development faces certain inevitable ambiguities that cannot be summed up neatly by some variant of "benefits" relative to costs. Furthermore, all of the cases are beset with the problem of "time," that vexatious variable which renders much of economic analysis especially complex. Since all of the benefits and costs do not occur simultaneously but are spread out into the future in widely varying amounts, making them comparable would require some rate of discount and some notion of the "value of time." No good evidence was presented in any of the cases on this point nor would an accurate estimate be easy to make, even if the same rate of discount could be expected to prevail in each future time period.

Difficult as this problem is, the fact that each case analyzes the situation for periods of only two or three to ten years after road construction is of greater significance. Still unanswered and subject to substantial guess work are the future prospects which are essential for final evaluation. Though a particular investment may not appear to have had much effect in economic terms immediately upon completion, it may have stimulated subtle changes that will later pave the way for rapid and sustainable growth. On the other hand, an immediate sharp increase in output and traffic may soon peter out if it fails to trigger other strategic changes essential for sustained dynamism. In every case it is necessary to raise the question whether a really fruitful succession or complex of changes has taken place or whether a marked dampening effect is to be expected. And to a large extent this is a product of exogenous circumstances such as government policy, natural phenomena, and changes in world markets. None of these circumstances is clearly predictable, particularly in terms of the impact on a regional distribution of economic activity that is predominantly agricultural. With adequate data, however, some meaningful interpretations and forecasts could be attempted and reaction patterns more reasonably assessed. Yet the paucity of reliable evidence precludes derivation of coefficients of various kinds and leaves the interpretation necessarily impressionistic.

The Problem of Statistics

It is a commonplace to complain about the unreliability and dearth of factual information for underdeveloped countries. Although most of them have national accounts, price and production data, these figures are frequently unreliable and are often revised at a later date without explanation. But rough as the statistics are that pertain to the nation as a whole, they are more so for regions. For example, the data in the Thailand cases dealing with agricultural production in the regions affected by the road were changed between the time of the initial investigation and a follow-up analysis one year later. Similar changes might well be found in a later follow-up of the other cases.

Political boundaries seldom coincide with economic regions, and even less coincidence is to be expected in the ill-defined region deemed to be "affected by" the new transport capacity. It is therefore not surprising that in few of the cases are computations of regional incomes on any basis attempted. It will be noted that many of them refer to volumes of production, usually in terms of weight, which has a rather ambiguous economic connotation. Nor, except for El Salvador, is there much evidence on additional investments, especially in the agricultural areas deemed to be most influenced by the new transport capacity.

Data on freight rates and costs of transportation are rough guesses in all of the cases. Even when rates were taken from published tariffs, the extent to which these are actually followed is unclear. In the Guatemalan case, for example, there was a strong suspicion that rebates were being given after the price accord between the railway and trucking interests. The information on costs is even more suspect and spotty. Thus functional relationships between volume handled and unit costs, even related to such crude units as ton-miles or passenger-miles, are conspicuous by their absence.

The profitability of the transport firms involved remains a significant unknown in any precise sense. Even for the railroads which parallel roads in several of the cases, the evidence is poor largely because the railroad accounts are kept on the basis of divisions, which do not coincide with the area under consideration. Where some evidence on these matters is presented, it is often based on heroic assumptions about average relationships found to pertain in a different context or on general impressions formed on the spot by the investigator.

Population estimates are likewise subject to an unknown degree of error, especially on the local or regional basis. Traffic along the highways has generally been estimated by traffic counts at particular points during the course of one or more days or weeks a year. They are subject to wide variation in interpretation particularly since little information on commodity flows or seasonality is given.

Finally, we may mention the well-known discrepancies between accounting data (that is, actual prices paid, costs incurred, and so on) and economic categories. While the existence of the former may be a necessary condition for estimating the latter, their equivalence cannot be assumed without close scrutiny. This is especially important where markets are highly imperfect and some forms of subsidy, tax, or protection are so distorting that they make product and factor prices inadequate measures of relative satisfactions and scarcity. Nor is there an adequate basis for estimating the extent of divergence between private and social costs. It is not possible, therefore, to determine the extent to which the picture presented in the cases is a valid portrayal of the actual situation. The general lack of reliable data (even of the private accounting type) capable of being checked through independent calculations creates an aura of speculation that is inevitable in this type of investigation. The evidence presented and its interpretation is heavily dependent upon who carries out the particular investigation.

Methodology of the Cases

Each of the cases utilizes a combination of cross-sectional and time-series analysis, with heavier emphasis on the latter. Each of these two general approaches has substantial, though different types of, shortcomings. In combination they may either offset or accentuate the difficulties of each taken separately.

The cross-sectional approach refers to all those comparisons with other regions or the nation as a whole. The main problem associated with cross-sectional analysis involves the question of the homogeneity of the regions compared in all aspects save those whose variance is being investigated. In the present study which attempts to assess the impact of transport on economic development the relationship sought takes the general form:

$$D = f(T)$$

where D refers to economic development and T refers to transport capacity. But in no instance where cross-sectional comparisons are involved were the regions homogeneous in every respect save transport. In Drewes' Peruvian study, the only one relying almost exclusively on this method, the areas differ in size, population, types of people, public policy, and to a lesser extent natural resources.

Indeed, one could make a case that the differences in population alone "explain" all the variables mentioned, except natural resources. The greater the number of people, the greater the ability to specialize, and the larger the total output; and, given the resource base, the greater the volume of exports and imports even on a per capita basis. The observed relationship between population growth and transport facilities does not, per se, demonstrate that improved transport causes population growth. It is equally plausible to argue that the greater the population, the more necessary it is to provide better access and the greater the incentive, on strictly economic grounds, to ensure accessibility. Since the decision to improve transportation is normally a political one, even if it is based on cost-benefit analysis, it is clear that causation is not one way and that both transport and population are interrelated as cause and consequence of each other. The isolation of Pozuzo in Peru is as much due to its small size as to its inaccessibility. It is thus economically undesirable and perhaps politically unnecessary to provide all-weather connections. The populaton growth and decline in response to the road situation in Satipo, Peru, might even be attributed to its small population which did not agitate vigorously for restoration of the road after its collapse.

Size and quality of population are both cause and consequence of all the other economic variables as well. Drewes' analysis recognizes this but tends to impute unidirectional causation to factors that are interdependent and *mutually* determining. It is well to recall with Alfred Marshall that no one of the balls in the bowl determines the position of them all. Furthermore, as has already been pointed out, the data are neither sufficiently reliable nor extensive to warrant computation of coefficients of determination using one or more explanatory variables. Even if they were, questions would still have to be faced as to the form of the regression function used as well as the fact that correlation does not prove causation and that quantitative measurement of some of the variables is difficult if not impossible.

In addition, extreme care must be used when a variable representing "attitudes, incentives, and abilities" is introduced. Since these qualities cannot be measured with any precision, it is always tempting to ascribe varying results which cannot be explained in terms of other quantifiable evidence to these amorphous factors. The whole discussion thereupon becomes tautological in the sense that observed variations in economic development, which itself is not subject to precise meaning or measurement, are ascribed to whatever is quantifiable and "everything else" which is then equated with "attitudes, incentives and abilities." In short, the analysis can be used to explain everything which means that it explains nothing.[1]

The two cases in Thailand compare specific types of production trends in "reference areas" with those in areas deemed to be affected by the two highways. Little attempt is made to assess the degree of comparability except for rainfall. The crucial difference is simply stated to be transport. No reference is made to relative population, geographical size, resources, freight rates, or the distribution of production by types in the reference areas. In terms of weight of production of, for example, upland crops and vegetables, there is a vast discrepancy in amount when each reference area is compared to the primary area affected by the highway. Since no figures on value of output or product distribution for the reference areas are given, it is difficult to interpret the economic significance of the fact that over a four or five year period, the *weight* of production in the reference areas grew more slowly than in the areas affected by the highways. The most that can validly be said, as in the Uganda case, is that increased output was associated with the expanded transportation capacity; that some un-

---

[1] Malthus' population thesis is subject to similar strictures, as is Rostow's notion of "preconditions" for take-off. As Kuznets says of the latter: "I do not know what a 'political, social, and institutional framework which exploits the impulses to expansion in the modern sector, etc.' is; or how to identify such a framework except by hindsight and conjecture; or how to specify the empirical evidence that would have to be brought to bear to ascertain whether such a framework is 'in existence or in quick emergence.' It seems to me that the passage just cited defines these social phenomena as a complex that produces the effect Professor Rostow wishes to explain; and then he treats this definition as if it were a meaningful identification." Simon Kuznets, "Notes on the Take-Off," Chapter 2 of W. W. Rostow, ed., *The Economics of Take-Off into Sustained Growth* (St. Martin's Press, 1963), p. 28.

specified relationship appears to exist, the nature of which requires further examination.

The other cases make cross-sectional comparisons on a less systematic basis, and for the most part they are used to support or modify conclusions already reached through time-series analysis.

Ideally, the time-series approach analyzes the economic conditions in a particular region over a period of time during which an exogenous factor, such as increased transportation capacity, is introduced. It then compares the conditions subsequent to the exogenous factor with those prevailing previously. If all other things remain equal, the differences are attributed to the exogenous factor. But it is precisely the stubborn refusal of other things to remain the same that complicates the imputation of causality to this exogenous factor. In the first place we cannot be sure that the earlier conditions would in fact have remained stable even if the exogenous factor had not been introduced. Some of the observed changes occurring later in time might well have taken place anyway, and the creation of new transport capacity might have either thwarted such changes or accentuated them. The relative significance of the investment is thus difficult to assess.

Again, during any long time period, there is usually more than one exogenous influence at work, and the observed changes are due to a complex of exogenous factors occurring within the given set of conditions. Attributing changes to any one of them is a very slippery endeavor, especially where reliable data are lacking. Indeed it is this weakness of time-series analysis that makes cross-sectional comparisons more appealing, just as the problem of homogeneity in the latter suggests the advantages of the former.

In short, both approaches have their own peculiar strengths and weaknesses. The decision as to which one to adopt is frequently a pragmatic one, especially in the present set of case studies, and is dictated by the kinds of evidence available. Where no usable time-series data exist, the only alternative, short of attempting to derive such data, is to study several areas at a particular time. On the other hand, when "reasonably comparable" regions are hard to find, investigators may use the time-series approach with whatever data are available. The choice of approach is less the result of compelling logic or careful calculation than of expediency. This consideration, along with the dearth of reliable evidence and problems of comparability, has led to the use of both approaches in the same case. The problem in combining the two is that one is never certain whether the result combines the best or the worst features of both.

Case Studies As a Method of Analysis

On a more general level some comments may be made on the virtues and defects of a case-study approach to an analysis of economic growth and transportation. In the Introduction, some of the weaknesses of excessive aggregation and emphasis on the nation as an economic unit were noted. Breaking down the totals and focusing on the "reality" of regional life may provide a helpful supplement to the broad approach which has been so heavily emphasized. If economic growth is really a question of people, then the aggregative, national approach might miss the essence of the process of development. Tying the analysis to specific industries and regions should permit a closer contact with individual response mechanisms, which is essential to a fuller comprehension of economic growth. The more microscopic approach gets closer to reality, to the way people live, behave, and react in specific circumstances. After all, economic and social activity takes place in particular locations, in specific industries and occupations, and with a particular set of social contacts. In a country with low mobility, these particularities are more real and vital to an individual than is the broader national society.

Therefore, planning sensible developmental strategy and, more important, implementing it, requires a disaggregated approach to determine what particular investments to make, where to locate them, and when to make them. As Albert Hirschman once put it, "generalizations involving large aggregates of the economic system have somehow seemed to be lacking in ready applicability to the specific problems that confront the practical planner."[2] Of

[2] Albert O. Hirschman in *Investment Criteria and Economic Growth*, Papers presented at a Conference sponsored by the Center for International Studies and the Social Science Research Council (Massachusetts Institute of Technology, December 1955), p. 36.

course, this is not the purpose of the general theory of economic growth. But it must be remembered that underdeveloped countries are seldom united, economically or politically, within a national boundary. One of the attributes of underdevelopment is a high degree of regional isolation, separateness, and self-sufficiency—to which national aggregates have little relevance. For these reasons, the case-study approach appeared to have great merit.

However, despite a closer contact with reality, as construed above, the case-study approach is beset with unique problems that are avoided at higher levels of aggregation. Aggregative analysis deals with a smaller number of variables. Individual differences often wash out in the process of aggregation, thereby facilitating discovery of meaningful relationships. Some degree of generalization and abstraction is necessary to avoid confronting the very diversity to be explained. Of course, the washing out of individual differences may preclude a useful analysis of the reasons for such diversity. As already observed, the composition of an aggregate may be as significant as its magnitude. Nor can one be especially satisfied with aggregative data that rely on the hope or assumption of compensating error in the subcomponents to enhance their accuracy. Nevertheless, it cannot be denied that important insights are obtained through aggregation that would be missed by alternative approaches. (The reverse is also true which suggests the virtue of both approaches, although for different reasons.)

Furthermore, a regional case study is beset with the problem of statistical gaps. Interregional transactions, for example, are not recorded on a regular basis with any such degree of precision as are international transactions. The same applies to population movements; though certainly no one would suggest that the same procedures that are followed in international transactions and population movements should be applied internally. But it should be recognized that the development of regional statistics is a more difficult and costly task than the development of national data. The preoccupation with aggregates is both cause and consequence of this fact.

Even if data are available, the knowledge gained from a single case study is relevant only to the set of conditions actually examined. There is, however, a predisposition on the part of those intimately acquainted with a particular situation to impute its characteristics to larger areas or to other circumstances where their relevance is remote. If we should be wary of applying aggregative relationships to specific instances, we should be equally wary of doing the reverse. A road may have facilitated significant development in Nicaragua or El Salvador but may have had little noticeable impact in Guatemala or Bolivia. In this sense each case is unique. As the cases imply, the selection of any one of them as generally applicable in other circumstances would be dangerously misleading in many respects.

But using a set of cases may suggest certain uniformities and permit a wider degree of generalization. As Gould suggests, "the more studies of transportation development . . . we have, the easier it will be to pick out some of the constantly recurring themes. . . ."[3] It is in this spirit that the cases are presented, despite their heterogeneity, difference in approach, and variation in the kind and quality of evidence. Nevertheless, there are weaknesses even in using a set of cases, as anthropologists and business historians are quick to acknowledge. The divergences between the case and aggregative approaches have been well summarized in the following comparison between anthropology and economics:

The method of anthropology—intensive, first-hand field study of small social units within the larger society—means that its primary contribution to the understanding of economic development must inevitably lie in a relatively microscopic and circumstantial analysis of a wide range of social processes as they appear in concrete form in this village, or that town, or the other social class; the theoretical framework of the economist almost as inevitably trains his interest on the society as a whole and on the aggregate implications for the entire economy of the processes the anthropologist studies in miniature. One result of this division of labor has been that anthropological studies of development have tended to consist of a set of more or less disconnected examples of the various social forces which "somehow" play a part in development with little or no indication as to how they play this part or how they affect the overall

[3] Peter R. Gould, *The Development of the Transportation Pattern in Ghana,* Studies in Geography, No. 5 (Northwestern University, April 1960), p. 163.

functioning of the economy; economic studies of development tend to consist of general statements about the implications of various sorts of relationships among technically defined aggregate economic variables for growth, with little or no indication of how the social forces determining the values of these variables can be expected to behave. On the one hand, you have a sociological eclecticism . . . , on the other, an economic formalism. . . .[4]

The next chapter will examine the constantly recurring themes from the unconnected cases and seek to chart a course some-were between eclecticism and formalism.

[4] Clifford Geertz, *Peddlers and Princes, Social Change and Economic Modernization in Two Indonesian Towns* (University of Chicago Press, 1963), pp. 4-5.

CHAPTER VII

What the Cases Show

GEORGE W. WILSON

THE CASES CONFIRM THE BELIEF that additional capital, whatever its form, may be a necessary but not a sufficient condition to induce economic growth. In every instance, even where rapid development ensued, it was a combination of circumstances which, in conjunction with the highway or road, occasioned the growth of output.

In North Borneo and Uganda, population increase induced the taking up of new land, and there is no doubt that with or without increased access, agricultural expansion would have resulted. Rising prices for cotton and rubber accentuated this trend, rendered all the more essential since the ability to increase yields on presently cultivated acreage is limited by the failure to use fertilizer, at least in Uganda. Furthermore, the ease of road construction in Uganda made the feeder road program a rather simple and natural response to the demand for land. The World Bank study of Uganda states that the ". . . spread of cotton cultivation . . . created a demand for roads, mainly secondary and feeder. . . ." and that their construction was made easier by the general availability of excellent roadbuilding material (murram) and an ". . . old tradition of road building [as well as] the application of *luwalo*, a customary law which gave the option to the African taxpayer to choose between payment of local government tax in cash or community work."[1] In the case of neither cotton nor rubber can the road facilities be considered to have "opened up" new areas; they were responses to a set of forces that would have led to new settlement and increased output in any event. The observed relationship between roads and production in Uganda does not imply that the

[1] International Bank for Reconstruction and Development, *The Economic Development of Uganda* (Johns Hopkins Press, 1962), p. 310.

174

roads were the cause of greater production. In fact, the opposite is more nearly the truth.

Leading Sectors and Preconditions for Take-Off

The same is only sightly less true in Nicaragua and El Salvador. In the region affected by the Pacific Littoral Highway in Nicaragua (the Departments of Chinandega and León), the area planted in cotton and total cotton output were both increasing well before the highway was completed. This trend would doubtless have continued without the road, because cotton prices were increasing and more efficient production techniques were adopted.

This situation has direct relevance to the notion of "leading sectors" and so-called "preconditions for take-off" as far as the role of transport is concerned. In these two cases, transport, instead of being a necessary precondition or even a leading sector, was a response to pressures generated both from without and within on account of rising commodity prices and growing population. Of course, the whole notion of take-off and stages of growth to which the "leading sectors" notion applies is fraught with ambiguity.[2]

The Land Access Factor

Bolivia is somewhat different despite population pressure in the highlands. New lands were not easily settled; hence the population pressure built up a need for new lands that could not be satisfied in the area, and movement out of the region was stifled by physical and perhaps psychological barriers. A kind of pent-up demand arose to which the highway was one form of response. But unlike the other cases mentioned, this response was to latent demands that otherwise would have been frustrated. In this sense

[2] W. W. Rostow (ed.), *The Economics of Take-Off into Sustained Growth* (St. Martin's Press, 1963), Introduction, Epilogue, Chapters 2 and 15.

the Bolivian road has more causal implications with respect to actual or potential development.

In other instances, the availability of easily exploitable natural resources was a necessary factor in the development following completion of the highway. For example, the East-West Highway in Thailand served to open up the lush Pasak Valley, especially to timber production. The Friendship Highway also passes through a region in which most of the land is suitable for agriculture as the sharp increases in output testify. In the Western Montaña of Central Peru, the close relationship of lumbering to road access is significant. The fact that the Guatemalan road (and to a lesser extent the Cochabamba-Santa Cruz highway in Bolivia) failed to generate much new traffic is in large part attributed to the dearth of natural resources along the right-of-way.

In several cases, including Bolivia, Guatemala, Peru, India, and the two areas in Thailand, whatever development there was would not have occurred without the highway. The highway, along with other investments, policies, and natural resources, did not merely facilitate a line of development that would have unfolded anyway. It was part of an initiating cluster of change and deserves recognition as one of the causal agents.

The existence of readily exploitable resources, even if they could be developed by using available skills and equipment, is not enough. A more basic prerequisite for development is a willingness and ability to identify and exploit a new economic opportunity. This is the great intangible which we shall examine explicitly at a later stage. The point here is that the stimulus to growth requires a set of conditions of which transport capacity is but one, even in those cases where it may be deemed causal in some degree.

The search for a single source of economic growth, for a particular catalyst that will work in every instance is doomed to failure. It is not merely a higher rate of savings and investment, or the creation of a class of entrepreneurs, or improved labor quality, or political stability, or "adequate" infrastructure—taken separately. It is all these things and more besides. Economic growth is due to a "combination of social, cultural, political and economic changes."[3] It is not possible to isolate a single prime mover and ascribe all else to it alone. A much more skeptical attitude toward transport appears essential, and far more attention needs to be devoted to the set of circumstances surrounding any expansion of transport capacity. The cases in the present volume illustrate this point despite the fact that most of them appear to be "successes" in one way or another.

Traffic Generation

In every case there was a rise in traffic along the new facility, which in most instances represented a net increase in total mobility, not merely a diversion. Where no previous connection existed, the traffic on the highway represented a net increase in movement. But in most instances, even where rail connections were paralleled, the rise in highway movement represented a net increase. For example, only 12 percent of the total traffic along the Friendship Highway was believed to have been diverted from the railway; and along the Ramnad-Mandapam road and on the coastal highway in El Salvador, rail freight traffic increased following its completion. Along the portion of the highway in Nicaragua closely paralleling the railroad, rail traffic declined, but the rise in trucking more than offset this. On the Guatemalan road, some net increase in mobility was recorded, although this was slight and attributable mainly to other factors.

In general the total volume of traffic in the region or country increased, and the extent of diversion from parallel facilities, other than indigenous forms of transport, was not significant compared to the growth along the new facility. Even where diversion occurred, it brought about what proved to be a more rational allocation of traffic. The decline of primitive forms of transport is illustrated in the Nicaraguan case. As late as 1954 almost all cargo to Telica was carried by oxcart. With the highway, trucks now carry all except strictly local traffic. A similar though less pronounced diversion is evident in the Ramnad-Mandapam road in India.

[3] P. T. Bauer and Basil Yamey, *The Economics of Under-Developed Countries* (University of Chicago Press, 1957), p. 128.

In every case, local traffic was almost completely captured by truck transport, except for heavy, bulky, low-valued commodities such as bricks, tiles, gravel, timber, etc., which continue to move by rail where this alternative is offered. In Guatemala, for example, local rail traffic is estimated to have declined by almost 50 percent. In Nicaragua local rail traffic fell sharply between 1954 and 1962. In this period it accounted for only one-third of total rail and truck short-haul or local traffic. We have already noted the decline of indigenous forms of transport which were entirely short-haul.

Longer-haul or through traffic also showed a shift to truck from rail, but traffic diverted from alternative forms of transport was relatively small compared to what was generated by the increased production of the region.

Passenger traffic, however, shifted dramatically to bus service once the road was completed. In Guatemala, bus service even replaced an airline between Guatemala City and Puerto Barrios. Large reductions in rail passenger traffic were generally reported despite a rise in total passenger movement. It is clear from the cases that bus transport captured much of the previous passenger business and was responsible for practically all of the increase.

Production

The net increase in mobility implied an increase in both the tonnage of freight and the number of people moved during any time period and, in some instances, a lengthening of the average distance traveled. As both a cause and a consequence of this, a sharp rise in production (mostly agricultural) took place, with a growing emphasis on production for the market rather than for subsistence. In other words, the rise in mobility did not mean simply movement over longer distances of existing annual volumes of production. In virtually every case, the greater mobility represented a net increase in physical output as well as a higher value of output per unit of weight. Higher-value crops were substituted for both low-value cash crops and subsistence crops.

Most of the increases in output constituted a net growth for the economy as a whole and did not represent simply a relocation of productive activity.

The substitution of cash for subsistence crops was especially apparent in North Borneo, El Salvador, Nicaragua, Thailand, the Santa Cruz area in Bolivia, and the Western Montaña in Peru. This implies not only a greater volume of output but a higher unit and total value as well. More importantly, it permits greater specialization and provides an essential integration of market-oriented economic activity over a more extensive area.

In most instances the transport facility served directly or indirectly to bring more land into productive use, although the extent of this varied widely. It obviously depended on the type and length of the road as well as on the quality of the soils or forests through which the road went or to which it provided easier access. Yet there is no relationship between the cost of the highway per mile and the developmental impact.

Excluding the highway in Venezuela, which is a very special case, the most expensive road was that constructed in Guatemala, which cost over $260,000 a mile. The East-West Highway in Thailand cost about $210,000 a mile, and the others in Latin America cost between $100,000 and $165,000 a mile. The Ramnad-Mandapam road and the unpaved roads in North Borneo cost less than $20,000 a mile. There is also no relationship between these amounts and traffic several years later which was estimated at less than 150 vehicles per day for the highway in Bolivia and the roads in North Borneo and Uganda, between 400 and 700 on the Guatemalan and East-West highways, and almost 1,000 on the Friendship Highway and portions of the coastal highway in El Salvador (see Table VII-1). There are several factors which make these cost estimates hard to compare, such as the degree of inflation (since the highways were constructed at different times), the variations in the exchange rate between local currencies and U. S. dollars, and, of course, the nature of the terrain and standard of road built. But even considering these sources of cost variation, the kind of road and its cost per mile is not associated with the degree of success, however it is measured.

TABLE VII-1. *Selected Data from the Cases*

	Vehicles per Day, 2 to 5 Years after Construction	*Average Annual Change in Production in Area Affected (Percent)*	Approximate Cost of Road per Mile (U. S. Dollars)
Bolivia	102–120	*20*	134,000
El Salvador	150–1200	*80*	165,000
Guatemala	400–700	*5*	261,000
India	Under 100	*5*	14,000
Nicaragua	770–1500	*45*	100,000
North Borneo	n.a.	*35*	10,000–17,000
Peru	n.a.	*75*	n.a.
Thailand:			
Friendship	700–1000	*40*	150,000
East-West	40–470	*50*	210,000
Uganda	n.a.	*65*	n.a.
Venezuela	Over 5,000	*30*	1,600,000

Sources: Case Studies. Data refer to simple average annual increases, not compound rates of growth, rounded to nearest 5 percent. The production estimates were derived as follows:
  Bolivia: tonnage of rice and sugar production, 1950–58.
  El Salvador: tonnage of cotton production, 1953–54 to 1963–64.
  Guatemala: estimated from tonnage handled at the ports influenced by the highway, 1953–62.
  India: weight of agricultural output excluding paddy, in the study area, 1954–55 to 1958–59.
  Nicaragua: average of weight of cotton and sugar output for Departments of Chinandega and León, 1951–52 to 1962–63.
  North Borneo: land demand, 1953–60.
  Peru: lumber production in the Chinchamayo-Oxapampa area, 1942–51.
  Thailand: Friendship, weight of output of upland crops and vegetables, in provinces affected, 1957–61.
          East-West, weight of output of upland crops and vegetables, in provinces affected, 1957–62.
  Uganda: average of weight of cotton output for Madi and Jonam, 1948–49 to 1955–56.
  Venezuela: production index average for Department of Aragua and Carabobo, 1954–60.

Rates and Service

The mechanism that served to stimulate additional output, cultivation of new lands, and more passenger travel was, in every case except that of El Salvador, a rather sharp decrease in freight and passenger charges as well as improved service. This, however, did not happen spontaneously. Moreover, some commodities and segments of the region benefited more than others, and there was wide variety in the extent of average rate decreases. As far as penetration facilities are concerned, it is not proper to speak of rate decreases since no previous service existed, but in most cases there were alternative connections, more or less devious, hazardous, and costly. Rough estimates suggest that rates for most of the commodities involved dropped by about 50 percent in the Guatemalan, Bolivian, and Indian cases and by even more than this on the Friendship and Nicaraguan Pacific Littoral highways. However, in El Salvador passenger and freight rates on the railroad which paralleled the road for part of its distance did not drop. Furthermore, it is estimated that the cost of moving maize from Korat to Bangkok is about the same whether by rail or by the Friendship Highway. It is not clear whether the rail rate prior to the highway was much higher than at present. Data on rates for the other cases are either not available or indicate a mixed pattern. These rate changes hide a wide variety of changes as among commodities: import rates, where relevant, fell more than export rates, and rates for local traffic declined more than those for through traffic.

The difference in the extent of rate reduction between imports and exports reflects the typical situation in an underdeveloped country. Bulky, low unit value agricultural commodities predominate among export commodities. High unit value manufactured goods constitute the major proportion of total imports. This meant that before road competition, the rail rate *from* the ports was significantly higher than the rate *to* the ports, since "value of service" rate-making principles typify most rail networks. Furthermore, the import traffic in general is more suited to truck transport than is the export traffic. Thus, the import rate by rail was especially vulnerable to truck competition. It is not surprising that when road facilities were made available, the prime target was the import traffic. In the Nicaraguan case, rail rates on imported goods declined by well over 50 percent, while export rates on cotton and coffee were reduced by only 11 and 19 percent respectively. The rail rates in the Atlantic Highway case showed a somewhat similar pattern. The export rates for sugar and coffee were reduced by about 10 and 50 percent, respectively, between 1958 and 1963, while import rates on competitive truck traffic were generally halved.

On the other hand, the even more drastic rate reduction for local traffic was not primarily the result of "excessive" rail rates where rail transport was an alternative. Rather, it was the high cost of indigenous forms of transport and vigorous competition among the large number of independent truckers who suddenly emerged.

For example, the short-haul cotton traffic from the field to the cotton gin in Nicaragua was estimated to cost 35 cents per ton kilometer by oxcart and only 10 cents by truck. In the Western Montaña of Central Peru, costs by mule per ton-mile are more than double those by air and many times higher than by truck, where these forms of transport are possible.

In places where rail competition existed, the rates on local traffic generally declined very sharply. In the Guatemalan case, the rail rate for general merchandise was reduced from almost $2.00 per hundredweight in 1957 to $0.40 in 1963. This put additional pressure on truck charges aside from what was caused by competition among the truckers themselves. The marked service advantage of motor transport over rail, especially for short hauls, meant that a substantial diversion from rail to truck could not be prevented. Indeed, the railway in Guatemala acknowledged that shippers prefer truck service for export cotton. Shorthaul truck rates up to 50 percent above the corresponding rail rate did not prevent the loss of local traffic to trucks.

But no downward rate change was possible without the creation of excess capacity in transport at the previous rate and relative freedom to set whatever rates seemed necessary. Where some type of restriction on entry into the trucking business was in force—for example, in Guatemala—the results were among the poorest although evasion of the law and lack of enforcement served to offset the importance of the restrictions. Again, in the Bolivian case part of the failure to reduce rates, at least during the early years, has been attributed to monopolistic tariffs imposed through ". . . restrictive practices of the Cochabamba and Santa Cruz road haulers' federations."[4]

Two preconditions for rate changes were the rise or expansion of entrepreneurial activity in the provision of transport service and the absence of direct or indirect restrictions. Despite a sharp decline in rates charged, new or existing transport firms still found it sufficiently profitable, at least in the short run, to initiate or expand service to the area served by the new right-of-way. In

[4] J. Colin Crossley, "Santa Cruz at the Cross-Roads, A Study of Development in Eastern Bolivia," *Tijdschrift voor Economische en Sociale Geographie* (August 1961), p. 204. The income from a round trip, Cochabamba to Santa Cruz, in 1958 was estimated at $185, while costs were only $110. *Ibid.*

all cases, the transport industry received an influx of small-scale operators in response to the new economic opportunity, and the low-level instability of rates and service typical of this kind of operation naturally ensued. Vehicle registrations in the areas directly affected increased more rapidly than the national average, and the number of vehicles utilizing the highway rose even faster as trucks, buses, and automobiles were diverted from other more costly routes.

In Nicaragua an economic slump occurred between 1957 and 1962, occasioned by declining coffee and cotton prices. Despite the fact that the slump led to a contraction in the purchase of vehicles, traffic along the completed portion of the Pacific Littoral Highway rose steadily from 277 vehicles a day (counted at a station 30 kilometers north of Managua) to 1200 in 1963. This suggests some diversion from other routes as well as increased utilization of the existing stock of vehicles.

Even in the less successful Guatemalan case, as soon as the paved highway was completed, trucking interests commenced to operate to and from the port, precipitating a serious rate war. Since there was no significant increase in the size of the country's vehicle fleet, this represented mainly a reallocation of motor transport in response to the increased profit potentials created by the highway. That the response was substantial is indicated by the fact that in 1963, eighteen bus companies were operating over the entire length of the highway, while eighty-nine others were licensed to operate over routes which required the use of portions of the road. Thirty-seven larger trucking firms used the highway, and although data are lacking, it is believed that several times this number operate as small independent truckers or owner-operators.

Vehicle registration in the provinces directly affected by the Friendship and East-West highways in Thailand showed markedly faster rates of growth than for all of Thailand. There is also evidence suggesting that the number of vehicles per day is continuing to rise, although no data are given on the number and type of transport firms operating along these highways.

Similar data are not available for all of the other cases, but it is clear that something of the same type of phenomenon must have occurred in response to production increases. At the same time that rates decreased, the service became faster, and accommodations for small shipments over relatively short distances were improved.

Transit Time and Flexibility of Service

Time in transit was sharply reduced, compared with previous alternatives, in almost all cases. Before the road in Bolivia was completed, travel between Cochabamba and Santa Cruz, even during the dry season, took two to four days. It now takes about half a day to a day during all seasons. On both the East-West and Friendship highways in Thailand, time savings of over 50 percent were achieved between important points, compared to the next best alternative. The same is true of the several areas in the Peruvian Western Montaña with respect to travel time to Lima. Time savings in the Nicaraguan case amount to about one-third, although this was not directly attributable to the road, since the railways had installed better equipment in 1955 which improved speeds by this amount.

Of greater importance, especially to local traffic and small entrepreneurs, is the increased flexibility of service and the ability to transport smaller amounts economically. Average loads, with few exceptions, run barely 4 to 10 tons, depending on the country and nature of the vehicle. Door-to-door service also eliminates the time and extra cost of transshipment.

Furthermore, truck transport is inherently more capable of tailoring service to specific needs, especially of small-scale producers. Not only is there more frequent scheduling of service or more service provided on demand but also truck drivers sometimes assist in loading and perform other services for small individual producers that a railroad could not. It is not surprising that the bulk of short-haul, local traffic now moves by truck in virtually all the cases examined. This is, of course, consistent with the technology and economics of road as compared with rail transportation.

Because of the nature of these changes, substantial benefits accrued to those located near the highway relatively close to the market as well as to middlemen who handle small quantities at any one time. Where the highway paralleled a rail connection, the relative advantage was even greater since there was no need to transship, and smaller loads could be moved more efficiently. In all such cases a more rational traffic allocation ensued. The less-than-carload, short-distance traffic which was assigned high rail rates was captured by the trucks. This permitted, or forced, the railroad to concentrate more on the type of traffic for which it has an "inherent advantage." The importance of this traffic shift was particularly pronounced in those instances where the railroad was operating at or beyond full economic capacity.

The effect of a net increase in mobility was to bring about improved utilization of an expanded transport capacity. Both the former users of alternative modes of transport as well as the new users benefited. At the same time, fewer resources were used than would otherwise have been the case. More traffic was carried at lower real cost per unit, as well as at lower rates, because of the new facility and the increased number of vehicles.

Population

Even in the absence of information concerning regional demographic trends, a positive relationship between new transport capacity and population was evident. For particular regions, transport facilities are both cause and consequence of population growth. When transport creates new economic opportunity, it attracts people to the area. Increases in output usually require more labor; higher incomes attract new settlers; and a demand for services, shops, and so on emerges. So long as markets remain favorable and the resource base undepleted, this process becomes self-reinforcing, and the rate of population growth in the region affected is accelerated.

One of the most striking illustrations of what improved access means in terms of population growth is provided by Drewes' comparison of the four areas in central Peru, although, as has already been noted, cause and effect are not readily separated. The slowest and steadiest growth of population was recorded in Pozuzo, which has been virtually isolated since 1900 and grew almost entirely without immigration. On the other hand, population grew sharply in the Tingo Maria-Pucallpa area after completion of the road connection to Lima. Satipo is an example of induced volatility. The population increased sharply after decades of stagnation after access was improved in 1940, and decreased just as sharply after the road was destroyed in 1947.

But the complexity of the interrelationships between improved access and population growth is suggested by the Bolivian and Guatemalan cases. It is true that the city of Santa Cruz grew at a rate well above the national average between 1950 and 1962, but this was due to a complex of factors, only one of which is the Cochabamba-Santa Cruz highway. Furthermore, the Department of Santa Cruz recorded a rate of population growth *below* the national average and only one-fourth that of the city of Santa Cruz. In the Guatemalan case, little migration has occurred and the overall demographic impact has been negligible.

Improvements in health, resettlement schemes, and relative economic potential of particular areas are more significant than access, per se, regardless of the fact that access of some sort is a necessary condition for effective attacks on disease and resettlement (for example, El Salvador), as well as exploitation of economic opportunity. Just as in the growth of production, population responds differently to new transport capacity depending upon a complex of conditions.

Conclusion

In every case, the extent of new traffic generated depended mainly upon the availability of easily exploitable natural resources. The lowest levels of traffic, omitting the earth roads in Uganda and North Borneo for which traffic estimates are lacking, were associated with highways traversing a territory poor in resources. The Guatemalan, Bolivian, and Indian experiences typify this situation.[5] The largest traffic volumes, or those growing most rapidly, involved highways through areas rich in forest reserves or with good soil conditions for cash crops. This was especially true in Nicaragua, El Salvador, Venezuela, Peru, and Thailand. Additional inducements to open up new lands were population pressure, rising prices for the crops concerned, reduced transport charges, and improved service. In short, the highest traffic volumes were fairly consistently associated with rising net receipts to producers of agricultural products. No adequate details of actual or possible profit prospects were provided, but the inference is clear that they created a powerful inducement to raise output and sell a greater proportion of it in local, sectional, or world markets. Some of the evidence on production changes is presented in Table VII-1. The data are not strictly comparable, nor can they be assumed accurate in all cases. Details of their

[5] A comparison of the Atlantic Highway in Guatemala with the Pacific highways in both Nicaragua and El Salvador is instructive. The major highway investment in Guatemala before 1960 was remote from the good cotton area on the Pacific Coast. Preoccupation with the Atlantic Highway thus delayed construction of a highway designed to tap the fertile Pacific littoral. In Nicaragua and El Salvador, on the other hand, the major highway expenditures were associated with the rising profit prospects for cotton as both cause and consequence. The evidence on physical cotton output and, more important, the value of cotton exports indicates clearly the opportunity cost to Guatemala of the Atlantic Highway. The big spurt in cotton occurred in Nicaragua in about 1953-54 and in El Salvador in 1955-56. The value of cotton exports had remained negligible up to these dates, at which time they roughly doubled. Exports continued to increase despite declines in cotton prices after 1956 and by 1963 were over six times the levels prevailing prior to 1953-54. In Guatemala, on the other hand, negligible exports of cotton prevailed until 1961, when they doubled and continued to grow rapidly, reaching a value in 1963 almost five times that prevailing in the best years before 1960. The take-off dates for cotton in each country coincide with the beginning of construction of highways designed to tap the fertile coastal area on the Pacific. (The data upon which the above was based are from Joseph H. Steveson, *Cotton Production in Central America*, [Cotton Division, Foreign Agricultural Service, U. S. Department of Agriculture, November, 1963]).

In other words, the delay in building a Pacific littoral highway in Guatemala, which was doubtless occasioned by, among other reasons, the difficulty surrounding the Atlantic Highway, prevented a full and early participation in the cotton boom. Thus, higher foreign exchange earnings and possibly overall economic growth as well were delayed some five or six years as a result of the decision to build the Atlantic Highway, which did little in a developmental sense. It is difficult not to conclude that Guatemala built the wrong highway at the wrong time, and, as shown in the case, for the wrong reasons.

computation are given in the notes to the table. But with all their weaknesses, they do suggest the radically different impact on production between the Guatemalan, Indian, and to some extent the Bolivian cases and all the others. With appropriate qualifications, these data may be construed as rough indicators of the relative degree of success. Using this criterion, even considering the costs per mile and amount of traffic, the least successful roads, up to the present, are those in the three countries just mentioned.

It cannot, however, be stressed too much that this evidence by itself, even ignoring its frail statistical basis, is inconclusive for the reasons already discussed. Nor has it been possible to deduce a consistent set of calculations yielding a meaningful and comparable benefit-cost ratio. But the inferences deduced from the behavior of production in the affected areas are consistent with the impressionistic evidence concerning relative profitability, which itself is closely associated with the availability of natural resources in the regions.

As far as causation is concerned, we have noted the role of the highways in Bolivia, Guatemala, and India (even if there was not much in the way of development according to production indicators), as well as in both areas in Thailand, and in Peru and probably El Salvador. For the other cases, the highway or road is best construed as a response to a development that would probably have occurred in any event, although not necessarily in the same way nor to the same extent. The role of transport in the latter cases was more one of facilitating a dynamism already underway. In the former group the road was at least a partial initiator, inducing a development that would not otherwise be expected to occur. The relative lack of success to date in three of these instances does not detract completely from the importance of the particular road. Indeed, in Guatemala not only was there a large expansion in truck transport, but a new type of transport using refrigeration equipment appeared, and its prospects appear bright. In Bolivia the future success of the colonization scheme lies partly in the existence of a good connection between the highlands and the Santa Cruz area, to say nothing of the political significance of tying together two regions of a country hitherto separated physically and psychologically. Even in the Indian case, the growing number of market areas, a narrowing of regional price differentials, and the rapid expansion of some key products might well pave the way for accelerated growth in the future. However, data are not available to show what has taken place more recently in the Ramnad-Mandapam area.

What these three examples suggest is that, given a relatively static or deteriorating situation prior to the new transportation capacity, along with few readily exploitable natural resources, the task of initiating sustainable growth is both more difficult and more protracted, which implies the necessity of combining transport investment with other measures if important changes are to occur.

Furthermore, the three countries with the slowest rates of overall growth, as indicated in Chapter 1, coincide with the three relatively unsuccessful cases just mentioned. This would suggest that where there is a *general* lack of dynamism, there is also a greater probability that a specific investment will not become much of a success. Where there is a high degree of overall dynamism, on the other hand, a specific investment is apt to become an apparent success for two reasons: (1) The greater the general rate of growth the more likely it is that any investment will appear as a necessary response to prevent or alleviate a bottleneck situation; or (2) even in the absence of an actual or incipient bottleneck, a rapid rate of expansion is associated with an environment where additional economic opportunity is not only more assiduously sought but more rigorously exploited. The reverse typifies a situation of persistent overall stagnation.

In the next chapter a more general interpretation of these apparent results is made. There follows an attempt to assess the broader implications of the importance of transportation to economic growth and what the cases suggest in terms of the theory of economic growth.

CHAPTER VIII

Toward a Theory of Transport and Development

GEORGE W. WILSON

THE VARIATION OF RESULTS in the cases examined may be explained by differences in two main factors: (1) the creation of economic opportunity and (2) the response to economic opportunity. The first depends upon the quality and quantity of resources in the regions served, the actual change in transport rates and service, and commodity price levels. The second depends upon an awareness of opportunity and what may be broadly defined as attitudes toward economic change.

Economic Opportunity

The extent of the economic opportunity created has two main dimensions, both of which are functions of natural resources and the rate and service changes in the transport sector. Human resources are ignored at this point and will be discussed later.

The Resource Base

In every case where a road opened up new territory, the soil or forest conditions in the area determined not only the type of activity but also much of the increase in output. The suitability of the soils when coupled with feeder roads is mainly responsible for the sharp increases in production that took place. Profit prospects for agriculture and forestry widened appreciably in most of the cases because of a combination of higher yields in the areas, rising prices, and declining freight rates. Even where prices of the major products were declining or stable over the period under review, the increase in yields, combined with reduced freight charges and improved service, increased growers' net receipts. For the most part, prices were determined in markets outside the local area which meant that rising local supplies exerted little or no influence on price. The general picture thus fits a model of perfect competition, with the demand schedule perfectly elastic at the externally determined, though variable, price. The stimulus to production was due to declining unit costs of production and distribution. The stimulus was accentuated in some cases by rising prices or partially offset by declining prices. Where prices were falling and yields not increasing, the key to development was the decline in transportation costs. In a situation with improving yields or rising prices, reduced freight rates merely provided a further stimulus, and the new transport capacity was permissive and responsive rather than causal.

The Transport Sector

The extent of apparent economic opportunity in both the transport and nontransport sectors is a direct function of the natural resources that are made more accessible. There may be divergent effects between the sectors, due to rate and quality changes. The extent of the negative impact on transport of lower rates depends upon the elasticity of demand for transport and the behavior of unit costs with changes in volume. Little is known about this in the situations investigated here. Except for local truck traffic, a high degree of demand elasticity for trucking is apparent. It is probably fair to say that the total amount of economic opportunity created varies inversely with rate levels, since the stimulus to increase production probably more than compensates for any possible increase in unit costs of providing transport service. If unit costs decline with volume, as seems likely, and assuming appropriately high demand elasticities, lower rates may benefit both producers of commodities and suppliers of transport. The immediate result, as is evident in most of the cases, was the creation of an excess capacity in vehicles which probably depressed rates below levels that would be sustainable over time. The very large number of owner-operated trucking firms gave rise to a level of rates that can only mean bankruptcy for many of them. Later upward revisions of rates can and are to be expected. This appears to have happened already in the Guatemalan situation.

The excess capacity may have a lasting advantage, however. First, it provides some experience in business enterprise that, while discouraging to some, might prove salutary to others. Second, the sharp stimulus to production and new settlement was due in most cases to other factors as well as to unduly low rates. The gains appear to be sustainable even in the face of later rate increases. It is even possible that lower net income per unit of agricultural output, once production was established, would induce a greater output to maintain the producer's overall income, although this is by no means certain. Better still, it might encourage the use of fertilizers or other improvements that lead to lower unit costs. These improvements would have a much more permanent influence on yields.

Responses to Economic Opportunity

Attitudes and awareness influence the response of individuals to the creation of economic opportunity. The response may be zero, negative, or positive in terms of developmental impact and is broadly bound up with aspects of culture, social relationships, individual psychology, and levels of well-being. It is here that the economist steps gingerly into that overflowing category of "other things" in the qualification "other things being equal." Formal economic models make little reference to these reactions and presume responses roughly applicable to institutions mainly relevant to western economic systems. Despite the serious misgivings of some economists,[1] the bulk of growth theory continues to be over-

---

[1] For example, "in those countries where growth seems most essential for human welfare, problems outside the conventional limits of economics are surely paramount. Indeed, a strong argument can be made that the problem of underdevelopment will not be solved until economics has achieved a more compatible marriage

ly schematic, general, and aggregative. Some economists have turned completely to noneconomic explanations or have raised serious questions whether economic development has much to do with economic matters at all, at least in the form of contemporary micro- and macro-analysis developed in the West.

The purpose here is not to analyze the growing guilt feelings of economists in understandably deemphasizing institutional factors but to suggest that a meaningful interpretation, especially of localized growth, cannot ignore them. In the case studies, several situations have been noted where ethnic differences appear crucial—for example, North Borneo and Peru. It cannot be assumed the other cases are immune from such influences.

In considering the question of attitudes that influence the response to economic or other types of change, the economist must tread warily. Yet tread he must if he is to derive relevant conclusions and make useful policy suggestions. Essentially the question is: under what circumstances and to what extent will economic opportunity be exploited in such a way that net output per capita rises? Additional transport capacity generates new opportunities for pecuniary gain. There is no apparent consistency in the extent to which such opportunities are seized or in the apparent consequences.

The main factors influencing the response to new transport capacity are: (a) awareness of its potential, (b) the availability of finance, and (c) the magnitude of the possible benefits relative to alternative investment options.

Awareness of the New Potential

Obviously, to evoke any response people must know that new economic opportunity has developed. The extent of awareness of the consequences of additional transport capacity depends in large part on the number of people who are directly influenced. The greater the population in the area through which the new or improved facility runs, the more extensive is the knowledge of what it might accomplish. More people can sense the fact that

than now prevails with other social sciences." Bert F. Hoselitz and others, *Theories of Economic Growth* (The Free Press of Glencoe, 1960), p. 242.

something new has happened that may be of benefit to them. In areas where communication is defective, this is obviously important. But beyond the mere numbers of people affected, there is the question of accessibility. A pipeline traversing a heavily populated area cannot evoke much response, whereas an unlimited-access road can. The unlimited access of roads in the early stages of development of any region has an awareness effect that serves to induce a larger number of people to take advantage of new economic potential. This contrasts with the direct economic stimulus of limited-access highways where congestion or local bottlenecks slow down traffic and raise the costs of transport. Indeed, it is this feature that underlies the frequent assertions that the indirect or spillover effects of road transport are more important than the direct reductions in user costs and faster transit.[2] The so-called "openness of roads"[3] acts as a kind of advertisement for its own economic potential, to which many individuals may respond since it is not a private nor a closed public facility accessible to only a handful of owners or employees.

Railroads are in a peculiar situation in this regard. To increase accessibility requires more stations along the line and hence shorter hauls and more frequent stops, which is inconsistent with economical operation. Increased accessibility for railroads is thus purchased at the expense of higher costs which in turn require higher rates if the facility is to be self-supporting. While increased accessibility is stimulating in itself, the higher rates reduce the magnitude of economic opportunity created and thereby offset to a greater or lesser extent the stimulus to development due to improved access. Railroads have been most successful in moving large amounts of goods over long distances from a specific region to a port or a major consuming center. The developmental impact along the right-of-way is generally far less than for facilities that are more open.

---

[2] For example, R. S. Millard argues that unlike developed countries, in overseas territories, "the benefits from road construction are almost entirely in the form of new development from the traffic which the new road will generate." R. S. Millard, "Road Development in the Overseas Territories," *Journal of the Royal Society of Arts* (March 1959), p. 275.

[3] This suggestive phrase is from Edwin T. Haefele, "Road Construction as a Means of Developing Areas Served," Document No. 57, *Ninth Pan American Highway Congress* (Organization of American States, May 6-18, 1963).

Effects of Different Kinds of Investment

In underdeveloped economies, there are important variations in the *kind* of impact to be expected from alternative investments in the field of transportation and elsewhere. Some types of capital formation have spillover effects, in addition to direct effects, that differ greatly from others. Indeed, it is precisely these varying possibilities that economic planners seek to exploit in attempting to maximize the rate of growth of output. But economic analysis ranks investment projects by some version of "expected rate of return" or benefit-cost ratio, both of which typically ignore many indirect and noneconomic effects. Yet the creation of economic capacity is only permissive. Effective utilization and augmentation require attitudes, abilities, and incentives that cannot be taken for granted in most underdeveloped economies. It has often been stressed that the key to sustainable economic growth is a change in attitudes toward work, business, thrift, and so on. Therefore, another way of ranking investment projects is by their effect on attitudes. In this respect, certain investments may provide a greater catalytic effect than others whose immediate payoff in increased output is far superior.

Thus investment outlets might usefully be construed in terms of their relative influence on attitudes vis-à-vis labor productivity through an increase in the capital-labor ratio. The first refers to a qualitative change in the labor input, while the latter refers to a quantitative change in the amount of capital relative to the quantity of labor. Both affect productivity, although in different ways. Changes in attitudes may positively influence productivity with no increase in physical capital, that is, by altering the duration and intensity of labor or stimulating entrepreneurial activity. Likewise, it is possible to raise efficiency by additional machinery without changing attitudes, through adaptation of the equipment to contemporary customs and attitudes. These are extremes, of course. In most instances some degree of change in attitude will be induced by additional equipment. That is, workers and management will have to adjust somewhat to new techniques or even to an extension of existing facilities, and these in turn may partly be arranged to suit existing attitudes.

But the point is that it is possible to array alternative investment possibilities in terms of their direct impact upon efficiency through their effects on the quantity of directly productive capital on the one hand and their influence on attitudes on the other.

Investments in health, education, and propaganda, for example, are direct attacks on attitudes and abilities that do not create capital for directly productive activities. At the other extreme is investment in a particular factory which may have no influence on attitudes or at best influence only those directly employed. It also appears that the overall incidence of these two extremes, in terms of numbers of people affected by the investments, is significantly different. Investments in directly productive facilities usually affect a far smaller number of people than investments in health, education, or general communications.

Between these two extremes are a series of other investment options that influence attitudes and either facilitate the development of directly productive activities or are a form of such activity themselves. We may therefore place particular kinds of investment along a continuum as portrayed in Figure VIII-1. At one extreme A are those investments that affect only attitudes but have no impact on efficiency directly, while at the other extreme are investments that only have such an impact. As one moves from A to B, the relative importance of the direct influence on efficiency through a change in the capital-labor ratio increases vis-à-vis the impact on attitudes, and conversely when moving from B to A. The particular investments arrayed on the scale are based on intuitive judgment for the most part. However, the discussion will examine the position of transport investments as a whole and the position of particular forms of transportation on this continuum.

This taxonomy does not suggest that if an investment is placed closer to B than to A, it necessarily loses much of its influence on attitudes. It is only the ratio that varies as one moves along the scale. There is no attempt to apply isoquant analysis nor to suggest the substitution possibilities between investments in qualitative change in labor inputs and quantitative change in (directly productive) equipment. The nature of the relative payoffs are too intangible and amorphous to warrant application of the isoquant approach. Furthermore, the isoquant approach is concerned with an efficient allocation of capital and other resources *a priori,* whereas the interest of the present study centers on the explanation of events following a given investment.

Harvey Leibenstein has adopted an approach bearing some affinity to the above, but since his interests were on optimal allocation criteria, his use of the distinctions between the two types of investment which he calls "human" and "capital goods" is quite different from that in this study. Leibenstein's critique of the "social marginal productivity" criteria is consistent with the views expressed above. However, his use of a standard involving effects on the supply of entrepreneurship, future savings habits, population growth, and so on in the form of the familiar isoquant approach implies a degree of possible quantification that seems unrealistic.[4] In this sense, Hirschman's comment that Leibenstein's "criticism seems likely to result in an agnostic 'it all depends' attitude since it seriously impairs the usefulness of the SMP [social marginal productivity] criterion without replacing it by a manageable new instrument" seems valid.[5] But Leibenstein's critique of SMP is valid enough—it is only his substitute criteria that seem defective.

Rosenberg has pointed to a classification roughly analogous to that in the text. For example, he argues that

> Economic growth is, in many important respects, a learning process, a process whereby the human factor acquires new skills, aptitudes, capabilities, and aspirations. And the pattern of resource use which may maximize output from a given stock of resources may or may not generate the qualitative changes in the human agent which are most conducive to the growth of output in subsequent time periods.

Neo-classical economics fails to capture much of the explanation for the growth in productivity because of the failure to consider a variety of feedback mechanisms. We fail to consider, for example, the impact upon productivity of certain kinds of economic activi-

---

[4] Harvey Leibenstein, *Economic Backwardness and Economic Growth* (John Wiley & Sons, 1957), Chapter 15.

[5] Albert O. Hirschman, *The Strategy of Economic Development* (Yale University Press, 1962), p. 77.

ties as opposed to others—such as manufacturing vs. agriculture. Different kinds of economic activities have different kinds of effects upon the productivity of the human agent. . . .[6]

The present aim is to analyze further the results of the case studies by examining the extent to which the investments influenced attitudes aside from their direct technical efficiency.

FIGURE VIII-1. *Investment Options and Attitudes*

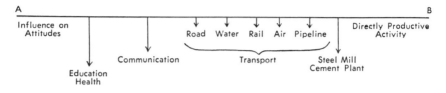

Figure VIII-1 implies that transport investments lie intermediate on the scale between *A* and *B*. This position requires some comment. Investments in transportation have a wider geographical dimension than almost any other. Therefore, they affect a far greater number of people and in a more intimate fashion than does a factory or other facility requiring a specific location.[7] Furthermore, access to the latter types of investment is limited mainly to employees, although their products may be widely distributed. But even wide distribution of products will not affect attitudes nor give rise to much additional economic opportunity unless the product is a producer's good, in which case it will be acquired mainly by people already "developed" in an entrepreneurial or business sense.[8]

[6] Nathan Rosenberg, "Neglected Dimensions in the Analysis of Economic Change," *Bulletin of the Oxford University Institute of Economics and Statistics*, Vol. 26, No. 1 (February 1964), p. 61.

[7] However, although an investment may affect large numbers of people, this does not guarantee that the impact will be favorable. Often such an impact will make certain people cling even more compulsively to traditional ways. Much depends on the magnitude and nature of the investment as well as on its geographical dispersion and the number of people directly influenced.

[8] However, we cannot argue confidently that a series of small factories whose total cost equals that of one major transport facility will necessarily have a smaller favorable impact than the facility itself. The discussion here is mainly heuristic and admittedly tentative. I am indebted to Professor E. E. Hagen for these and other caveats regarding this section of the manuscript.

Perhaps location in a densely populated area may increase the exposure of a new investment. However, it is in urban areas that one finds a dense population and the greatest degree of development and the widest range of economic opportunity already existing. It is in the more traditional rural areas that change is urgently needed since generally the bulk of the population is rural. Thus a steel mill in an urban complex will not have much influence on attitudes despite the fact that large numbers of people are aware of it. Transport facilities, on the other hand, not only can be used directly by many people but when extended into rural areas can bring a greater proportion of the most traditional aspects of a society into direct contact with new phenomena. Transport investment brings greater opportunity to extensive areas most in need of it. If freight rates and passenger fares are reduced substantially, transport can, and in most cases does, stimulate use—as the case studies amply demonstrate. At the same time an acute awareness of new capabilities is communicated to a large number of people, possibly more than from any other form of investment.

The point of this kind of classification is to emphasize a different set of options from the ones traditional theory distinguishes and to stress the point that investments differ in the extent to which they affect *both* attitudes and technical productivity. Yields from an investment that affect mainly productivity are specific and quantifiable and may be substantial and immediate. On the other hand, the payoff from education, for example, is diffuse. It may also be substantial, but it is normally remote in time and nonquantifiable. Since it is agreed that for sustainable economic growth attitudes must change and efficiency of employed resources must rise (the two being related in an as yet ill-understood fashion), economic planners in reality have a much broader range of investment and expenditure options than that implied in the traditional rate-of-return calculus.

TRANSPORT AND ACCESSIBILITY. Since our main concern in this study is with transportation investment, it is important to stress the degree to which the several forms of transport influence both attitudes and directly productive activities. In general, the extent of awareness of new investments and their potential noneconomic effects are a direct function of the degree of accessibility to them.

Within the range of possible transport investments we have at one extreme pipelines which have a geographic dimension but have few effects of the indirect type indicated above. Indeed, a pipeline is better viewed as part of the investment in the industry it serves; it is part of a directly productive activity. At the other extreme is investment in road right-of-way.

Because of a higher degree of accessibility, a road permits use of relatively small and inexpensive units of capital (trucks, buses, cars) under independent ownership without serious economic penalty, since the evidence tends to support the belief that there are no economies of scale in motor transport.[9] There is little need for, and less possibility of, large-scale, remote, or alien ownership of trucking facilities than is the case with other modes of transport. This permits a greater number of small, local entrepreneurs to enter the industry and provides experience in management that may be widely shared and readily grasped. Motor transport has few of the problems associated with persistent income remission to other areas or resentment of a foreign-owned enterprise. Repair and maintenance of vehicles is not technically difficult and can be learned quickly by almost anyone willing to make the attempt.[10] The ability to transport small shipments more efficiently than other modes of transport is especially important in the early stages of development, when trading is highly individualized and individual sales are relatively small. The greater number of participants in the trucking industry implies a more competitive outcome with the result that cost reductions are passed on to shippers to a greater extent than for other, more monopolistic transport enterprises. There is also contact with other types of business which may broaden the trucker's horizons and induce entry into new fields.

[9] A qualification is needed here, however. In many underdeveloped countries there is a general absence of ancillary facilities which requires producers to supply these themselves. Thus in motor transport there may be scale economies where substantial investments are needed in maintenance and repair facilities but which are not worthwhile for companies or individuals having only a few vehicles.

[10] For example, Farmer reports that "the Saudis have easily taken to mechanical transport, and while their illiteracy occasionally creates operating problems, driving ability is a widespread skill in the area." Richard N. Farmer, "Inland Freight Transportation Pricing in Eastern Saudi Arabia," *The Journal of Industrial Economics* (July 1962), p. 177.

There are other advantages of a political and social nature. Centralized control of the highway system is not required to the same extent as in the case of rail, water, air, and pipelines. This permits a higher degree of local participation in both construction and maintenance. Local participation has its special problems, but it imparts experience in administration and control. Socially and culturally, road transport permits, and usually generates, a higher degree of personal contact than trains that pass or planes that fly overhead. As Haefele puts it, "the combination of rail and trail holds far less promise for social development than does a road net. . . . Trains go by and trucks stop—an essential difference when viewed as carriers of culture instead of freight."[11]

Thus the technology of road transport is such that it has greater potential for involving more people in a wider variety of endeavors than any other form of transport. It therefore has an influence on attitudes and abilities that cannot be captured in any calculation of net benefits. In the final analysis this may be more important than the direct economic benefits.

Others have pointed out the possible "teaching" effect of motor carriers. A statement from the Pan American Union argues that road transportation is

> . . . a medium that can be organized into small companies, thereby helping to create . . . a group of entrepreneurs worthy of consideration. In this connection, the carrier with small resources is distinguished from the small tradesman in that, whereas the latter is concerned only with the use of working capital, the former, because he is using fixed capital, has to cope with the more complex problems relating to depreciation, obsolescence, and maintenance. That is why the small carrier has been assigned considerable importance as a future industrial entrepreneur.[12]

The implication is that the greater the accessibility or openness and the more people directly influenced by the facility, the greater the probability of development, so long as costs of transport are substantially reduced. This does not mean that rail or other facilities designed to exploit a large mineral deposit or extensive

[11] *Op. cit.*, p. 7.
[12] Pan American Union, *General Problems of Transportation in Latin America* (Washington, 1963), p. 31.

plantations do not have significant effects. Rather, in such cases, much of the railroad investment is better construed as part of the overall investment associated with exploitation of a relatively localized productive activity.

Classification of Transport Investments

Lumping all transport capacity together under the heading of social overhead capital may be seriously misleading. Some portion of each form of transportation is specific in the sense that in reality it is geared to a particular industry; its developmental potential is then intimately associated with the industry in question. In such cases it is no more meaningful to talk about the relationship of transportation to economic development than it is to refer to the relationship of any industry to growth. It is frequently suggested that transport facilities serve a wide variety of industries and it is this aspect that leads people to regard them as social overhead. Indeed this leads to the common carrier obligation. On an aggregative basis this is no doubt valid, but in the process of disaggregation, the validity of this aspect of transport is considerably reduced. In an underdeveloped economy with a small undiversified manufacturing sector and a large agricultural sector specializing in one or a few crops, the transportation facilities are bound to be far more specific and less social. At the same time, the carriers function less as common carriers regardless of their legal status. In general, the lower the level of economic development, the higher the degree of transport specificity. This is true for modes that in other more developed and diversified economies are in fact, as well as by law, common carriers.

In short, it seems preferable to treat much of transport capacity as part of the main industry it serves, especially in underdeveloped economies. An oil pipeline is an obvious example, but a railway or road that passes through barren territory to connect an isolated natural resource to a local market or port is not very different. The social nature of any transport facility increases as the degree of resource isolation diminishes and the territory along the right-of-way improves; that is to say, as the level and extent of potential or actual economic development rises. In the cases examined here, virtually all the roads serve a single sector—agriculture—and even within that sector the major traffic is in one or two export crops. Generally the longer the highway, the less specific it is, depending on the nature of the territory along the right-of-way, which will influence the extent and diversity of possible ribbon development. Likewise the higher the level of economic development, the less specific the highway. The Friendship Highway in Thailand contrasts sharply with the Ramnad-Mandapam road and the penetration roads in Uganda and North Borneo.

As soon as a distinction is made among types of transport in terms of degree of attachment to a particular industry or product, it can be decided whether it is preferable to lump the transport investment with the industry, then examine the developmental impact of that industry, or assign the investment to transport in general. As Cootner puts it, ". . . instead of lumping all railroad investment in social overhead capital, we can treat the construction of transcontinental railroads separately from investment which involves short spur lines to serve additional plants at lower cost, or double tracking, or new equipment. A new farm in a settled area need not be treated as identical with a farm on the frontier which depends on the construction of a railroad to be profitable."[13]

The roads that have been classified as merely permissive and responsive to already established trends represent part of the investment in the particular industries whose activity induced their construction. In the other, noncausal situations, road construction, being responsive to already rising profit prospects, is uniquely associated with them. As far as awareness in these cases is concerned, accessibility and numbers of people, while still important, are not the strategic factors in inducing favorable economic responses. The awareness was already there. In the other cases,

[13] Paul H. Cootner, "Social Overhead Capital and Economic Growth," in W. W. Rostow (ed.), *The Economics of Take-Off into Sustained Growth* (St. Martin's Press, 1963), p. 267. In another context, I have urged restraint in treating all aspects of investment in transport, even in a particular mode of transport, as a homogeneous whole. See my *Essays on Some Unsettled Questions in the Economics of Transportation*, Foundation for Economic and Business Studies (Indiana University, 1962), pp. 142-43. From a developmental point of view, this disaggregation seems particularly relevant.

these factors are much more significant as inducements to change.

Of course, the degree of attachment to a particular industry or type of economic activity would naturally be substantial at the outset. If further development follows, this specificity would be expected to decline in most cases. In the case of road transport, where the motive equipment itself is not generally specialized nor irrevocably committed to specific commodities or regions, there is much less long-range connection. Trucking firms established in response to, say, a sharp rise in cotton production might merely turn elsewhere in the event of a subsequent contraction. The ability of other modes to do this is more restricted.

THE PROBLEM OF ENTREPRENEURSHIP. Aside from the extent of awareness, which may be taken as a direct function of numbers of people affected and degree of access, there is the further problem of the kind of people influenced. This raises the issue of entrepreneurship and its distribution among both geographic areas and population groups according to ethnic distinctions, income, or education. Few of the cases here presented other than very impressionistic evidence on any of these points, and indeed there is no general agreement on the distribution of entrepreneurial talent.

In the literature on development there are frequent references to "pariah entrepreneurship," which attribute great significance to alien minorities, such as the Chinese and Indian traders in Southeast Asia, the Lebanese and Indians in Africa, and the Jews in Western Europe and the United States during various periods of history. The universality of such pariah entrepreneurship and its peculiar incidence among minority groups is often debated. This study makes no contribution to this debate but simply notes that divergent opinion persists.

But in almost all the present cases, the transport facilities directly affected rural environments, and, except for the examples in Peru, Bolivia, and North Borneo, there was no apparent ethnic or cultural divergence among those living in or near the affected localities. There were doubtless important differences in income distribution which may correlate in some fashion with both willingness and ability to respond to economic opportunity,[14] but no good evidence of this appeared. Therefore, as far as the present set of cases is concerned it seems reasonable to assume that among them the receptivity of and responses to new economic opportunities does not differ significantly. If this is a valid inference, it follows that as far as the response is concerned, we may interpret this strictly in terms of "awareness," which we have already equated with accessibility and numbers of people.

Yet there remain nagging doubts about such a cavalier dismissal. The fact that few specific examples show up in the cases does not prove uniformity of attitudes. Furthermore, the different effects earlier ascribed to the technologies of rail and road may not be completely technological after all. In almost all underdeveloped countries the railroads are owned by the government with key positions held by members of the dominant ethnic group. In some countries access to positions of responsibility is denied to minority groups. In the realm of transport this encourages the latter, who frequently are far more aggressive, to enter the trucking business where individual enterprise is more feasible anyway. There is accordingly in some countries an ethnic distinction in terms of ownership and operation of different modes of transport that correlates with variations in the degree of initiative, aggressiveness, and success. Some part of the observed developmental impact of road versus rail is doubtless attributable to this kind of ethnic phenomenon, especially in Thailand, and possibly, although to a lesser extent, in parts of Africa and Latin America. The dearth of evidence on this score, both within and beyond the transport sector, impels us to neglect its significance as far as the cases are concerned. The point is raised to suggest that this may be of some importance in particular regions and worthy of more careful investigation.[15]

[14] See George M. Foster, *Traditional Cultures and the Impact of Technological Change* (Harper, 1962), who argues that the people who are most receptive to new economic opportunity "are neither at the top nor the bottom of the local socio-economic scale," p. 172; Everett E. Hagen, *On the Theory of Social Change* (Dorsey Press, 1962), p. 30; and Max F. Millikan and Donald L. M. Blackmer, *The Emerging Nations, Their Growth and United States Policy* (Little Brown & Co., 1961), p. 38, also suggest something akin to Foster's view.

[15] The situation is all the more intriguing since somewhat similar disparities

The Availability of Finance

It is one thing to argue that knowledge of economic opportunity is intimately related to accessibility and numbers of people. It can be done by assuming that entrepreneurial talents are randomly distributed, or that in any given population the proportion of those responsive is roughly comparable. It is quite another matter to suggest that the ability exists to make the necessary investments either in providing transport or in expanding nontransport capacity. In the transport sector, the extension of service was usually undertaken by nonresidents of the area affected. Similarly, since part of the resources in the region were owned by nonresidents, the expansion of regional productive capacity likewise depended on the awareness and financial position of extraregional entrepreneurs. In Nicaragua, El Salvador, and Bolivia, there is direct evidence that much of the development was due to nonresident, either public or private, responses to economic opportunity. A simple relationship between numbers of people in or near the region and response is not to be expected. Yet in every economy, regardless of how poor or underdeveloped, there are always some people with the means to respond to new opportunities wherever they may be located. As in the case of public investment, the crucial consideration in such cases is the productivity, private or social, of the opportunity created by additional transport relative to other alternatives. Without a knowledge of the entire set of investment outlets, it is impossible to predict the importance of nonresident or exogenous responses in a particular region.

Furthermore, it is unlikely that the total response will come from such sources, although in some instances it may be very significant in inducing further development of the area along

---

between rail and road exist in countries without serious ethnic problems. India is an example, although the role of caste may lead to a kind of exclusiveness having the above-mentioned consequences. More generally it may be a question of private versus public ownership exacerbated in many cases by racial or caste differences, especially where rail transport is used as a broad instrument of social policy, in which case efficient use of rail facilities may be sacrificed for other purposes while truck transport is relatively immune from such social purpose functions.

lines suggested by Schumpeter's "herd of imitators." While the number of people aware of new opportunities and capable of responding may be widely dispersed geographically, it has not been possible from the cases analyzed here, to account for this in any general sense. The model thus relies mainly on the variables of accessibility and population affected, as measured by some index of regional population. That variations may exist due to nonresident participation is freely acknowledged and indeed is exemplified by the "agricultural entrepreneurs" in El Salvador.

But in a more general developmental sense, the availability of finance, like so much else, is permissive only. If those possessing the liquid capital choose to purchase land for speculation or to acquire existing assets or foreign securities, there will be no development stimulated in the country where they live. What is required is a set of arrangements designed to induce productive use of supernumerary income or wealth. If governments invest in transportation facilities in the hope of developing particular regions, it is then incumbent upon them to create favorable conditions for success. Governments may do this themselves or, if this is not possible or desirable, provide inducements that make private entrepreneurs respond in the desired fashion. The latter method may take the form either of making unattractive the use of funds that have no productive value to the nation or region or of increasing the profitability of private investments of the productive type. Certainly the use of new highways should not be restrained by high user charges, heavy taxation, or restriction on imports of vehicles, parts, or other capital equipment that is needed for effective exploitation of whatever new potential is created. Bold, daring entrepreneurs with wealth may devote their energies, time, talents, and money to a wide variety of activities which do almost nothing to raise the net national product but which are privately rewarding in prestige or money. As has been said, "What may be a source of income creation for the individual need not be a means of income creation as seen by the community at large."[16] The function of any public policy not totally committed to a goal of *public* enterprise is to create those arrangements that make "private vice" coalesce with "public virtue," as

---

[16] Leibenstein, *op. cit.*, p. 113.

Adam Smith long ago argued. The mere existence of economic surplus does not dictate that it will be used productively in an economic sense. Much depends on the set of options, and their costs, available to those with the ability to undertake them.

The Magnitude of Benefits

The problem of determining the amount of potential benefit has been discussed earlier. At this point it is worth stressing that unless potential benefit is large compared to existing alternatives, it is unlikely to evoke much response. Regardless of motivation, little can be expected in the way of development unless relatively large profit prospects are made available. In this sense, response to economic opportunity is closely related to its amount.

Disturbance of Existing Institutions

It has frequently been suggested that investments that involve the least change in institutions or, what is the same thing, investments that are readily adaptable to present techniques, abilities, and incentives, have the greatest likelihood of success.[17] A. E. Kahn argues that "modest projects which employ relatively little capital and attempt . . . a minimal disruption of settled habits of thinking and living are more likely to succeed than those which involve a mass frontal assault on nonwestern patterns of culture."[18]

On the other hand, without a change in institutions or even in people themselves,[19] there are few prospects of achieving sustainable growth. What is required, therefore, is something intermediate between a massive assault on culture and those investments that leave all else completely unchanged. This has direct relevance to road transport. In almost every case, the accessibility of roads, the ease of entry into trucking, as well as the prestige aspects of vehicle ownership, largely account for the sudden

[17] Foster, op. cit., p. 145.

[18] A. E. Kahn, "Investment Criteria in Development Program," Quarterly Journal of Economics (February 1951), p. 51.

[19] Leibenstein, op. cit., p. 113; Millikan and Blackmer, op. cit., p. 23; Hagen, op. cit.

growth of motorized for-hire transport which tends to insure that lower costs of transport are passed on to users.

In the final analysis it seems to be the rate of required adaptation that is crucial, and this is related to the extent to which efficient exploitation of new economic opportunity requires a radical departure from existing practices. Sudden changes are apt to be resisted strenuously. Since truck transport is less different from most forms of traditional transport than railroads or aircraft and the operating skills required more readily learned, the impact is less likely to evoke resistance.[20]

There is another aspect to the issue of institutional disturbance —the reaction of those whose economic and even social position may be undercut by the new transport capacity. If such groups are unable to impede the use of the new facility, the probability of its success is sharply increased. Yet resistance to technological change has been manifest in all societies in the past and has achieved varying degrees of success over fairly long periods of time. There is no reason to expect that such resistance will be any less vigorous in the future, especially in underdeveloped countries, where neither the range of alternatives nor the resources for compensation are very substantial.

In none of the cases was there any major assault on habits or institutional arrangements. But the impact on economic positions of some types of occupation was substantial. Alternative forms of transport, notably rail and bullock carts, immediately come to mind. Bullock cart owners were in no position to protest effectively, however, and except in Guatemala, the railways were not seriously threatened by the new highways. No important non-transportation enterprise with the power to block or impede highway use appears in any of the cases, so the problem of institu-

---

[20] This does not rule out the possibility that a dramatic challenge to existing institutions may be beneficial in the sense that it evokes positive responses by creating tensions that necessitate some activity. It is not inevitably the case that such responses are merely those which strengthen prior attitudes. In this instance, as in so many others discussed in the present chapter, the ability to predict behavioral responses to particular events is seriously deficient. Yet to ignore the effects of attitudes, as previously suggested, is to leave the matter grossly one-sided. The economist is thus torn between saying nothing in this area or attempting some crude generalizations. I have chosen the latter in the hope that behavioral naivete may be heuristic.

tional disturbance may be neglected in the present discussion. This is especially true of penetration facilities.

Conclusion

The general explanation of the divergent results is to be found in the extent of economic opportunity created. Following are some of the implications of the cases with respect to the economic analysis of development.

1. Investment options might usefully be analyzed in terms not only of their direct economic payoff but also in terms of their influence on attitudes. This is relevant to the manner in which rates of return, even using the social marginal productivity concept, are typically computed. Furthermore, in every case, the actual results are correctly ascribed to a cluster of investments, ignoring policies, natural resources, and attitudes. This means that attributing any portion of the increased production solely to the highway is not only spurious, but regularly overstates net benefits relative to costs. *All* of the investments must enter the denominator, and any attribution of the total productive result to one of them is as economically unsound as finding the cost of each of two or more joint products.

2. The educational and other spillover effects of road transportation appear to be greater than those of other modes of transport. This is especially significant at low levels of development.

3. All transportation capacity is not "social overhead" in any meaningful sense of that elusive phrase. Rather the social nature of transportation depends on the extent to which it is specific to a particular industry or generally available to a wide variety of industries or has educational or spillover effects.

4. The issue of ethnic distinctions, although not apparently decisive in the present cases, should not be avoided by economists out of a desire not to offend or for any other similar motive however well intentioned. The Chinese in Malaysia, for example, are important in imparting the peculiar dynamism to that country. To ignore this as a fact of economic as well as political and social consequence, is to create a distorted image of reality already blurred by the usual economic approach to growth.

5. The number of elements in the growth process that are designated as "necessary but not sufficient" is substantial. They include the following: capital in general and transport investment in particular; appropriate psychological attitudes toward economic activity and change; entrepreneurial abilities; technical abilities and education; the legal, social and political environment; the kind and amount of natural resources. In short, the phrase "necessary but not sufficient" has become a kind of grand developmental cliché applied to so many separate notions that it might well be expunged from the literature.

Some Lessons for Policy

This section concerns the lessons that can be learned from the cases so that past failures can be avoided in the future and successes improved upon. The lessons of greatest relevance are, therefore, those pertaining to preinvestment surveys.

The Significance of Prior Dynamism

The probability of success of a transportation investment is obviously dependent on the existence of prior dynamism in the region or nation as a whole. If a particular region is growing rapidly in terms of population, output, and so forth, the probability is very great that existing transport facilities will soon constitute a true bottleneck even if there is some excess capacity at the moment. The discovery of such dynamic areas not only suggests where additional capacity should be located but also is a good indicator that heavy utilization may be expected.

If the nation as a whole is growing rapidly, the probability of making a successful transport investment is high even in a region which is not growing so long as it possesses some reasonably good economic potential. The existence of overall dynamism implies among other things an environment in which economic opportunity tends to be sought and quickly exploited when found. Thus in any circumstance of local or general dynamism both the need for new transport capacity and the probability of success is very great.

But where there is no initial growth or development, a single transportation project cannot be expected to accomplish much. It is in this type of situation that a coordinated set of investments, inducements, and policies is most essential and where the prospects of success from a single project of any kind are very low. The *initiation* of growth is a fundamentally different and more difficult task than its facilitation and normally requires a more careful appraisal of noneconomic factors as well.

These considerations have obvious implications for the nature of preinvestment transportation surveys. In a dynamic context, there is less need for a comprehensive, all-inclusive economic report than would be the case in a static situation. Transport economists alone would probably suffice for the economic appraisal of transport in the former case, while more broadly trained economists and others would be needed in the latter. The degree of prior dynamism obviously conditions the length and nature of the economic feasibility report.

But in every instance there is need for rather thorough information regarding soils, forests, minerals, and so on. If the region involved has already been carefully analyzed in terms of these natural features, the economist's job is rendered not only easier but potentially more fruitful.

What this suggests is that the role of transport specialists, either as economists or transport engineers, is or should be secondary. In particular, detailed engineering estimates that purport to give the costs of the transportation facility in very specific terms are not essential until *after* the decision to go ahead has been made. Rough and ready cost estimates are good enough in advance to compare with the anticipated economic benefits. The latter must be estimated first on the basis of prior natural resource potential estimates. In terms of so-called "economic" feasibility studies, most of which are now concerned mainly with the engineering aspects of the transport facility, this could mean a greatly simplified and less costly survey prior to the decision to go ahead with the project.

Government Policy Toward New Highway Capacity

One of the important ingredients in inducing increased production was a sharp reduction in rates usually associated with an expansion of vehicle capacity. In other words, the coming into existence of a highly competitive motor transport industry was the mechanism whereby the cost savings in transport were passed on to producers.

There are several ways in which this stimulus can be blunted or eliminated: (a) by the imposition of high user taxes or tolls, (b) entry restrictions into motor transport, (c) rate regulation or rate agreements among the firms, (d) the prohibition of, or high duties on, imports of new vehicles, (e) weight and size limitations beyond those necessary to protect the highway with adequate maintenance.

Since such taxes or tolls reduce the extent of sustainable rate reductions, it is important that they be limited to those amounts strictly associated with the revenues needed to maintain the highway and to pay interest and principal on whatever loans were incurred in its construction. Alternatively, since the developmental impact of rate reductions is generally high, a tax on land values along the right-of-way, which generally rise with improved transportation, might be preferable on economic grounds and could be set at such a level that at least interest and principal on the highway loans involved could be covered. User taxes could then be limited to amounts necessary to finance those costs directly associated with use, namely maintenance and repair not caused by weather or other natural phenomena.

As a general rule in most underdeveloped countries, there should be no restriction on entry at all unless a definite safety need emerges. We have noted the substantial learning effect of widespread participation in motor transport, which suggests that the natural ease of entry should not be reduced without compelling reason. Furthermore, the more firms in existence in the absence of rate agreements, the more likely that competition will exert a downward pressure on rates. Similarly weight and size limitations for vehicles should be limited strictly to the capacity of an adequately maintained highway. The latter is important since failure to maintain highways adequately increases the apparent damage done by heavier vehicles. Such damage, which encourages imposition of stringent restrictions, is more properly related to inadequate maintenance.

Rate regulation of motor transport requires a degree of administrative overhead that is out of the question in most underdeveloped countries. Public rate regulation generally serves chiefly to prevent rate reductions and thus in developing countries may blunt the incentive to expand production in the area. Where private rate agreements emerge among the various firms supplying transport, these should be eliminated. Motor transport markets seem to be effectively competitive in many underdeveloped economies, even where knowledge of operating costs is lacking and where practices with respect to depreciation, maintenance, and repair leave much to be desired. For example, Farmer concludes, in two cases investigated, Lebanon and Eastern Saudi Arabia, that ". . . without creating vast government bureaucracies controlling transport, the Lebanese [and Saudis] have evolved a workable transport system free from large or clearly unjust inequities."[21]

Because truck markets seem workably competitive, and there is a scarcity of literate people who could effectively regulate such an industry, the opportunity cost of establishing, administering, and enforcing a detailed set of regulatory constraints is particularly high.

As far as developmental loans for transport are concerned, a general policy favoring entry and rate freedom in motor transport might usefully become part of the contract conditions when highway construction is under consideration.

The problem of import restrictions or excessive duties on vehicles is closely associated with existing vehicle supply and the foreign exchange position. If a highway is to be built and if the present vehicle supply is inadequate to meet the expected increase in output, then the whole question revolves around the availability of foreign exchange. If there are difficulties here, ve-

[21] Richard N. Farmer, "Motor-Vehicle Transport Pricing in Lebanon," *The Journal of Industrial Economics* (July 1959), p. 205. See also his article "Inland Freight Transportation Pricing in Eastern Saudi Arabia," *The Journal of Industrial Economics* (July 1962), pp. 174-87.

hicle imports may have to be curbed. But there is still room for maneuvering in the sense that private passenger cars can be prohibited while trucks may be imported with few restrictions up to the numbers considered necessary.

Regular Analysis of Past Investments

There should be initiated a series of case studies in various parts of the underdeveloped world. In the first place, it is important to check the actual results of any major investment against those anticipated beforehand. If there are serious discrepancies, an analysis of why they occurred is important to improve future decision-making. Follow-up studies of particular investments provide the only reliable, factual guide to what may reasonably be expected under given conditions in the future. This is particularly important for lending agencies continuously required to make project appraisals. Yet there is no systematic provision for detailed reporting on what actually happened after a major transport improvement nor a careful evaluation of why certain things happened and other things did not. If any significant improvement in prior appraisal of transport projects is to take place, a continuing collection of the results of past projects would seem to be indispensable.

As already argued, a case study approach is a healthy and, in my opinion, long overdue supplement to the heavy reliance upon national aggregates. More attention to regional and local situations by economists is clearly warranted in countries yet to develop a high degree of national integration and typified by islands of relative isolation and independence. A case study approach of the type presented in this volume uniquely fits this need. Furthermore, we have much to learn about the growth process and studies of this sort which seek to explain why the effects were as they were, adds considerable insight into the appropriate set of conditions whose concurrence would raise the probability of success.

But there are other reasons for recommending initiation of a continuing case study program. A careful study will necessarily develop data or make estimates that would not otherwise be available and would thus help to reduce the size of the "information gap." Indeed, a continuing analysis would provide the basis for a number of time series of economic data at the regional level. Much of the leg work of a case study should be done by local people, students, or the "educated unemployed" and would provide a valuable training ground in research techniques.

A research program of this type, however, is not to be entered upon lightly. The Brookings program, being experimental, encountered several difficulties. A few suggestions which the Brookings experience has shown to be important follow:

CASE SELECTION. The criteria for selection are many, but the major reasons for selecting a particular project are (1) its relative importance and (2) the availability of good prior information. World Bank or A.I.D. financed projects normally fit both of these criteria. Some effort should be made to select cases involving different modes of transport and providing a regionally balanced selection. The Brookings cases were unable to do this without concentrating excessively in one country. Nor were there many cases involving other than road transport that appeared to be suitable at the time for careful study. The case selection thus sacrificed modal diversity and regional balance within one country for single cases from a variety of countries. World Bank or A.I.D. missions could more readily remedy these defects.

PERSONNEL. Qualified people are hard to find in any country and even harder to hire. Although we were fortunate in obtaining a first-rate research staff, we cannot claim to have been completely successful. This suggests the need for a careful study format which specifies in substantial detail the type of data to be gathered as well as some alternative techniques for obtaining information such as sample surveys, traffic counts, personal interviews and so on. Much of the analysis of what the data means can be performed by people more skilled in economic analysis. Thus the number of trained personnel can be reduced.

The people involved should be familiar not only with the country in general but with the region and the situation as it existed prior to the new investment. Once again World Bank and A.I.D. field staffs are uniquely situated in this regard. But the importance of encouraging native personnel to perform or even initiate such work cannot be stressed too much. To obtain a broad spectrum of cases in many countries requires participation of the national planning commissions both for needed support and to provide experience in research techniques so the program can become self-sustaining and an integral part of the planning process itself. There is often an automatic turning to outside experts without an awareness that many people in the various national agencies or universities are fully capable of conducting research of this kind. Yet these skilled people are otherwise not fully or effectively employed or, in some cases, not even familiar with particular regional problems. The case study approach can thus satisfy a large number of needs.

TIME. The investigators should be able to obtain all the information required for a thorough assessment of results and their explanation. Important information is frequently lacking. It is true, of course, that some information can never be obtained regardless of how much time and money the researcher has, but more of the relevant information can be gotten if there is enough time available to spend in the area of investigation. As far as the cases presented here are concerned, the wonder is not that some pertinent information is lacking but that so much was gathered and analyzed in a short period of time.

We recommend that agencies in the field utilize their own personnel along with as much local help as is obtainable and useful to initiate a continuing program of follow-up case studies. This should be done for carefully selected projects involving several modes of transport at regular intervals over a period of years. A systematic and consistent set of data at the local and regional level should be accumulated and made available to all interested persons. For all new projects, procedures for a regular review of their effects should be established prior to completion.

Epilogue

Analysis of transportation is an exercise in applied economic analysis. Yet separation of transport into a distinct area of study has generated the appearance of uniqueness which has in turn supported a belief in what Fogel calls the "axiom of indispensability."[22] The present study suggests that there are, in fact, few magical properties in transport investments that warrant the excessive attention frequently paid to them. Transportation is merely another industry or industries; transport investment is like any other and should be judged on grounds applicable to other forms of economic activity and capital formation. The role of transport investment in economic growth is similarly not unique. Transport investment is no more an initiator of growth than any other form of investment or deliberate policy. Under some conditions it may turn out to be strategic but the same can be said about any specific investment or policy. The essential message of the present volume is that policy makers and analysts take a more agnostic view of transportation operations and investment. The plea for more case studies of transportation and development is designed to isolate the conditions under which transportation may in fact be strategic. If the present volume has succeeded in tempering some of the ill-founded enthusiasm with which investments in transportation facilities are made, it will have served its purpose.

[22] Robert W. Fogel, *Railroads and American Economic Growth: Essays in Econometric History* (Johns Hopkins Press, 1964).

Index

Index*

Accessibility: and transport modes, 199-202

Africa, 205. *See also* Uganda

Aggregative approach, 1*n*, 2, 4-6, 170-72, 203*n*, 215

Agriculture: and Bolivian road, 20, *27*, 30, 34-39, 47, 53-54, 179, *180;* and Guatemalan road, 57, 74, 80, 82-83; and Indian road, 136, 137; in North Borneo, 137; and Nicaraguan road, 143, 144, 146-49; in Peru, 149, 151-54; and Salvadorean road, 88, 92-93, 96-104, 114, 120, 165, 207; and Thailand roads, 130-31, 134, 179; and transport, 164, 174, 178-80, 202, 203; and Venezuelan road, 160

AID. *See* U. S. Agency for International Development

Air transport, 60, 72, 178, 182, *198*, 209

Anthropology, 172-73

Arbenz regime, 60

Argentina, 21, 22*n*

Aswan Dam strategy, 12, 26, 53

Atlantic Highway (Guatemala): costs of, 61-63, 79; evaluation of, 63-75, 76-81, 83-85, 172, 176-81, 183, 186-88, 192; and railroad, 55, 58-60, 65-69, 113, 129, 165, 178, 181, 182, 209

Attitudes: and transport investments, 168, 190, 191-92, 198-99, 209-11

Automobiles. *See* Bus transport; Passenger travel; Trucking

Awareness, 190, 191-92, 193-94, 199, 203

Backwash. *See* Regionalism

* Reference to tables and charts are in italics.

Balance of payments, 44-45, 47, 162. *See also* Foreign trade

Balderrama, Alfonso, 34*n*

Balsam of Peru, 98, 106

Bananas: in Guatemala, 57-59, 62, 71, 77; in Venezuela, 156

Bauer, P. T., 177*n*

Blackmer, Donald L. M., 205*n*, 208*n*

Bolivia: background information on, 17-23, 29; development strategy of, 22-28, 53-54; *maps,* 18, 19; statistics on, *13, 14, 15,* 16, *20, 24, 39, 46, 180. See also* Cochabamba-Santa Cruz Highway

Bonney, R. S. P., 137*n*, 139, 140, 141

Brown, Robert T., vii, 9, 11, 17*n*, 21, 22*n*

Bus transport: 111-13, 129, 135, 200; on Atlantic Highway, 71, 72, 80-81, 178; on Pacific Littoral, 145-46, 148. *See also* Passenger travel

Capacity, 162

Capital: 74-75, 195; and economic development, 1-5, 42-43, 122, 159-60, 174, 200, 211

Casas, Antonio, vii

Case study approach, 5-6, 16, 162-64, 166-73, 215-17

Cattle, 80, 92-93, 97, 104, 156

Central American Research Institute for Industry, 112-13

Chile, 21

Clarke, John H. T., 90

Cochabamba-Santa Cruz Highway (Bolivia): cost-benefit analysis of, 30-33, 45-54; developmental effects of, 172-77, 179, *180,* 181, 184, 186, 188, 206; financing of, 31-33; rates on, *36,* 182; and regional development, 28-31, 34-44; traffic on, *32, 33, 34*